CREATING NEW LANGUAGES OF RESISTANCE

Omid Tofighian has been engaged in collaborative philosophical, artistic and political work with displaced, exiled and incarcerated peoples for 25 years. These interdisciplinary and transdisciplinary collaborations include co-authoring different genres of writing in English; co-creation and translation into English; and shared intellectual and artistic projects. The most notable example is his translation and collaboration in Behrouz Boochani's award-winning book *No Friend but the Mountains: Writing from Manus Prison* (2018).

Creating New Languages of Resistance is an intellectual and personal reflection on creative resistance; it addresses critical issues pertaining to epistemic injustice, kyriarchy and border violence. Incorporating scholarship, different literary genres, exclusive interviews, media articles and notes on translation, this rigorous and accessible study examines the 'shared philosophical activity' Tofighian participates in with different collaborators. It suggests experimental and collaborative ways for producing and analysing similar texts and cultural productions; creates new spaces and frameworks for thinking about displacement and exile; and raises compelling questions and issues for people interested in researching and working to end border violence, bordering and intersectional discrimination.

Presenting a special rationale and philosophical vision about collaboration and co-creation in extreme situations, this is key reading for students, scholars and general readers interested in critical and cultural border studies, translation studies, public philosophy, literatures of resistance, coloniality and decoloniality, identity and positionality.

Omid Tofighian is an Adjunct Lecturer at the University of New South Wales, Australia. His publications include *Myth and Philosophy in Platonic Dialogues* (2016) and his translation of Behrouz Boochani's *No Friend but the Mountains: Writing from Manus Prison* (2018).

Translation, Politics and Society

Translation is increasingly becoming a broad topic of scholarly reflection in the social sciences. In disciplines like sociology, anthropology, international relations, policy studies and human rights studies a new concern with the significance of translation in social life is emerging among interdisciplinary scholars who productively draw from accounts developed in postcolonial studies, translation studies, and science and technology studies. This heterogeneous body of research shares the following distinctive traits:

- An association of translation with movement and transformation.
- An attention to the key intervention of local actors and to spaces of contestation and resistance to the global diffusion of practices and norms.
- A broad view of translation as relating not just to texts but to emerging social relations between previously unconnected people, materials and things.
- A critical call to rethinking their disciplines through translation.

Translation, Politics and Society is a series providing an interdisciplinary space where different approximations to the role of translation in contemporary politics and society can flourish and productively interconnect, becoming more widely visible. The series publishes broad-ranging, accessible titles that will be of interest to advanced students and researchers with disciplinary backgrounds in sociology, political science, anthropology, international relations, human rights studies, cultural studies and translation studies.

Series Editor:
Esperança Bielsa is Associate Professor and ICREA Academia Fellow at the Department of Sociology of the Universitat Autònoma de Barcelona. Her most recent books are *The Routledge Handbook of Translation and Media* (ed. 2022) and *The Routledge Handbook of Translation and Globalization* (with D. Kapsaskis, eds. 2021).

Creating New Languages of Resistance
Translation, Public Philosophy and Border Violence
Omid Tofighian

For more information about this series, please visit: www.routledge.com/Translation-Politics-and-Society/book-series/TPS

"It is rare that a book emerges that generates a distinctive approach to a topic that has consistently piqued the interest of scholars, academics and the professions."
— **Linda Briskman**, *Western Sydney University*

"Compellingly written, unflinching and inspiring, this book is the product of Tofighian's reflective translation practice, scholarly expertise, and relentless commitment to co-creating a more just society."
— **Emma Cunliffe**, *University of British Columbia*

"Translation has at once a colonial history and an emancipatory potential. Omid Tofighian's translation practice is everywhere engaged in stretching toward the latter."
— **Michael R. Griffiths**, *University of Wollongong*

"In this truly intellectual and illuminating endeavour, Tofighian's 'voice' is present as much as his profound and engaging scholarly knowledge. And this is simply brilliant."
— **Sajad Kabgani**, *Deakin University*

"Tofighian's vision for a collaborative public philosophy is exciting, radical, and clear."
— **Bri Lee**, *award-winning author, academic, and activist*

"Tofighian's book is a wide-ranging and well-timed intervention, written in a very skilful and accessible prose."
— **Ali Mirsepassi**, *New York University*

"An incisive and deeply moving interrogation of Australia's brutal border-industrial complex. We have needed a new language to express the horrors of the carceral-border nation-state. Tofighian has given us one in this deeply humane book – that of the refugee."
— **Kristina Olsson**, *writer and member of Sisters Inside*

"Centering co-creation and relationship-building, his work of translation reveals how he and his collaborators have innovated 'new languages of resistance' out of necessity, breaking through not only the physical separation of camps and borders, but also the social imaginary saturated with dehumanizing representations of migrants."
— **A. Naomi Paik**, author of *Rightlessness: Testimony & Redress in US Prison Camps Since World War II*

"Omid Tofighian offers a master class in intelligent, concerted activism. His work as a translator embraces the full extent of cultural translation, combing language transfer with facilitation, media change, adaptation, elaboration, explanation, political promotion, and interventions in public philosophy."
– **Anthony Pym,** *The University of Melbourne*

"Here is an important contribution in a multilingual world in desperate need of more cultural bridges."
– **Hessom Razavi,** *eye surgeon, essayist and poet*

"… the metaphilosophy running through Tofighian's work is not individualistic or merely passive and academic, but a collaborative practice engaging exiled, incacerated, 'illegal' refugees riddled with cares and passions, pushing philosophy beyond the well-guarded borders of the profession towards unchartered territory promising new languages of creative resistance and alternate forms of knowledge production. This is the philosophy of the future."
– **N. N. Trakakis,** *Australian Catholic University*

"This book takes forward Omid Tofighian's existing work on new languages of creative resistance emerging from Australia's carceral-border archipelago in the Pacific. It envisages a unique public philosophy emerging from this collective intellectual, artistic and political work, a shared philosophical activity that engages with the lived experience of those held in indefinite detention."
– **Gillian Whitlock,** author of *Refugee Lives in the Archives. A Pacific Imaginary*

CREATING NEW LANGUAGES OF RESISTANCE

Translation, Public Philosophy and Border Violence

Omid Tofighian

LONDON AND NEW YORK

Designed cover image: Parviz Agharokh, 'I Journey On' / 'Dar Safaram'.
Original sketch 2006 / oil on canvas 2007 – Isfahan, Iran; 100cmx70cm.

First published 2025
by Routledge
4 Park Square, Milton Park, Abingdon, Oxon OX14 4RN

and by Routledge
605 Third Avenue, New York, NY 10158

Routledge is an imprint of the Taylor & Francis Group, an informa business

© 2025 Omid Tofighian

The right of Omid Tofighian to be identified as author of this work has been asserted in accordance with sections 77 and 78 of the Copyright, Designs and Patents Act 1988.

All rights reserved. No part of this book may be reprinted or reproduced or utilised in any form or by any electronic, mechanical, or other means, now known or hereafter invented, including photocopying and recording, or in any information storage or retrieval system, without permission in writing from the publishers.

Trademark notice: Product or corporate names may be trademarks or registered trademarks, and are used only for identification and explanation without intent to infringe.

British Library Cataloguing-in-Publication Data
A catalogue record for this book is available from the British Library

Library of Congress Cataloging-in-Publication Data
Names: Tofighian, Omid, author.
Title: Creating new languages of resistance : translation, public philosophy and border violence / Omid Tofighian.
Description: Abingdon, Oxon ; New York, NY : Routledge, 2025. |
Series: Translation, politics and society | Includes bibliographical references and index. |
Identifiers: LCCN 2024036835 (print) | LCCN 2024036836 (ebook) |
ISBN 9781032596273 (hardback) | ISBN 9781032596266 (paperback) |
ISBN 9781003455493 (ebook)
Subjects: LCSH: Translating and interpreting.
Classification: LCC P306 .T59 2025 (print) | LCC P306 (ebook) |
DDC 418/.0201–dc23/eng/20241212
LC record available at https://lccn.loc.gov/2024036835
LC ebook record available at https://lccn.loc.gov/2024036836

ISBN: 978-1-032-59627-3 (hbk)
ISBN: 978-1-032-59626-6 (pbk)
ISBN: 978-1-003-45549-3 (ebk)

DOI: 10.4324/9781003455493

Typeset in Sabon
by Newgen Publishing UK

For my mother and father,
Akhtar and Manoutchehr

For my nephews,
Kian and Roan

CONTENTS

Preface   *xi*

Introduction: Translation practice and public philosophy/
creative resistance and collective knowledge   1

   *A shared philosophical activity and the potential for
     public philosophy 4*
   *Translation as political and philosophical rendering:
     new languages of resistance vs kyriocentric language 10*
   *The border-industrial complex: the refugee industry and
     pro-refugee/anti-refugee disposition 14*
   The two islands thought experiment 18

1 Translation as resistance: Creating new languages
   through collaboration   26

   Stories of translation plans, processes and products 26
   Crossing borders and arriving at translation 33
   Representing and translating carceral-border narratives 42
   Notes on translation 45
   Appendix 49

2 Translation as public philosophy: Creating new
   knowledges   57

   *Creative resistance from inside the prison camps:
   The role of collaborators and translators 57*

Damaging narratives, damaging tropes/new narratives, new languages 66
Notes on translation 75
Appendix 78

3 Collaboration, activism, translation and storytelling: Revisiting the 23-day siege on Manus Prison   91

Collective knowledge and resisting border violence 91
Translating interweaving narratives, combining diverse creations 97
Personal communication and reception within the siege narrative 102
Epistolic networks and legacies: writing and translating letters about a tragedy 105
The final visit to Manus Prison 111
Notes on translation 115
Appendix 1 117
Appendix 2 122

4 Translation, public philosophy and collective work   137

Translation and knowledge production: knowing border violence 137
Translation and experimentation 149
The reception to No Friend but the Mountains 152
Notes on translation 155
Appendix 156

5 Border-industrial complex   171

Storytelling, cultural memory and experimentation 171
Synecdoche: part/whole relationships of border violence 178
Identifying kyriarchy, exposing the kyriarchal system 184
Notes on translation 191
Appendix 192

Conclusion: More translator's reflections   206

Index   221

PREFACE

The painting that adorns the cover paperback and digital editions of this book (see Figure 0.1) was created by my relative and respected Iranian artist, the master painter from Isfahan, Parviz Agharokh. The artwork is an example of intersemiotic translation; an image created by interpreting poetry published in Persian/Farsi. The painting was inspired by Ahmad Shamlou's translation of Margot Bickel's poetry – Parviz was influenced by one stanza in particular: see Figure 0.2. Shamlou's translation is from German to Persian.

FIGURE 0.1 Parviz Agharokh, 'I Journey On' / 'Dar Safaram'. Original sketch 2006 / oil on canvas 2007 – Isfahan, Iran; 100cmx70cm.

Auf meiner Reise zu dir /	در سفرم به سوی تو	In search of you, I journey on /
Auf meiner Reise zu mir /	به سوی خود	In search of self /
Auf meiner Reise zu Gott/	به سوی خدا	In search of God /
Deren Wege uneben sind /	که راهیست ناشناخته	The passages are unknown /
Deren Wege dornig sind /	پر خار	Passages full of barbs /
Deren Wege ich kaum kenne /	ناهموار	Fragmented, jagged /
Die ich aber antreten will /	راهی که باری در آن گام میگذارم	Passages oft travelled /
Die ich schon angetreten habe /	که قدم نهاده ام	Passages already traversed /
Die ich nicht abbrechen will	و سر بازگشت ندارم	From which I cannot return

The painting is an intersemiotic translation of Shamlou's Persian translation of Bickel's poetry in German, in particular the stanza which appears directly above in three languages (Shamlou is also the subject of the painting). The three stanzas: first is the original in German; second is the Persian translation; third is my collective or 'synoptic' translation of the German and Persian texts and the painting considered all together. The English translation is an experimental amalgamation of interlinguistic and intersemiotic translations designed to correspond directly with the message, purpose and reception of this new book.

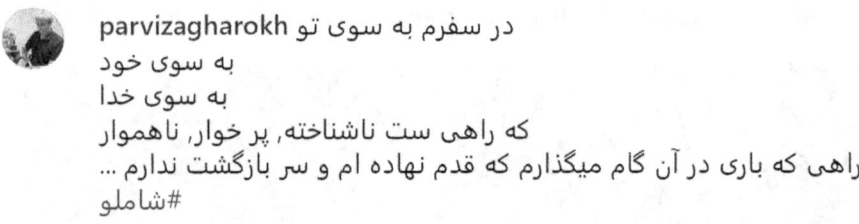

FIGURE 0.2 The cover design is an artwork by Parviz Agharokh; when posting an image of the work on Instagram he commented with a stanza from Ahmad Shamlou's translation of a Margot Bickel poem (German to Persian). Posted to Instagram on 24 April 2021.

After submitting the final draft of the manuscript I began thinking about the most appropriate cover design for this publication. The stories behind my choice of Parviz's painting, his lived experience of persecution and border crossing, and the character and identity of the master artist and teacher-mentor, have uncanny connections with the philosophy and spirit of the book. All these combined elements pertaining to the cover reflect what I refer to in my research as horrific surrealism.

Collaboration, activism, translation and storytelling constitute the most prominent features of this book. They also characterise its theoretical framework, and the principles and values I espouse throughout its pages. In addition to collaboration, activism, translation and storytelling the book foregrounds the way fragmentation, disruption, disjointedness, shattered experiences and phenomena determine and shape the structure, content and interpretive vision. All these features and factors also pertain to the cover design and the events leading up to its selection.

When the time came to decide on the artwork I contacted my mother to discuss the possibility of selecting a work by one of the master artists we knew from Isfahan. My mother recommended Parviz for reasons related to genre and style (realism and hyperrealism). I concurred, especially after reflecting on the lengthy discussions I had with Parviz when I visited his gallery in Isfahan over twelve years ago. During our conversations he described the persecution and discrimination he faced because of the political activities he was involved in when he was younger.

He was imprisoned as a sixteen-year-old and remained incarcerated for four years during which he was tortured and acquired serious eye injuries. Parviz was forced to flee Iran the day after his release. When I visited Parviz he narrated tales about living in exile, first journeying throughout the borderlands of Afghanistan and Pakistan before traveling to other places, including Europe. I was captivated by stories about those twelve years of displacement; the people he met and the places he moved between during that precarious time; about his search for safety and freedom. No one had heard from him during those years – he could not risk putting his loved ones in danger by communicating with them. After twelve difficult and dangerous years in exile he devised a plan to re-enter Iran upon receiving news about his father's death. He also returned with a passion for contributing to the art and culture of his homeland, a passion for teaching and mentoring a new generation of artists. Crossing the border had its own difficulties and dangers, and he was apprehended by Iranian border guards and interrogated in custody.

Parviz was released but was targeted and suppressed by the state in so many ways. For instance, he was summoned to return to Tehran regularly for interview within the first few years after returning. And his art practice was always under scrutiny and censorship. The multiple layers of meaning in his art, his complex and experimental use of metaphors and other tropes, are profoundly political and nonconformist. *Parviz created new languages of resistance*. He lived a life deprived of many rights in Iran, always under surveillance and always struggling against systemic discrimination.

After my phone conversation with my mother I called ▮▮▮▮ who was Parviz' student back in Iran. I explained my decision regarding the book cover and requested his number. ▮ supported the idea and we began discussing the best way forward. Then ▮ paused. ▮ remembered that his phone is monitored by state authorities. There was no way I could call him to discuss anything related to the content of my book. There were also other factors that complicated this potential collaboration. Potential risks emerged after publication of the edited translation of Behrouz Boochani's *No Friend but the Mountains* in 2018, the subsequent global attention, and later the publication of the Persian edition in Iran in 2020 (*Hich Doosti be joz Kouhestān*). This was compounded by my own background as a minority; that is, my association with a stigmatised and persecuted group based on socio-religious status (I tell different stories about these aspects and my family's forced migration throughout the book). In relation to the cover art, we decided that it was best if I explain my request by WhatsApp voice text and then we could ask ▮▮▮▮ to share it with Parviz in person.

Very early the next morning I could not sleep for some reason. I was travelling at the time and decided to drive to a nearby beach. As I was taking pictures and videos of the sunrise I opened a voice message from ▮▮▮▮ sent a few hours earlier while I was asleep.

Parviz was no longer with us. His death was sudden and unexpected – he was only sixty years old. He had died just several hours before the idea came to me about engaging with him for the book cover.

Parviz was buried a few days later. The Iranian authorities originally refused permission for burial within the prestigious artists' quarter at Isfahan's main cemetery (Bāgh-e Rezvān). After a great deal of urgent campaigning by numerous artist communities his resting place amongst his fellow creatives was approved. Even in death exclusion and systemic discrimination continue.

The short stories in this preface are stark reminders of the insidious and unrelenting ways that borders and bordering practices operate. Carceral-borders expand, multiply and reinforce systems of violence; they are an integral part of what I refer to in this book as the kyriarchal system. Borders and bordering practices are produced and become ingrained as habits of the state and society; and they forever mark bodies, families, communities, and the natural environment.

Carceral-borders relentlessly control the lives of people like Parviz. They dominate the lives of human beings who are either internally displaced; left waiting in limbo while transiting; forced to return to danger by deportation or other pressures; granted some form of temporary status in a third country or granted permanent protection when released from detention. Carceral-borders represent perpetual violence; they cause damage and death.

INTRODUCTION

Translation practice and public philosophy/creative resistance and collective knowledge

For twenty-five years my scholarship, activism and community work has involved rich and dynamic collaborations with displaced, exiled and incarcerated peoples. Our transnational relationships have forged interconnected political and cultural spaces; a critical ethos and anti-colonial imaginary; creative acts of defiance; and new discourses. Together we have created new languages of resistance. Small collectives of people with lived experience of displacement and intersectional discrimination worked collaboratively to develop ecosystems of knowledge and cultural productions. We formed relationships based on shared visions of freedom, a commitment to struggle, and an agreed understanding of collective organising. Over the last fifteen years in particular my academic and activist work has been mostly dedicated to challenging Australia's border regime with many of my translation projects and joint intellectual/cultural/political initiatives involving people targeted by the immigration detention industry: people held illegally in carceral sites in Papua New Guinea (Manus Island and Port Moresby), the Republic of Nauru, Australian-funded detention facilities in Indonesia, the Australian territory of Christmas Island and the mainland – what I call Australia's carceral-border archipelago.[1]

The different chapters in this book engage with this more recent period of my research and political activities, and the kyriarchal realities of the carceral-border archipelago – locations used for imprisonment, punishment, and financial and political profit (for examples see Tofighian, 2018b, 2020; Tofighian, Boochani, Mira and Zivardar, 2022; Tofighian and Zivardar, 2024). The themes, topics and concerns have global dimensions and international relevance; the border-industrial complex is a transnational phenomenon and critiques and challenges in the Australian context require responses that

DOI: 10.4324/9781003455493-1

address systemic injustices and related phenomena beyond narrowly defined territorial boundaries, specific national ideologies, or political/cultural situations limited by single sociohistorical periods and geographies (Miller, 2019, 2021; Loyd, Mitchelson and Burridge, 2012; Godin, 2021; Akkerman, 2023; Isaac, 2024; Paik, 2016; Mitropoulos and Kiem, 2015; Nethery, 2021; Tofighian, 2020; Tazreiter and Tofighian, with Boochani, 2022).

I have referred to my work with displaced, exiled and incarcerated peoples as a 'shared philosophical activity' (Tofighian, 2018a; Tofighian, 2018d; Tofighian, 2020; Boochani and Tofighian, 2019; Tofighian, Boochani, Mira and Zivardar, 2022; Tofighian and Zivardar, 2024; Zivardar and Tofighian, forthcoming). Many of the outcomes of these political, artistic and intellectual projects have inspired this book and provide examples and critical discussion points. The diverse products from our collaborations feature throughout the five chapters, in addition to the stories, intellectual exchanges and artistic practices involved in preparing and producing them. In addition to examples of collective work, each chapter also presents examples from scholarship I produced on my own over the past fifteen years. I draw from and build on these previous scholarly articles and other writing (these examples of my own published works interweave comments, ideas and narratives from collaborators). In addition, I draw from and build on ideas, arguments and insights from talks, seminars, workshops and dialogues related to the collaborative work (some significant and exclusive examples appear in the appendixes for each chapter, which I explain below). And every chapter provides examples, explanation and analysis of my translation work and multilingual consultation and planning.

In addition to critical commentary, reflections on my previous collaborations, and new research, each chapter is followed by an appendix which offers valuable insight regarding translation *plans*, *processes* and *products*. The inclusion of these appendixes is vital for several reasons:

First, they represent the public dimension of this work and support the idea that these collaborations create epistemic resources; second, they show the beginnings of a unique kind of public philosophy; third, they illustrate the dialectical nature of the collaborations and the important role of reception; fourth, they demonstrate how many ideas and approaches evolve from dialogues and dialectical relationships pertaining to collaborative projects; and fifth, they emphasise the importance of multilingualism and translation within the plans, processes and products addressed in this book.

While mostly focused on my edited translation and collaboration in Behrouz Boochani's *No Friend but the Mountains: Writing from Manus Prison* (Picador-Pan Macmillan, 2018; Tofighian 2018a and 2018c) the interviews and dialogues in the appendixes represent major features and factors related to the majority of the collaborative works with Boochani and others. The important exchanges with interviewers and interlocutors that make up the appendixes were conducted after the edited translation and 2018 release of the multi-award-winning book and enhance the arguments within each chapter of this book. The appendixes also help situate *No Friend but the Mountains* and other projects within transnational interactions and organising; they help interpret the projects in connection to activities by local and global communities and cultural networks; they reflect the public dimensions of the creative resistance; and they illuminate the crucial role of diverse audiences for our collaborations.

All these nuances related to the appendixes are discussed in further detail throughout the chapters of this book. The interviews and discussions that make up the appendixes are also framed by introductory comments about the context, role and significance of each dialogue. While the accompanying appendixes are situated at the end of each chapter, they are referenced throughout the book in order to illustrate crucial linkages; the connections I make demonstrate how arguments, research and translation interweave with public engagement, with various cultural communities, and with political action. The interactions and insights in the appendixes relate directly to the central themes and issues in the chapters, with several quotations and citation of key points throughout. This method helps portray the unique experiences and trajectories associated with multiple projects, and the urgency and tension involved in working with displaced, exiled and incarcerated peoples. The appendixes are not available in print or online form (however, some are transcripts from radio interviews), and a number of them have been translated from Persian/Farsi for the first time by me for this publication.

The five chapters and appendixes provide exclusive information and narratives about the important events, activities and perspectives regarding my edited translation work and joint projects with people who have experienced indefinite detention. I discuss the edited translations and collaborations in this book with a focus on *No Friend but the Mountains*, the success it achieved, and the other projects it followed, coincided with, influenced or inspired. At different times during 2019 the edited translation won the 2019 Victorian Prize for Literature and the award for nonfiction at the 2019 Victorian Premier's Literary Awards; the Special Award and Highly Commended for the Translation Prize at the 2019 NSW Premier's Literary Awards; the 2019 National Biography Award; the General Non-Fiction Book of the Year at the 2019 Australian Book Industry Awards (ABIA); and other prestigious awards. In 2020 *No Friend but the Mountains* won ABIA Audiobook of the Year.

Chapter 1 connects central issues of translation and collaboration by addressing what it means for us to create new languages of resistance. I explore the significance of storytelling in direct relation to translation plans, processes and products. In order to explain the significance of narrative for the intellectual, cultural and activist work I have been doing I reflect on the relationship between my own experiences of crossing borders, displacement, exile and migration; how I was drawn to translation work; and the development of my critical perspectives and skillset. I also examine pivotal questions pertaining to representation and translation in the context of Australia's carceral-borders.

In Chapter 2 I consider the ways translation practice can transform into forms of public philosophy. Engaging with translation planning, processes and products through a philosophical lens opens up possibilities for new knowledges, especially in the context of Australia's carceral-borders and the collaborative work necessary to understand and challenge it. I consider creative resistance by incarcerated refugees and their complex transnational networks with supporters such as translators. I also address issues pertaining to narratives, tropes and the need for new languages of resistance.

Chapter 3 involves a comprehensive case study of the translations produced in relation to the 2017 23-day siege in Manus Prison. The role of storytelling is central to this analysis, as is the expanding shared philosophical activity involved in producing a wide range of translation products. I also reflect on the role of reception as an integral part of the translation planning, processes and products. The importance of mobile phones, personal and public communication through messaging applications, and social media is factored in. Finally, I present several significant points about my activist practices and collaborative work through the narrative associated with my third visit to Manus Prison.

In Chapter 4 I expand on the connections between translation work and public philosophy by considering questions about terminology and theory. I discuss the unique ways that translation work and collaboration produce knowledge relevant to challenging border regimes with a focus on Australia's carceral-borders. I return to the issue of reception as it relates to *No Friend but the Mountains*. And I reflect on the significance of experimentation and narrative within these contexts.

Chapter 5 delves deeper into several pivotal points about the philosophical framework and epistemic issues of translation and collaboration in the context of Australia's carceral-borders. First, I examine the notion of the border-industrial complex and the philosophical and political influences behind it. And I explore different features of kyriarchy and the kyriarchal system.

A shared philosophical activity and the potential for public philosophy

One of the aims of this book is to define what I mean by shared philosophical activity, explain how it works, give examples of how it has been practiced, and discuss the significance of some of the outcomes it has produced. The most important results of this collective intellectual, artistic and political work are

Introduction 5

the public forms of philosophy it has produced. The shared philosophical activity is fundamental to the examples of creative resistance I describe – unique political projects that involve collaborative theoretical and imaginative work, and can be leveraged to render accessible and important philosophical questions and ideas, contribute to philosophical discourses, and stimulate philosophical discovery. I argue that the forms of public philosophy we have been aiming to introduce are distinct due to the *interdependent* nature of interactions within the process, the *positionalities* involved and the range of lived experiences, the extraordinary *political conditions*, the multitude of *discourses* we have had to contend with and produce, and our *methods* and *mode of production*.

In the following list I have tried to sum up some of the many existing approaches and perspectives pertaining to public philosophy. These include philosophers:

1) repurposing their theories and arguments for a general non-specialist audience;
2) producing work targeted specifically at a general non-specialist audience;
3) responding to requests, questions and concerns from a general non-specialist audience;
4) devising and introducing questions and ideas in order to encourage engagement from a general non-specialist audience;
5) identifying artistic and cultural productions, and questions and concerns in popular culture and public discourse, as worthy of philosophical investigation and elaboration;
6) identifying artistic and cultural productions, and questions and concerns in popular culture and public discourse, as different forms of doing philosophy;
7) commenting/critiquing issues that arise in different public contexts and which were originally discussed and debated amongst general non-specialist audiences.

All these modes centre and prioritise the philosopher as the leader, main expert, guide, initiator and adjudicator.

There is another model that has not been explored sufficiently:

8) philosophy produced in *collaboration* with non-specialist individuals, groups and audiences.

The collaborative work I have been doing with displaced, exiled and incarcerated peoples reflects this last model. This is what I have described as a *shared philosophical activity*. It involves both philosophers and non-specialists working together to identify and invigorate the philosophical potency of collaborative artistic and cultural work; translation projects; public engagement and its documentation; political organising and relational forms of theorising. These partnerships include devising and enhancing the questions and concerns that evolve during planning and process, and then with the presentation and evaluation of products. It also entails co-creating philosophical work, and working together to arrive at philosophical discovery by collaborating on translation projects and scholarship (traditional scholarly and non-traditional scholarly writing, and forms of academic and public engagement).

Shared philosophical activity also involves people formally trained in philosophy and non-specialists co-creating new collaborative translation, artistic and cultural productions with philosophical resonance; exploring new collective forms of doing philosophy; and introducing new co-devised philosophical questions, concerns, terminology, theories and critiques. The collaborations I have been part of are with people incarcerated in (or recently released from) Australia's carceral-border archipelago (Manus Island/Port Moresby in Papua New Guinea, the Republic of Nauru, Christmas Island and the Australian mainland, and Indonesia): each collaboration is distinct because of different *interdependent* interactions within the process; the diverse *positionalities* involved and their specific lived experiences; the shifting and accumulative *political conditions*; the multiple *discourses* that change and combine at every stage in the different collaborations; and the separate *methods* we devise together in each project, and vicissitudes pertaining to their *modes of production*.

My collaborative work with displaced, exiled and incarcerated peoples first began just before the establishment of the Pacific Solution (phase 1) in 2001. However, the introduction of widespread and accessible communication technology (in particular, smart phones, messaging applications and social media platforms) – in addition to gaining more experience, improved skills and knowledge – meant that over the last decade there has been greater attention and success for the work I have been involved in. In particular, mobile phone messaging applications and social media have enabled the groups of collaborators to network and promote our 'new languages of resistance' globally and in unprecedented ways. The work I have been engaged in since Australia intensified its border regime in 2012 (with the inception of the second phase of the Pacific Solution, then followed by the introduction of Operation Sovereign Borders in 2013) has elevated our collaborative and creative resistance to unexpected levels, to new platforms, and to wider audiences. Examples of this work have been acknowledged in prestigious institutions and diverse community spaces around the world. Many of us are now connected to global audiences; to scholars, creatives and activists from all over the world; to international institutions such as universities and literary festivals; and to transnational political and cultural movements and campaigns. In fact, the opportunity to publish this book with Routledge, after first meeting and collaborating with the series editor and translation scholar Esperança Bielsa, is one such example (see Bielsa 2023, pp. 23–26).

The chapters in this book explain and analyse the significance of our collaborations, the development of our ideas and theories, the impact of our achievements, the difficulties faced and the ingenuity involved. They also explore the afterlife of these projects and their different dimensions, including the shared visions and hopes for where and how they might develop in the future. This book is another outcome of our collective resistance, a new addition to a journey aimed at dismantling the border-industrial complex. It is also a contribution to the fight against epistemic injustice.

Rather than subjects of inquiry or case studies for research, our friends, colleagues and collaborators have established themselves (to different degrees) as knowledge producers and creatives. As leaders and experts within struggles against border violence, their work has attracted global attention and gained special recognition; they have asserted themselves as contributors with special insights into border regimes and as significant multidimensional analysts of state violence in various intersecting contexts. Based on experiences of marginalisation, oppression and stigmatisation – and also a dedication to creativity, ideas and systemic change – we formed bonds that have evolved into unique political, philosophical and aesthetic offerings.

Our collective work also represents a profoundly unique and indispensable historical archive. My aim in this book is to honour the translation planning, processes and products and provide readers with narratives and arguments that can help them imagine the profundity, vitality and exploration involved. Also, my hope is that this book can provide models for similar collaborations – we wish to suggest models that can inspire other collective political, intellectual and artistic endeavours in which the subjects of oppression, domination and subjugation occupy key roles as knowledge generators, creative producers and pivotal agents in making contributions to political change.

Our activist work and cultural advocacy developed organically as all collaborators consulted and shared ideas and experiences. As a result, we have been invited to participate in about 300 Australian and international events and activities. In many instances we used our own networks, resources and collective will to create new platforms and opportunities. Communication technology was essential since many people involved were incarcerated, or formerly incarcerated but still targeted relentlessly by Australia's border regime. Whether it was issues related to mobility restrictions, connectivity, bureaucracy, lack of or no funding, little or no institutional support, transport, translation/interpreting, or the many instances of intersectional discrimination, these projects were always at risk of failure. The border-industrial complex operates in many violent, debilitating and unpredictable ways – our events and activities have been hindered by harsh political and economic realities, but they also suffer from dismissal, disregard and divestment ... they face epistemic injustice. As the examples explored in this book prove, we were somehow always able to overcome most obstacles.

I recorded many of the dialogues and talks, or used notes from these events and activities, as a basis to write either my own or co-authored articles – many of which are discussed in this book (many of these dialogues, talks, seminars and workshops share similarities with the appendixes at the end of each chapter). Incorporating these audio recordings (of everyone involved in the events and activities) and notes (in most cases my own research and reflections) involved a lot of ingenuity and experimentation, in addition to close collaboration, consultation and sharing to ensure that the voices and intentions of everyone was respected, honoured, supported and represented/translated accurately. While working to create these examples of literature and scholarship – most of them experimental and unconventional – I realised that new ideas, terminology, strategies, techniques and theoretical frameworks were forming. These all became fertile ground for engaging in public philosophy in rich, original and collaborative ways; a public philosophy committed to debordering in every way. In the following chapters, I discuss the importance of examples such as our work on the shared philosophical activity, border-industrial complex, the carceral-border, Manus Prison Theory, Nauru Prison Theory, Nauru Imprisoned Exiles Collective, the kyriarchal system, architecture of torture, weaponisation to time, weaponisation of identity, weaponisation of space, weaponisation of design, abode for serenity (which is my translation of *ārāmsāyesh gāh* a concept related to Elahe Zivardar's architectural work; see Tofighian, Boochani, Mira and Zivardar, 2022, pp. 135–136), and more.

> During this most recent period, I have been translating, co-writing, facilitating publications, consulting, supporting writing and art projects, organizing politically, and more.
>
> I have engaged with all of these not individually, but as a shared philosophical activity. I describe the significance of this briefly in my translator's note to Behrouz Boochani's 2018 book, *No Friend but the Mountains: Writing from Manus Prison* (Tofighian 2018a), and related articles, interviews, talks and seminars. While editing and translating the many rough text messages that made up the book, Behrouz and I had daily conversations. This shared philosophical activity, together with other examples of our creative resistance, helped form what we refer to as Manus Prison Theory – similar collaborative projects produced with [Elahe] Zivardar and explored in this paper have developed into Nauru Prison Theory. The writing and translation processes for *No Friend*

but the Mountains were co-creative in many ways; one example is the discussions and debates that took place, not just with Behrouz but also with the translation consultants Moones Mansoubi (a community and cultural development worker who collected most of the text messages and is Behrouz's first translator) and Sajad Kabgani (who is a researcher specialising in literature, education, psychoanalysis and posthumanism). I worked with both during the process and, like I did with Behrouz, we had philosophical conversations that would sometimes last hours and focus on just one word or concept, one sentence or one passage. There were other people we interacted with and received feedback from, but this core team was vital to the creation, development and formation of the book, and its central messages and layers of meaning. We were all working towards the same goal and thinking about the project in very similar ways. Our individual preparations, contributions and ruminations would combine harmoniously when we met, our individual input validated and enhanced the contributions of other collaborators in uncanny ways; this occurred whenever I met with each one to work on the book and only grew and strengthened as we continued working. It was almost like we were one identity, many bodies.

(Tofighian and Zivardar, 2024, p. 24)

In relation to the translation consultants for *No Friend but the Mountains*, Mansoubi brought a wide range of experience, ideas and expertise (especially related to Iran and Australia) especially from her community and cultural development work since she has translated and interpreted for many refugees for over a decade in addition to Boochani (see Mansoubi 2021, 2023; Abood and Mansoubi, 2021). And Kabgani, in addition to his research specialisations and knowledge of both Western and Iranian philosophy and literature and diverse cultures and societies in Iran, has also translated numerous books and articles from English to Persian (see Kabgani 2023, 2024).

The processes, endeavours and encounters pertaining to my edited translation work and our collaborative projects are rich examples for philosophical, literary and other forms of scholarly and aesthetic examination and learning. Throughout the chapters in this book I reflect on and suggest ways that this shared philosophical activity pertains to questions and discourses in metaphysics (particularly personal identity), social epistemology (particularly epistemic justice), political and social philosophy, aesthetics, philosophy of literature and philosophy of translation. There are already many examples of scholars engaging with our work in meaningful and complex ways – I address many of these examples, incorporate them into my own arguments, and build on their important contributions. Some of the aims of this book are to convey the importance of the translation plans, processes and products; to invite new interlocutors and collaborators to our shared philosophical activity; and to inspire larger and more impactful projects, including new and innovative forms of public philosophy.

Translation as political and philosophical rendering: new languages of resistance vs kyriocentric language

Translating work written/spoken by people subjected to border violence and collaborating with them requires experimental and philosophical visions that understand and confront interlocking systems of oppression, domination and subjugation. This form of translation and collaboration creates new languages of resistance. Whether creative writing, analytical writing or visual art such as design, painting or cinema, our work requires a critical approach that exposes the kyriarchal relations of domination inherent in the language, forms and frameworks established to represent and interpret border violence. This critical approach draws power from lived experiences and builds on culturally-situated histories of resistance, and complex intellectual and aesthetic traditions to combat the intersecting systems of violence and nuanced strategies associated with the border-industrial complex. In combination, it is also necessary to transform the socio-cultural, political and economic infrastructures that have excluded refugees from dominant discourses about displacement and exile.

> The term 'kyriarchy' was first coined in 1992 by Elisabeth Schüssler Fiorenza to describe a theory of interconnected social systems established for the purposes of domination, oppression and submission. We have applied this term for the purposes of labelling the complex structure underlying Australia's detention regime.
> *(Tofighian in Boochani, 2018, p. 124, fn 6;*
> *also see Schüssler Fiorenza, 1992)*

Schüssler Fiorenza argues that the category of patriarchy (and also the dualistic category of gender) is insufficient for a critical analysis of power. She coined the term kyriarchy: 'a new analytic category that could understand gender in terms of the interstructuredness of oppressions.' (Schüssler Fiorenza, 2020, pp. 5–6, also see pp. 9–10)

Building on Schüssler Fiorenza's scholarship for the purposes of critically analysing Australian border violence, I have explained how kyriarchy '… encompasses multiple, interlocking kinds of stigmatisation and oppression, including racism, heteronormativity, economic discrimination, class-based violence, faith-based discrimination, coloniality, Indigenous genocide, anti-Blackness, militarism and xenophobia.' (Tofighian, 2018c, p. 370) Kyriarchy has been vital to my own theorising and activism and our collaborative work because of the way it accommodates the specificities and peculiarities of the border-industrial complex and the individual and collective experiences and thinking by people subject to Australian border violence. In particular, the term captures nuances about the situations and narratives that are otherwise difficult to convey. For instance, it has inspired me to interpret the nature of border violence in relation to colonialism, militarism and racial capitalism and elaborate on how intersecting systems are characterised by oppression, domination and submission. Also, kyriarchy helped me elaborate on the important way that systems of violence are perpetually reinforced and replicated within the complicated context of Australia's carceral-borders and their connection to the nation and its citizens. 'This important aspect connects the prison with Australian colonial history and fundamental factors plaguing contemporary Australian society, culture and politics.' (Tofighian, 2018c, p. 370)

Schüssler Fiorenza's ground-breaking studies on kyriarchy also help illuminate the relationship between language and the different levels of violence pervading socio-political spheres; she explains in the context of her radical feminist hermeneutics of the bible:

> But language is not only active-performative; it is also always already political and normative. Kyriocentric language shapes and at the same time is shaped by existing ideas of reality and relationships of kyriarchy. Kyriocentric language about G*d such as Lord, King, Almighty serves kyriarchal interests and, in turn, kyriarchal interests determine the content of kyriocentric language about the divine. Hence, an intra- and intertextual analysis of language and text are insufficient. They must be laid open by a critical systematic analysis of religio-political structures of kyriarchy that practice violence and exclusion in order to be revealed as legitimating domination or critically questioning it.
> *(Schüssler Fiorenza, 2011, pp. 222–223)*

Kyriarchal relations are described as a pyramidal system of oppression, domination and submission in which agents occupy fluid and shifting positionalities; in the kyriarchal system one can be oppressed and also contribute to the oppression of others (Schüssler Fiorenza, 2020, p. 10). I have argued that in relation to Australia's border-nation nexus, the interlocking and multiplicative systems of violence self-replicate, constantly reproduce, and expand to create new vulnerabilities and victims. The violence is further intensified, internalised and directed toward other/new targets – even within one's own intimate circles (Tofighian, 2020; Tazreiter and Tofighian, with Boochani, 2022).

Within the kyriarchal system, therefore, everyone loses. The languages necessary to reflect the absurdly complex and insatiable brutality of kyriarchy must address the intersecting systems of violence, their multiplicative nature, and the perpetual multiplication of new systems of violence in relation to carceral-borders – and also within the nation-state. Since the kyriarchal system is characterised by socio-political and cultural relations of subordination, rule and exploitation, it requires obedience and submission not only to its practices but its ideology or kyriocentric logics. The languages of kyriarchy produce artifacts and ideas and distribute them strategically throughout socio-cultural spaces, and these artifacts and ideas help build order, influence decisions and interpretations, and establish perspectives dependent on kyriarchal frameworks, discourses and relationships that have intergenerational and cross-cultural reverberations. Different materials produced about refugees take the form of damaging representations through images and narratives, and reductive and dehumanising interpretations about the displaced and exiled. These representations are inscribed by the dominant subject positions of those who create them. Constructed artifacts and ideas are dangerous and saturate the social imaginary; therefore, they are intimately connected to the societies and epistemologies that help produce, reproduce, exhibit, interpret, evaluate and share them. These same societies and epistemologies also exploit, dismiss and devalue the refugees through manipulation and construction of images, language and narratives. When translating, supporting and co-producing, it is important for me to consider content, style and form. However, it is also essential that the power structures and histories pertaining to border violence and colonialism are investigated; one must examine how border violence has shaped and is shaped by social, political, economic and philosophical languages and the narratives they operate within. A critical analysis of kyriocentric language is key. Telling and representing (through translation, research, narrative or art) means contributing to and being influenced by the political economy of knowledge production. In the face of neoliberal globalisation, growing authoritarianism and populism, and the border-industrial complex, it is vital that translation and other collaborative projects challenge the way kyriarchy has been legitimised through the languages and narratives inherent to the capitalist and racist structures that determine dominant forms of knowledge production.

The translation work and the other collaborative projects we have been involved in have always had to contend with these barriers, remaining steadfast to a decolonial and liberatory vision. Kyriarchy has masked itself through mechanisms of detached analysis and neutrality – and even euphemistic language. Therefore, kyriocentrism must be confronted and transformed through collective organising and new languages of consciousness raising and action. 'While kyriarchy theoretically names the imperial-master intertwined power structures of the ancient and modern male-determined pyramid of domination, kyriocentrism is its ideological legitimation, necessary wherever the radical democratic ethos of "the equal power of the many" (Hannah

Arendt) challenges kyriarchy fundamentally. Since democracy claims equal power and dignity for the many, but historically has been largely limited to a male elite, that is, to propertied, educated gentlemen (Greek kyrioi), the ideological and the*logical legitimation of kyriarchy became again and again necessary.' (Schüssler Fiorenza, 2011, p. 226)

I argue that Australia's border regime represents one of the most violent examples of contemporary kyriarchy and involves an increasingly high number of intersecting systems of violence and vulnerable groups. That is, it is also characterised by a higher multiplicative frequency. Australia's detention industry also practices a rapid form of multiplication and replication, constantly creating new groups of vulnerable people and new and improved technologies of oppression, domination and submission to use against them. 'The elite will come to tyrannize over the majority until it brings the majority to tyrannize over itself' (Kukathas, 2021, p. 8). As I will argue in line with the work of Chandran Kukathas in *Immigration and Freedom*, these expanding vulnerabilities and kyriarchal technologies are also applied against citizens and residents, who by extension are also victims of the accompanying kyriocentric logics. Building on Kukathas' arguments, I emphasise the epistemic impact of border regimes and bordering practices on Australian citizens; the wide-ranging impact of the symbolic aesthetic that constitutes the border-industrial complex and affects Australian public discourse and civil society; and the interconnected legacies connecting carceral-borders with coloniality (viewing them as parts of a unified whole), an interplay that conditions the social imaginary.

An important approach to creating new languages of resistance has been the development of appropriate concepts, theoretical frameworks and heuristic devices for unpacking and challenging border violence. I introduced the notion of 'horrific surrealism' as a hermeneutical schema for interpreting the multidimensional and multilayered aspects of the work I have been involved in.

> The term, concept and expression of horrific surrealism emerged and diversified as part of my collaboration with Behrouz Boochani in making his book *No Friend but the Mountains*; it was part of Behrouz's writing and my translation process (Boochani 2018; Tofighian 2018a, 2018b). Engaging with him in different forms of resistance against the carceral border regime that kept him interned in Manus Island for over six years required extensive research and consistent critical analysis and reinterpretation. Our shared storytelling traditions (from the Middle East and Western literature) helped us connect on different levels, but what I was confronted with in Farsi (his second language after Kurdish) was extremely unique; I had to make the translation equally unique. The situation was, and is, unique – it is a neo-colonial experiment. I had to

constantly look for new concepts, new literary languages, styles and tropes and new ideas and theories. I even had to create new things, sometimes by merging various elements together (from different genres, cultures, languages, contexts), and sometimes by experimenting and inventing my own. This form of knowledge production and transmission is not unlike the collaborations I have been involved in with other refugees in offshore detention, in the Australian-run detention facilities in Indonesia, and in onshore and community detention.

(Tofighian, 2021, p. 309)

Horrific surrealism is a generative notion and interpretative lens that operates like an aggregation function to capture the absurd and tragic dimensions of the border-industrial complex and its historical ties with colonialism. This hermeneutical schema helps to understand global border regimes, in general, and Australian border violence, in particular. It also assists in drawing connections between different border regimes and illuminates the positionalities of displaced and exiled peoples within them. The conditions that give rise to and shape the relationships and conflicts between incarcerated refugees and citizens are uncanny and paradoxical in many ways, and horrific surrealism can be applied to form a more lucid picture of how these dynamics develop and what they mean in the context of our grossly unjust globalised world. Horrific surrealism also extends to understanding the structure and content of work produced, the methods and mode of production involved, and the reception. In relation to Australia, horrific surrealism is also reflected in the inseparable ties between the carceral-border and settler colonial society. Key features of this hermeneutical schema include 'fragmentation, disruption, disjointedness, shattered experiences and interpretations, paradox and incongruous juxtapositions, and free flow of the subconscious, especially through dream visions.' (Tofighian, 2023, pp. 78–79)

The border-industrial complex: the refugee industry and pro-refugee/anti-refugee disposition

Engaging in these spaces strategically as a scholar and activist requires an acute awareness of the 'refugee industry' and employing a diversity of tactics to challenge it. The border-industrial complex operates in multifarious ways; politics, economy and the media operate interdependently with social, cultural and intellectual structures. In some cases, individuals, groups and organisations participate in the construction, representation and enactment of particular 'victim-saviour' dynamics which transform acts of resistance into commodities for exchange and for public consumption. Producing/reproducing these roles and formations lock displaced, exiled and incarcerated peoples into narratives and discourses of liberal humanitarianism (see Kaus,

2019) in which identities are reduced to limited stereotypical constructions that depict deficit models and are primarily designed to evoke only sympathy or empathy (in relation to the systematic torture of indefinite detention is empathy at all possible?). In these instances, refugees are encouraged to perform representations of refugeehood that distort and marginalise agential powers and centre the contributions of certain supporters with citizen privilege. The refugee industry is pervasive and its generally attractive packaging appeals to diverse publics (right across the political spectrum).

Our shared philosophical activity is always conscious of these difficulties and diversions and avoids becoming part of them. We have spent a great deal of time and energy working to create new languages of resistance that circumvent being contained and exploited within the border-industrial complex (from its programs of dehumanisation and destruction, to its liberal humanitarianism and exoticisation), which creates and governs the refugee industry. Rather than employing an essentialist approach by imagining and constructing fixed 'authentic' identities based on the structures and systems of kyriarchy, our work prioritises the histories of resistance and knowledge systems that have shaped and inspired people before, during and after their experiences of displacement, exile and incarceration. We are careful when engaging with and incorporating state language, Western political discourses and conventional philosophical traditions, and networks of activism and creativity particular to settler societies. Instead, we aim to enhance and introduce compelling and vigorous subject positions by focusing on the identities, experiences and epistemic resources of people with lived experience of oppression, domination and submission. That is, we aim to empower and promote people at the forefront in the confrontation with kyriarchy. For refugees, their past experiences, ecosystems of knowledge, aesthetic influences, and unique connections with natural and built environments, have played key roles in the construction of their subjectivity.

Therefore, our work is dedicated to the complex and riveting intellectual, artistic and political worlds of the displaced, exiled and incarcerated. These principles and methodologies of empowerment are transformed into projects that envision and try to implement structural changes (political, epistemic and symbolic) as opposed to outcomes that simply highlight and promote individual experiences and identities primarily as a spectacle, or a human-interest story. By engaging in different projects using approaches dedicated to empowerment and debordering, refugees become leaders in activist spaces, acquire genuine feelings of belonging in new transnational communities, exercise decision-making powers and creative autonomy, and experience a radical form of equality within groups which they had key roles in establishing.

In 'Translator's Reflections' accompanying my edited translation of *No Friend but the Mountains* I introduce what I have called the 'pro-refugee/anti-refugee disposition'. I employ this idea to identify and help understand the precarious and multifaceted terrain in which all forms of pro-refugee activism and support operate. The term is not to be interpreted as an oxymoron, but it is designed to align with the notion of paradox central to horrific surrealism. I was inspired to develop this idea by the philosopher George Yancy who incorporates the notion of the 'antiracist racist' within his critical analysis of the white embedded and embodied self (see Yancy 2012, p. 166 and 175; Yancy 2008, Chapter 7; also see Clark 2015). In an interview with Maria Del Guadalupe Davidson (2016, pp. 12–13) he explains the purpose and meaning of the term as it pertains to white antiracism:

Maria Davidson: *In the conclusion to* Look, a White!, *you distinguish yourself from those theorists who assert that the "white antiracist" is an oxymoron. You raise a crucial nuance where you argue that being a white antiracist and yet being racist is not mutually exclusive. How can we change academic epistemologies for the better, i.e., exactly as you suggest, academic disciplines based on mythological notions of "whiteness" as neutral, invisible? Should they be forced to name themselves? If it were up to you, where would you want to see changes first and foremost – and why? Put another way, for those white readers inspired by your call to join the fight against entrenched racism, where would you encourage them to focus?*

George Yancy: The idea of the antiracist racist is a way of theorizing the complexity of what is involved in "undoing" whiteness. This is what I meant previously about the rebirthing process being one that is penultimate. The white antiracist is not a noun, but more like a verb, which means that the antiracist is always in process, always making a decision, choosing her life, as best she can, through an antiracist lens. Yet, I theorize this existential freedom within the context of heteronomous and structural forces. It is at this point that many whites with whom I've shared my work begin to retreat and want to hold on to the idea that they are neoliberal selves who are not bound by contextual, historical, or psychic forces, who are not racists.

(Yancy [with Davison], 2016, p. 12)

Yancy's arguments and his use of paradox in exploring this nuanced phenomenon, influenced my own thinking pertaining to the 'pro-refugee/anti-refugee disposition'. Paradox and absurdity pervade all facets and structures of the border-industrial complex, in general, and the refugee industry, in particular. Yancy argues that racialised bodies are delegitimised through both erasure and obfuscation: one's humanity is stripped when their experience is erased, and then the denier's mode of living in bad faith is obfuscated. It is especially relevant for our study also to consider Orisanmi Burton's clarification: 'As a mode of social life, whiteness is not exclusively tied to white bodies. To the contrary, whiteness is all-too-often desired, pursued, and even inhabited (albeit tenuously) by phenotypically non-white people. In other words, white supremacy is a multicultural project'. (Burton, 2015, p. 41)

Reflecting on Yancy's philosophical analysis, how do we erase and obfuscate while we try to *do something* to support displaced, exiled and incarcerated peoples? Do we conceal from view the reality of our own racism and other kinds of bordering in our relationships and encounters with refugees? What is our own vicinity to violence? How do we participate in practices of exploitation and exotification of bodies? The open insult and brutal policy are not the only ways to enact border violence.

> My recent work thinks about incarceration as a bordering practice. I consider borders to be physical, symbolic and epistemic and build on scholarship that moves beyond the notion of borders and bordering as things and interprets them as evolving processes and institutions. 'Practices of bordering' refers to the demarcation of spaces, processes of territorialization and the multiple dimensions of boundaries—all of these perpetually subject to contingent events and ideas. In this context, borders are part of broad, interweaving processes in which they are used to assign and sustain meaning and control movement. Borders and bordering also exist and function within complex, fluid and multiplying networks of oppression and carceral technologies. In addition, my work explores and suggests ways of debordering, and working towards abolition, particularly in the context of immigration detention.
>
> (Davari, Tofighian, Nikpour and Mansoori, 2020)

Securing borders is part of complex, wide-reaching and multidimensional processes; it depends on bordering practices that interweave throughout our societies, in our minds. Borders also mark our bodies and socio-cultural environments. Borders and bordering practices are part of one and the same nexus; they are physical, epistemic and symbolic. Borders and bordering are continually reproduced in language, ideas and images – they are etched into language, ideas and images simultaneously.

The notion of a pro-refugee/anti-refugee disposition seems to be an oxymoron. However, I use it to try and articulate how the kyriarchal system has created conditions in which we are all – to different degrees – both pro-refugee and anti-refugee at the same time. Reflecting on this idea it may become clearer how activists and supporters can create, display and disseminate images and relationships that reinforce absurd forms of violence; how offers to help demand, and reinforce, damaging performances of refugeehood. This critique also addresses the exploitative nature of the refugee industry by evaluating people, projects and campaigns that aim to *do something* but ultimately result in benefiting people with citizen privilege and disadvantaging or harming displaced and exiled peoples. Both pro-refugee and anti-refugee: activism with and for refugees, and then its afterlife without and against refugees. The refugee industry embodies this paradoxical disposition.

When dissecting race and racism, Yancy uses metaphors such as 'ambush', 'ensnare' and 'trap' to elucidate how oppression operates. Whiteness *ensnares* even as one resists against it. He issues a warning by quoting Shannon Sullivan: "Rather than rest assured that she is effectively fighting white privilege, when engaging in resistance a person needs to continually be questioning the effects of her activism on both self and world." (Yancy 2017 [2008], p. 219, quote from Sullivan 2006, p. 197)

Also in 'Translator's Reflections', I list a number of damaging tropes that sustain and extend the deficit/surplus dichotomy that is often used to distinguish refugee from citizen (Tofighian, 2018c, p. 365):

- Caged person – escape to the West
- Desperate supplicant
- Struggling overcomer – the battler
- Tragic and miserable victim
- Broken human being
- Mystic sage – quirky and mysterious, a trickster

Against these rhetorical strategies used to essentialise displaced, exiled and incarcerated peoples (sometimes the tropes are used in combination) we need new images and terms of empowerment, new languages of resistance (Ibid, p. 366). The kyriarchal system works on different levels including manipulation through language; within a symbolic aesthetic; within social and political structures; in cultural spaces; throughout family and community networks; and it is inflicted on bodies. These and many other manifestations of kyriarchy operate simultaneously and enhance and invigorate each other, they are multiplicative and multiply to form new manifestations of oppression, domination and subordination. In this way, kyriarchy amplifies violence against victims and expands by perpetually creating new targets and new aggressive relationships of ruthless competition, enmity and hate.

The two islands thought experiment

An indicative feature and regulating force throughout my research and activism is the critical analysis of the inseparable interplay between border control and the control of citizens. The theories and concepts that have emerged from the collective fight against Australia's neocolonial experiments (e.g. shared philosophical activity, kyriarchal system, the carceral-border, Manus Prison Theory and Nauru Prison Theory) and the projects and methodologies created in collaboration with refugees are dedicated to outlining the symmetrical, fluid, randomly interchangeable and uncanny relationship that Australia's border regime has with the nation and its citizens. The construction of carceral-borders – whether located offshore or onshore, whether hidden in bureaucracy or socio-culture spaces, whether in our minds and bodies, whether in the past or present – is determined by the nation-state which has its origins in the establishment of a penal colony, an offshore island prison set up by the British Empire. Therefore, the carceral character and history of the nation-state determines the everchanging realities and direction of the carceral-border. And in turn, the exile and imprisonment of refugees on extraterritorial islands, their containment in prison facilities within the Australian community, the stripping away of basic rights and pathways to freedom and security, their exclusion from the rule of law in fundamental ways inside and outside detention, their demonisation in the social/colonial imaginary, are determinant factors that impact the settler colonial state and its operations. In this symmetrical way, the carceral-border and the nation-state are interlinked in a fluid, random and mutually reinforcing exchange – the two islands condition, govern and deteriorate each other.

Illegal incarceration within and beyond territorial borders is interconnected with the control of citizens/residents within Australian society. An inside/outside dynamic manifests in pervasive and concealed ways, constantly changing and developing strategies to resist scrutiny and avoid accountability. The detention industry is intertwined with innumerable forms of bordering that affect all kinds of immigrants and citizens/residents: people in offshore and onshore detention, people in community detention, people on temporary visas, people suffering from the prolonged liminality associated with gaining residency, people subject to intersectional discrimination, citizens who cannot enjoy full citizen rights and who experience systemic exclusion, people excluded from belonging and contributing in meaningful ways, and many other examples.

> "… the guns face inwards more often than they face out, and the guards are to be found not merely well within the boundaries of the state but in every part of society. As we have tried to erect a fortress, so have we managed to build a prison. We have become used to living under surveillance, just as we are also getting used to monitoring each other in a panopticon of the people. Whether or not we fully realize it, we are no longer at ease, and rely upon a policy and a system that threatens rather than secures our freedom."
>
> *(Kukathas, 2021, p. 4)*

This inside/outside dynamic is addressed in numerous places throughout this book. In particular, the thought experiment I devised in 'Translator's Reflections' accompanying my edited translation of *No Friend but the Mountains* (also see appendix to Chapter 2). There I suggest how this interdependent relationship between the carceral-border and the nation-state has political, socio-cultural and epistemic consequences. The thought experiment is discussed in different chapters of this book where I situate it within my philosophical influences and explain how it helps elucidate the visceral and far-reaching impact of border violence.

In an article published just before the publication of *No Friend but the Mountains* I describe part of what inspired me to create my own thought experiment (Tofighian 2018d, pp. 538-539). The thought experiment was about to appear in my 'Translator's Reflections' together with my edited translation of the book and I critically discuss it in the article. After encountering Charles Mills' interpretation of W.E.B. Du Bois' use of metaphor for examining the positionality of Black Americans living in a white supremacist nation, I began to reflect on the epistemic standpoint of people subject to indefinite detention and the way narrative (through the use of a thought experiment) can work to elicit intuitions about their circumstances and convey something of their perspective regarding Australia's carceral-border and colonial imaginary.

> In his analysis of segregation and the epistemic standpoint of the black community described in W.E.B. Du Bois' *Souls of Black Folk* (1903), Charles Mills explains the contempt Du Bois has for the white cognitive world that excludes him. Entering this world would mean living in a permanent state of 'double-consciousness'; that is, seeing himself through the cognitive lens of white supremacy, seeing himself as a problem, the subject of contempt and pity (Mills 2017, p. 107).5 For Du Bois and Mills, black communities in America have a *meta-perspective*. They have the potential for 'second-sight' or to see through the misconceptions, manipulations and machinations of white communities in America and acquire an epistemically privileged position. In this situation, it is the dominant culture that is disadvantaged and blind to the functions of racism and to the structures and operations of a socio-political world divided on racial grounds. Mills argues that there is no possibility for reconciliation of epistemologies here: total resistance is the only approach when up against white supremacy (Mills 2017, p. 106–107; see also Medina 2012).
>
> Mills also discusses Du Bois' modification of Plato's Allegory of the Cave (Du Bois uses the metaphor of the veil). Du Bois situates those kept in the darkness, black Americans, as people with access to the social truth, and white Americans as ignorant even though they dwell in the light (Mills 2017, p. 108).

As examples of shared philosophical activity, Zivardar and I have written about collaborative projects involving people who have experienced border violence and described them as examples of knowledge production. In a co-authored article for *The Philosopher* we discuss Nauru Prison Theory as a form of public philosophy; in her contribution to this piece she confirms the core idea I discussed above. Zivardar analyses her epistemic standpoint in connection with the six-years she was incarcerated in Nauru:

> Now that I have been released from the island prison, my encounter with the world has led to new understandings. My horrific and surreal experiences have given me the capacity to compare our world before and after my detention. The period that I was detained in Nauru (2013 to 2019) was significant in terms of technological advances. While detained, we could never imagine how the world outside the island was changing. I believe I now have, ironically, a valuable and unique perspective. I can see things that many cannot see because, for most people, change occurred slowly and over a whole decade. It did not take long for me to realise what was missing in a world where technology had advanced at a rapid pace and with far-reaching impact – the world according to me after leaving the island prison. After living in purgatory for so long, I now find myself at a new threshold in my life.
> (Tofighian and Zivardar 2024, pp. 28–29)

The future for the kind of collaborative work discussed in this book must exhibit a combination of epistemic debordering, the creation of new liberatory knowledges, creative experimentation, and political praxis. Within these projects refugees need to be positioned as leaders and generators of knowledge and creativity; as creators and articulators of new languages of resistance. How we narrate the history of knowledge production about border violence shapes the identities of refugees and citizens. It is important to tell this history in ways that centre refugees and honours the collaborative processes involved; that is, creating conditions where refugees reclaim, determine and guide the narrative. This also requires encouraging and supporting responses to this work by other refugees with the aim of forming influential discourses dedicated to ethical kinds of reception. This work must not only be oriented towards the academy and other elite intellectual and creative institutions and communities. I argue that we transform this space into something more democratic, something radically egalitarian, and make places primarily dedicated to communities of struggle and their languages of resistance.

Note

1 Here the term archipelago is used both literally and metaphorically; it describes the connection between the varying locations within Australia's expansive

immigration detention estate, and the fact that the estate consists of offshore prisons situated on islands in addition to carceral sites within the nation-state, which is itself comprised of islands. The term archipelago is also part of the subtitle for the special issue of *Southerly* (2021) dedicated to writing and art from many locations within the carceral-border archipelago.

Combining the words carceral and border using a hyphen is intended to emphasise the complex and evolving ways that the border industry and detention industry (also the military and surveillance industries) function together and have become inseparable. For examples of the complex and fluid ways imprisonment, migration and other sectors interconnect in the Australian context see Arvin 2020, 2020, 2020, 2020; McNevin 2019; Davidson 2019; Knaus and Davidson (2019); Davidson and Boochani (2019); Zivardar and Tofighian (2021); Dana (2018, pp. 26-28); Galbraith, Abdile, Tofighian, Boochani (2021, pp. 13-20); Verma and John (2024). I have also used the term carceral-border for identifying and critically analysing examples of cultural production, see Tofighian (2019).

References

Abood, P. and Mansoubi, M. (2021) 'On being: creativity in the pursuit of justice', *Southerly – Writing Through Fences: Archipelago of Letters* 79(2): pp. 245–254. www.southerlylitmag.com.au/shop/writing-through-fences-archipelago-of-letters/

Akkerman, M. (2023) 'Global Spending on Immigration Enforcement is Higher than Ever and Rising', *Migration Policy Institute*. www.migrationpolicy.org/article/immigration-enforcement-spending-rising

Arvin, M. (2020) 'Navid vs Australia's Border Regime: Wrestling against Indefinite Detention'. Translated by O. Tofighian. *Overland*. www.overland.org.au/2020/12/navid/

Arvin, M. (2020) 'From Manus to Melbourne: We Do Not Even Know What We Are Being Punished for'. Translated by O. Tofighian. *The Guardian*. www.theguardian.com/commentisfree/2020/aug/08/from-manus-island-to-melbourne-we-do-not-even-know-what-we-are-being-punished-for

Arvin, M. (2020) 'This is My Eighth Christmas Locked in Immigration Detention. Next Year I Hope to Celebrate as a Free Man'. Translated by O. Tofighian. *The Guardian*. www.theguardian.com/commentisfree/2020/dec/24/this-is-my-eighth-christmas-locked-up-in-immigration-detention-next-year-i-hope-to-celebrate-as-a-free-man

Arvin, M. (2020) 'Australians Complain About Weeks in Quarantine. I've Been in Immigration Detention for Almost Eight Years'. Translated by O. Tofighian. *The Guardian*. www.theguardian.com/australia-news/commentisfree/2020/sep/14/australians-complain-about-weeks-in-quarantine-ive-been-in-immigration-detention-for-almost-eight-years

Bielsa, E. (2023) *A translational sociology: interdisciplinary perspectives on politics and society*. London: Routledge.

Boochani, B. (2018) *No Friend but the mountains: Writing from Manus Prison*, translated by Tofighian, O. Sydney: Picador-Pan Macmillan.

Boochani, B. and Tofighian, O. (2019) 'In conversation. Manus Prison theory: borders, incarceration and collective agency', *Griffith Review* 65: pp. 275–288. www.griffithreview.com/articles/manus-prison-theory/

Burton, O. (2015) 'To protect and serve whiteness', *Noth American Dialogue* 18(2): 38–50.

Clark, C. (2015) 'But Aren't We Good White People?', *Christine Sleeter* . www.christinesleeter.org/good-white-people

Dana, E. (2018) 'Indefinite Detention: Caring for Refugees in Indonesia as Performance'. Translated by O. Tofighian. *International Charles Town Maroons Conference & Festival Magazine*. www.maroons-jamaica.com/wp-content/uploads/flipbook/6/files/basic-html/page29.html

Davari, A., Omid T., Golnar, N. and Naveed M. "Is Abolition Global? Iran, Iranians, and Prison Politics. (Part 1)" Jadaliyya, 2 Sept. 2020, www.jadaliyya.com/Details/41658

Davidson, H. (2019) 'Asylum Seekers Moved to a Prison Complex in PNG', *The Guardian*. www.theguardian.com/australia-news/2019/aug/12/asylum-seekers-moved-to-a-prison-complex-in-png

Davidson, H. and Boochani, B. (2019) 'Asylum Seekers Approved for Medevac Transfers Detained in Port Moresby', *The Guardian*. www.theguardian.com/australia-news/2019/oct/10/asylum-seekers-approved-for-medevac-transfers-detained-in-port-moresby

Galbraith, J., Abdile, H., Tofighian, O. and Boochani, B. (2021) *Southerly – Writing Through Fences: Archipelago of Letters* 79(2). www.southerlylitmag.com.au/shop/writing-through-fences-archipelago-of-letters/

Galbraith, J., Abdile, H., Tofighian, O. and Boochani, B. (2021) 'Editorial', *Southerly – Writing Through Fences: Archipelago of Letters* 79(2): pp. 13–20.

Godin, M. (2021) 'The Rise of the Border and Surveillance Industry and Why You Should be Concerned', *OpenDemocracy*. www.opendemocracy.net/en/pandemic-border/rise-border-and-surveillance-industry-and-why-you-should-be-concerned/

Isaac, A. (2024) 'The price of mobility on the border industrial complex and the role of private industry in enforcing migration restrictions', *Spectrum* 12: 1–11. https://doi.org/10.29173/spectrum185

Kabgani, S. (2023) 'Time and Border, Policy and Lived Experience', in Boochani, B. (ed), *Freedom, only Freedom: the prison writings of Behrouz Boochani*, translated and edited by Tofighian, O. and Mansoubi, M. London: Bloomsbury Academic, pp. 59–61.

Kaus, A. (2019) 'Liberal humanitarianism: obscuring US culpability in James Disco and Susan Clark's *Echoes of the Lost Boys of Sudan* and Dave Eggers's *what is the what*', *Contemporary Literature* 60(2): pp. 198–226. www.muse.jhu.edu/article/757960

Knaus, C. and Davidson, H. (2019) 'Australia's Offshore Contracts: How Millions Were Spent Dubious Outcomes', *The Guardian*. www.theguardian.com/australia-news/2019/feb/23/australias-offshore-contracts-how-millions-were-spent-for-dubious-outcomes

Kukathas, C. (2021) *Immigration and Freedom*. Princeton and Oxford: Princeton University Press.

Loyd, J. M., Mitchelson, M. and Burridge, A. (2012) *Beyond walls and cages: Prisons, borders, and global crisis*. Athens: University of Georgia Press.

Mansoubi, M. (2021) 'On translation', *Southerly – Writing Through Fences: Archipelago of Letters* 79(2): pp. 92–94. www.southerlylitmag.com.au/shop/writing-through-fences-archipelago-of-letters/

Mansoubi, M. (2023) 'Translating Manus and Nauru: Refugee Writing', in Boochani, B. (ed), *Freedom, only Freedom: the prison writings of Behrouz Boochani*, translated and edited by Tofighian, O. and Mansoubi, M. London: Bloomsbury Academic, pp. 11–19.

McNevin, A. (2019) 'From Offshore Detention of Refugees to Indigenous Incarceration', *Public Seminar*. www.publicseminar.org/essays/from-offshore-detention-of-refugees-to-indigenous-incarceration/

Miller, T. (2019) *Empire of borders: how the US is expanding its border around the world*. London: Verso.

Miller, T. (2021) *Build bridges, not walls*. San Franscisco: City Lights Books.

Mitropoulos, A. and Kiem, M. (2015) 'Cross-Border Operations', *The New Inquiry*. www.thenewinquiry.com/cross-border-operations/

Nethery, A. (2021) 'Incarceration, classification and control: administrative detention in settler colonial Australia', *Political Geography* 89: 1–10. https://doi.org/10.1016/j.polgeo.2021.102457

Paik, A. N. (2016) *Rightlessness: testimony and redress in U.S. prison camps since World War II*. Chapel Hill: The University of North Carolina Press.

Sajad, K. (2024) 'The unknowable other and ethics of ungraspability: education through the irrational', *Educational Philosophy and Theory*: pp. 1–11. https://doi.org/10.1080/00131857.2024.2348806

Schüssler Fiorenza, E. (1992) *But She Said: feminist practices of biblical interpretation*. Boston: Beacon Press.

Schüssler Fiorenza, E. (2011) *Transforming vision: explorations in Feminist The*logy*. Minneapolis: Fortress Press.

Schüssler Fiorenza, E. (2020) 'Biblical Interpretation and Kyriarchal Globalization', in Scholz, S. (ed), *The Oxford Handbook of Feminist approaches to the Hebrew Bible*. Oxford: Oxford University Press, pp. 2–20. https://doi.org/10.1093/oxfordhb/9780190462673.013.1

Sullivan, S. (2006) *Revealing whiteness: the unconscious habits of racial privilege*. Bloomington: Indiana University Press.

Tazreiter, C. and Tofighian, O. with Boochani, B. (2022) 'Spectres of Subjugation/Inter-Subjugation/Resubjugation of People Seeking Asylum: the kyriarchal system in Australia's necropoleis', in Billings, P. (ed), *Regulating Refugee protection through social welfare: law, policy and praxis*. London: Routledge, pp. 68–90.

Tofighian, O. (2018a) 'Translator's Tale: A Window to the Mountains', in Boochani, B. (ed), *No Friend but the Mountains: Writing from Manus Prison*, translated by O. Tofighian. Sydney: Picador-Pan Macmillan, pp. xiii–xxxvi.

Tofighian, O. (2018b) 'Black bodies for political profit: Sudanese and Somali standpoints on Australia's racialised border regime', *Transition* 126: pp. 5–18. www.muse.jhu.edu/article/702736.

Tofighian, O. (2018c) 'Translator's Reflections', in Boochani, B. (ed), *No Friend but the Mountains: Writing from Manus Prison*, translated by O. Tofighian. Sydney: Picador-Pan Macmillan, pp. 359–374.

Tofighian, O. (2018d) 'Behrouz Boochani and the Manus Prison narratives: merging translation with philosophical reading', *Continuum: Journal of Media & Cultural Studies* 32(4): 532–540. https://doi.org/10.1080/10304312.2018.1494942

Tofighian, O. (2019) 'Carceral-border Cinema: A film from Manus Prison: introduction', *Alphaville: Journal of Film and Screen Media* 18, pp. 183–184. https://doi.org/10.33178/alpha.18.14

Tofighian, O. (2020) 'Introducing Manus Prison theory: knowing border violence', *Globalizations* 17(7): pp. 1138–1156. https://doi.org/10.1080/14747731.2020.1713547

Tofighian, O. (2021). Horrific Surrealism: New Storytelling for Australia's Carceral-Border Archipelago. Marrugeku: Telling That Story— 25 years of Trans-Indigenous and Intercultural Performance, edited by Helen Gilbert, Dalisa Pigram and Rachael Swain, 306-319. Wales: Performance Research Books.

Tofighian, O. (2023) 'Manus Island and Manus Prison Theory', in Braidotti, R., Klumbyte, G. and Jones, E. (eds), *More posthuman glossary*. London: Bloomsbury, pp. 77–80.

Tofighian, O., Boochani, B., Mira and Zivardar, E. (2022) 'Narratives of Resistance from Indefinite Detention: Manus Prison Theory and Nauru Imprisoned Exiles Collective', in Gordon, J. (ed), *The big anxiety: taking care of mental health in times of crisis*. London: Bloomsbury Academic, pp. 125–138

Tofighian, O. and Zivardar, E. (2024) 'Nauru prison theory as public philosophy: displacement, exile and creative resistance against border violence', *The Philosopher* 112(1): pp. 23–31.

Verma, S. and John, L. (2024) 'Labor's Deportation Bill Will Only Create An Endless Roundabout between Immigration Detention and Prison', *The Guardian*. www.theguardian.com/commentisfree/2024/mar/27/labor-deportation-bill-immigration-detention-prison

Yancy, G. (2017 [2008]). *Black bodies, white gazes: the continuing significance of race in America*. Second Edition. New York: Rowman & Littlefield.

Yancy, G. (2012) *Look, a white! Philosophical essays on whiteness*. Philadelphia: Temple University Press.

Yancy, G. (with Davidson, M. D. G.) (2016) 'Thinking about race, history, and identity: an interview with George Yancy', *The Western Journal of Black Studies* 40(1): pp. 1–13.

Zivardar, E. and Tofighian, O. (2021) 'The Torture of Australia's Offshore Immigration Detention System', *OpenDemocracy*. www.opendemocracy.net/en/beyond-trafficking-and-slavery/the-torture-of-australias-offshore-immigration-detention-system/

Zivardar, E and Tofighian, O. (forthcoming) 'Foundations for Nauru Prison Theory: Elahe Zivardar and Omid Tofighian on Australian Border Violence, Art and Knowledge Production', in Hawas, M. and Robbins, B. (eds), *Teaching Politically*. New York: Fordham University Press.

1
TRANSLATION AS RESISTANCE

Creating new languages through collaboration

Stories of translation plans, processes and products

Translations hold stories. The translation of anything written or spoken includes layers of stories; illuminating, instructive and multidimensional narratives which in most cases remain untold. What I mean by this is that every work of translation (or act of interpretation for speech), regardless of the genre, involves interlacing tales that inform us about the context in which some writing or speech act was reforged in another language. These stories both predate and arise during the *translation plan*, they are integral to the *translation process*, and they proceed from the *translation product*.

There are numerous factors that can assist us in disclosing the stories that describe the lead up to a *translation plan*, and then inform the actual moments and phases when the translation is being devised. Eugene Nida's functionalist approach identifies three basic factors that help distinguish between types of translation: the nature of the message; the purpose/s of both the author and translator; and issues pertaining to reception (Nida, 1964, p. 156). His research in Latin America, Africa and Asia relating to the translation of the Bible argues that the approaches employed by translators depend on their purpose, thus opening up the possibility for innumerable ways of translating (Tymoczko, 2014 [2007], p. 34). Considering a more critical approach to the issue of purpose, colonial domination and missionary aims intersect when one unpacks translation plans associated with vernacular translations of the Bible. Andrew Mbuvi examines how translation of the Bible's message was inextricably linked with colonisation (Mbuvi, 2023). Stories related to a translation plan render the evolving translation process and product as inherently political.

> Translations during the colonial period, we know, were an expression of the cultural power of the colonizer. Missionaries, anthropologists, learned Orientalists chose to translate the texts which corresponded to the image of the subjugated world which they wished to construct. Translations materialized modes of interpretation whose terms were rarely questioned. The title of the volume in honour of the celebrated British social anthropologist Evans-Pritchard, *Translating Culture* (1962), comes to represent a whole range of interpretive activities whose final meaning rested exclusively within the colonizers' language. Colonized cultures were texts whose vast spaces were contained within the hermeneutic frames of Western knowledge. "Translation" refers not only to the transfer of specific texts into European languages, but to all the practices whose aim was to compact and reduce an alien reality into the terms imposed by a triumphant Western culture.
>
> *(Simon, 2000, pp. 10–11)*

Esperança Bielsa questions the 'straightforwardness' of the *translation process* in the context of policy transfer. She draws attention to the ambiguity associated with the adoption of translated policies or norms and explains how the innovation and creativity of translators position them as vital non-state actors in policy diffusion and policy learning at the local level (Bielsa, 2023, p. 99).

And if, according to Walter Benjamin's view, a source text survives through translation then the *translation product* represents the afterlife of the work (Benjamin, 1996, pp. 254–256). Therefore, every product emerges as a new continuing life force, each with their own set of living stories.

Stories about the translator's relationship to the new work are indispensable to understanding the source text, the target text and all the movements through which the former is formed into the latter. Sometimes the *plan, process* and *product* blend into each other, or there exist different movements between them at various periods. Sometimes they do not appear in a linear fashion but as fragments arising randomly at different temporal points, which complicates the narratives and many basic and commonplace expectations regarding the translator's tale.

In some cases, the re-creation in the target language is better interpreted as more of a *co-creation* between author and translator. In other instances, the translation of the source text – conditioned by the translator's training, methodology, techniques, influences, positionality, and stages of editing work – requires reconfiguring the original to such an extent that the result blurs the boundaries between conventional notions of target text and a rewritten work.

Approaching translation by acknowledging the wide range of ambiguous, uncertain and complex features and factors involved, and appreciating the unfinished nature of translation plans, processes and products, "requires a reconceptualisation of the notion of translation away from both a narrow definition that conceives it strictly in terms of an interlingual transfer… and vague, metaphorical uses of the concept which forget its linguistic dimensions." (Bielsa, 2023, pp. 1–2) According to André Lefevre, the distinctions between a translation and other forms of rewriting are indistinct. The characteristics of translation – like the characteristics of other types of rewritings or metatexts – represent many significant features about its nature, function and social status. In fact, translations share common features with rewritings such as anthologies, abridgements, histories of literature, works of literary criticism, editions, children's versions, film and musical adaptations, cartoon and graphic versions, etc. (Tymoczko, 2014 [2007], p. 82).

Rather than reducing all translations to a simple case of language transfer, analysis of translation should invite critical and complex dialogues and re-evaluations that address the socio-cultural, political, aesthetic, personal and relational dimensions of translation plans, processes and products. Since translation work is a creative and intellectual (and often personal) endeavour that occupies many functions and has layered meanings for practitioners, it may be more appropriate, first and foremost, to prioritise narratives; that is, how translators narrate their own tangled and intricate approaches, activities, relationships and mixed reflections.

In this book I explore the possibilities of this approach by engaging with and unpacking my own translation experiences in addition to theorising and applying concepts and analytical tools. My approach has been inspired by scholarship from translation studies in which authors reflect on, analyse and incorporate their own personal translation experiences and explain how and why they arrived at conducting research on translation: these include Esperança Bielsa's *A Translational Sociology: interdisciplinary perspectives on politics and society* (particularly "Part III: Translation and Experience" [2023]); Maria Tymoczko's *Enlarging Translation, Empowering Translators* (particularly in her introduction [2014]); Edith Grossman's *Why Translation Matters* (2010); and the contributions to Mona Baker's *Translating Dissent: voices from and with the Egyptian Revolution* (2016).

As a category, the standard notion of translation as a form of linguistic transfer is insufficient and raises many questions and difficulties when applied to specific examples from around the world and throughout history. Most definitions seem inaccurate when considering the stories associated with different aspects of translation; interpreted as the result of a socially engaged human practice, the works we identify as translations consist of features and factors that often render them indefinable. Most translations can never be reduced to basic and easy versions of the mechanical definition of translation (or "a mechanical and transparent process of word substitution from one language to another" [Bielsa, 2023, p. 57]). The view of translations as stories may be a helpful move towards reaching some clarity about the most appropriate and enriching ways to describe and define them. Stories can establish a more intimate relationship with something or someone, they can help us work through confusion, inspire us when confronted with complexity, correct inaccurate descriptions and help us develop more appropriate definitions. The perspective that translation is defined by its related stories, in fact, corresponds closely with the reasons why we value and need the art of translation. We seek and welcome translations because we instinctually desire and depend on an abundance of heterogeneous and otherwise inaccessible tales.

Most of the untold stories connected to translation plans, processes and products are profoundly important and can reveal or teach us things that do not appear in what was written or said; in fact, they usually have little or nothing to do with the content that is translated. These narrative tapestries disclose unnoticed, marginalised or suppressed dimensions about collectives, identities, cultures, histories, societies, politics, ideas, representations and so much more. Translations are knowledge. They do not merely communicate knowledge from one language to another. Translation work itself produces its own knowledge and requires an appropriate epistemological lens to illuminate it, and an appropriate socio-political lens to clarify, empower and share that same knowledge.

Where does the story behind a translation begin? Clearly there is a moment when a decision is made by a translator to undertake a project. That is one story, or one narrative thread. A translator brings so many things to a translation project – language skills are only one element. How does a translator arrive at this moment? What influenced them to become a translator and why choose this project? What else have they translated? When did they begin translation work, for what purpose, and what else were they involved in before and during their translation practices? What is their relationship to the author/speaker, how was the connection made, and in what ways does that bond (or lack of it) inform the translation? What do they plan to do after their current/next translation project, and what are their expectations for the translated work? What do they anticipate from audiences? How do they reflect on the process, and do they have or are they developing a theory of translation? What techniques and approaches are used and in what ways, where and how were they acquired? Are they like other translators, how do they differ? What is it about themselves that is reflected in their translations, how do they appear in the work? Every thoughtful response to the above questions is a story, a lesson and a way of knowing.

Translators and their creations, translation practice and translation theory are part of long traditions; in fact, translation is an essential component of all histories and all cultures. Grossman highlights these facts in relation to the European Renaissance: 'The "rebirth" we all have studied at one time or another began as the translation into Latin and then the vernacular languages of the ancient Greek philosophy and science that had been lost to Christian Europe for centuries.' (p. 13) She continues by indicating the respect for and value of translation for poets and the diverse ways it was incorporated into their works: 'Poets of the late fifteenth, sixteenth, and seventeenth centuries – for example, the Spaniards Garcilaso de la Vega and Fray Luis de León – routinely translated and adapted classical and then Italian works, and these versions of Horace or Virgil or Petrarch were included as a matter of course in collections of their original poems.' (p. 13) Peter Adamson explains how during the early Middle Ages, the eastern part of the Roman Empire (Greek-speaking Byzantines) and throughout the Islamicate World (thanks to the highly funded and visionary translation movement under the patronage of the Abbasid caliphate, and the efforts of people like al-Kindi [died circa 870CE]) readers had access to the Hellenic intellectual heritage to about the same degree that readers of English do now (Adamson, 2016).

Sara Khalili's translations of Shahriar Mandanipour's novels share several common elements with many of my own translation projects. In her book-length collaborations with Mandanipour the writing and translation occurred simultaneously and the source texts she worked with have never been published, nor are there plans for their publication. Regarding my own edited translation of *No Friend but the Mountains*, Behrouz Boochani did eventually decide to publish the book in Persian/Farsi in Iran two years after my English edited translation was published (Boochani, 2020). After coming to an agreement with the publisher he edited the source text – an accumulation of text messages from the first five years he was imprisoned in Manus Island – on his own (I was not involved in this publication). He edited his own writing in Persian and engaged with the publisher and Persian editor via WhatsApp. There are many complex and unique details related to this issue that require unpacking. Araz Barseghian's review (2020) provides an overview of some of the details and complexities associated with its publication. He examines many significant features of Boochani's published book; however, in this case the edited Persian edition seems to be an intralingual translation. The edited Persian edition could be interpreted as a new target text (of intralingual translation), and the original text messages constitute the source text. Barseghian conducts an evaluation by contrasting the published Persian book with my English edited translation (however, he did not have access to the original mobile phone messages; for analysis of these WhatsApp texts see notes on translation at the end of this chapter, also examples of the original text messages in the notes on translation at the end of subsequent chapters). I will return to this topic in other parts of this book, but for the first analyses of my edited translation in the context of Barseghian's review see Kebsi, 2024 and In press (which references key points in Barseghian's review such as collaboration, the literary dimensions and word length). No other source text by Boochani or by others whose work I translated into English have been published.

Khalili's reflections on her decision to undertake translation work, to become a full-time translator, and other features of her practice reinforce the view I proposed earlier about the significance of stories related to translation plans, processes and products. I have included an excerpt here from a dialogue with translator and scholar Ilan Stavans in which they discuss important and revealing elements pertaining to the complex experiences, decisions and emotions that translators undergo at various stages.

Sara Khalili: I was coaxed into becoming a translator, but it didn't take long for me to find myself wanting to do nothing else. I am, or I should say, I was, a financial journalist and worked in my field for many years. I only thought about translation when the late Karim Emami would tell me, yet again, that I was wasting my time, that I should instead dedicate myself to translating Persian literature. He believed I had a talent for it.

IS: Emami translated from Persian to English and back again. He rendered Scott Fitzgerald's *The Great Gatsby* (1925) for Iranian readers, as well as four volumes of *The Adventures of Sherlock Holmes* (1993–1998). And he also translated into English seventy-two quatrains of poetry by Omar Khayyam in the *The Wine of Nishapur* (1997).

SK: Karim was one of Iran's most celebrated literary translators, as well as a renowned editor and literary critic. To me, he was also a dear friend and close relative.

IS: I know he was a lexicographer, too. I wished I had met him.

SK: Karim's arguments for, and my arguments against what he was urging me to do, went on for several years, until in 2004, when he suggested I work with him on the translation of a short story for an anthology of Iranian literature that PEN was publishing. I agreed, thinking it would be an interesting exercise. As we worked together, Karim in Tehran and me in New York, he patiently educated me on the art of translation. I was captivated. Needless to say, I finally did what he had hoped I would do.

(Khalili and Stavans, Spring 2019)

In an interview with Poupeh Missaghi, Khalili again explains her collaboration with Mandanipour. Some aspects of her experience resonate with me as they relate to my collaboration with Boochani during my edited translation of *No Friend but the Mountains*. There exist several illuminating similarities and important differences. Khalili's experiences are worth noting here and I will address these related issues in other points throughout this book.

During the interview, Missaghi asks Khalili about her reflections on translating Mandanipour's latest book in contrast to the first time she translated a book by the same author:

PM: How was translating this new work different, or not, from translating Shahriar's previous work, <u>Censoring an Iranian Love Story</u>? Now that you have had a longer-term author-translator relationship and thus come to know his style better, how did you two work on the translation? Can you speak a bit about the specifics and benefits of such long-term collaboration?

SK: Shahriar and I worked in tandem on both *Censoring an Iranian Love Story* and *Moon Brow*. I translated as he wrote. It certainly was not the conventional way of going about it. But despite its complications, the feeling of being in the trenches together created a much greater sense of collaboration between us.

The most palpable difference in my experience with *Moon Brow* was that by then we knew each other much better and I felt more confident in my understanding and interpretation of his style, his language, and the underlying intent in his prose. I was also less daunted by his intricate constructs. Peeling away the layers and disentangling the webs he weaves had become somewhat easier.

For me, the most valuable gift of my long-term working relationship with Shahriar is the trust that has developed between us. In our case, this trust is even more imperative because neither *Censoring* nor *Moon Brow* have ever been published in their original Persian, and all translations into other languages are based on my English rendition. This makes the stakes much higher for Shahriar as the writer, and the weight of the responsibility much greater for me as the translator.

I think today as Shahriar writes, he is less worried whether I can recreate his work in English. And I translate feeling less anxious of whether I am doing his work justice.

Of course, we still have our long discussions and occasional arguments, but each in our own way, we have more confidence and faith in the other's work, in the choices and decisions that the other makes.

(Missaghi, 2018)

Bielsa highlights the simultaneity of the planning, writing, co-creation and translation process for *No Friend but the Mountains* (referring to my notion of a shared philosophical activity) and the presentness of the realities described. She points out that these features distinguish Boochani's book from other forms of writing by people who experienced incarceration; she acknowledges the co-createdness of the book and identifies it as "a prime example of born-translated literature", the idea that the book comes into being with my English version (Bielsa 2023, pp. 23–24; also see Walkowitz, 2015; Zhang, 2016). Bielsa also suggests an alternative to the politics of identity through an analysis of the politics of translation. Interpreting the complicated and multidimensional work I was involved in when translating the book, she emphasises important features such as collaboration, relationality, respect, solidarity, positionality, creative resistance and experimentation (pp. 25–26). She presents her critical analysis of identity politics and a politics of translation in the context of the debate pertaining to the translation of Amanda Gorman's poetry (Bielsa, 2023, Chapter 1; also see my comments on this debate when interviewed by Erlend Wichne: Tofighian, 2022).

Crossing borders and arriving at translation

My own trajectory as a translator led me to ask the long list of questions I introduced in the previous section; inquiries into my own experiences and those of family and friends. My investigation and self-reflection also relate to aspects of the planning, processes and products of translation. Writing about and translating narratives of forced migration are inseparable from my own personal narrative, my own complicated history of displacement and exile. The dimensions of my story and lived experiences are embedded, for instance, in important modern histories of persecution in Iranian society and politics; oppression based on socio-religious status and amplified by events around the 1979 Iranian Revolution. My upbringing was directly fashioned by numerous global dynamics and inseparable from relatively recent events in the US and then Australia. Gradually, I became linked to other histories, other cultures, and other encounters involving marginalisation and suppression.

While becoming familiar with diverse structures of discrimination and oppression in different parts of the world that I lived in or visited, I was also uplifted by both local and transnational struggles for freedom, empowerment and dignity. I became connected with different societies and cultures and drawn to certain collectives and movements which inspired and helped build my own language of resistance. Narratives about inequality and injustice are incomplete without foregrounding acts of dissent and defiance; that is, the refusal to accept the status quo and the discriminatory and oppressive circumstances one is faced with. I grew to understand the significance of different expressions of disobedience and subversion regardless of their variety, method, degree or frequency. A variety of contexts and events introduced me to diverse languages of resistance, and they in turn inspired me to form my own.

The first opportunity for me to translate something for publication emerged nearly fifteen years ago in the context of collaborating with people in Australian immigration detention centres, and others who had been recently released. After spending nearly seven years abroad I returned to Australia in late 2010 and immediately began working with groups of refugees inside and outside detention, something I had been involved in before leaving and which I continued while overseas. Soon after resuming my activism I started working with colleagues on a special issue of the journal *Literature and Aesthetics* (volume 21, June 2011). My interpreting and translation work, dialogues, collective organising, and forms of knowledge sharing with refugees from this time informed the two articles I wrote for the special issue: "Iranians Continue to be Persecuted after Fleeing Iran: Australia's Human Rights Dilemma" (pp. 20–22) and "Prolonged Liminality and Comparative Examples of Rioting 'Down Under'" (pp. 97–103). For the first article, for instance, I translated commentary by a Kurdish Iranian man (a Feyli Kurd who spoke Kurdish, Persian and Arabic) which I imbedded in the following passage:

> This is one example of the tragedy that can result from living in an immigration detention centre in Australia. One detainee expressed the irony of detention in a developed and free country such as Australia by saying '*When they execute someone in Iran at least they don't make you carry the dead body away... at least you're not forced to live with the individual and get to know him before they kill him.*' The death of the Iraqi man followed the suicide of a Fijian man a month earlier. Shortly after the loss of the Iraqi man a young English man took his own life after being in detention for a short time.
>
> *(2011, p. 21, emphasis added here)*

The publication showcased many examples of art, many of which were produced by people seeking asylum inside and outside detention. Many women, children and men contributed artwork for both the journal and future exhibitions. In 2010 and 2011 I visited detention centres in Sydney, Melbourne and Weipa in Far North Queensland, and was in contact with refugees from around the country. However, there are many important stories leading up to the planning stage for these examples of writing, translation and organising.

At the end of 2010 I returned to Australia after years of living and researching in Europe and the Middle East. I was introduced to a very broad range of people from local and international communities. I also interacted with and learned from displaced and exiled peoples living in different cities. In the years I was abroad I visited many countries, met interesting and insightful people and groups, and collaborated with scholars, artists, writers, activists and others.

Through the people I met while travelling abroad between 2003 and 2010 I acquired knowledge of diverse, creative methods and visions. These approaches, perspectives and practices were associated with many kinds of local and transnational activists, movements, campaigns and traditions of resistance. I incorporated these experiences, ways of understanding and new skills into my own work upon my return to Australia. Border violence in Australia was constantly changing and expanding and after spending time overseas I realised that I wanted to collaborate with and support people in new and innovative ways – I wanted to bring together everything that I had learnt and experienced from around the world and in different contexts. After completing a PhD in philosophy, enhancing my research and writing abilities, acquiring a better grasp of academic and non-academic publishing, engaging with art and popular culture, and exploring the possibilities available through interdisciplinary and transdisciplinary work, I was well placed to merge scholarship with activism, cultural and community work.

By the time I was back in Australia and pursuing new academic ambitions and activist commitments, I was already motivated by the uprisings in the Middle East and North Africa from 2009 to 2010 – especially in Iran, Tunisia and Egypt. Added to this were the many profound and insightful encounters with displaced and exiled peoples in the different places I had visited, lived and researched and my experiences visiting family and family friends in Iran (after being away for twenty-five years) and in diaspora – all of whom introduced me to many more people and groups which expanded my perspective and understanding in invaluable ways.

When I returned to activism, cultural and community work in Australia I decided that I wanted to explore possibilities by drawing on my international and transnational experiences and ideas. I was not sure about engaging with the same approaches to activism and community advocacy that I had been involved in before leaving Australia in 2003, I now felt that I had something different to offer. The activities and events I was part of during 2010 and 2011, after coming back, were an important re-entry into the situation in Australia and an excellent way to build new relationships and initiate different practices. During this period I especially began to understand better the power and experimental potential of translation.

In 2014 I was introduced to a collaboration between two Sydney-based hip-hop artists. At the time I would interpret for Mamali, aka Mohammad Ali Gholami, aka Silas – his Christian name, in his interactions with Izzy, aka Jacob Ballard. Later I translated some of Mamali's lyrics, some of which appear in an online article I published in *The Conversation* (2014; see Figure 1.1). My piece discusses the lived experiences and lyrics of the two artists, the political topics and contexts they rap about, and their relationship. In the online article I draw from their stories and art to write about colonialism, the oppression and resistance of Indigenous peoples in Australia, and connect these themes and issues to people seeking asylum, Australian policies of indefinite immigration detention, and oppression in Iran. In the article I emphasise race and Australian identity in the context of Australian hip-hop, and I consider transnational hip-hop initiatives (I also translated a line by Iranian rapper Hichkas).

The translation of Mamali's lyrics was conditioned and led by the themes he was expressing and his personal experiences, but also by the themes and personal experiences represented in Izzy's lyrics in the same track. The translation would not have been the same if I had translated the same lines removed from the collaborative track. That is, if the translation was done in a different context; if I had not been friends with and interacted with the two artists; and if I had not witnessed the development of the final product. The themes of colonial violence against First Nations peoples in Australia, state violence in Iran, and Australian border violence come together to characterise the translation decisions and strategy.

Following publication of the article the three of us were invited by ABC Radio (we were joined by King Ali, aka Ali Razivand, another hip-hop collaborator [a beatmaker and producer] who came to Australia from Iran with Mamali) for an interview where I interpreted for Mamali and discussed my own research, cultural interests and activism (ABC, 2014). Mamali and King Ali have recently formed G-Funktion, a music movement created by the two of them. They have plans to collaborate with Izzy on a new album in future.

When considering the journey that brought me to the art and philosophy of translation, and informed my practice and vision, I must incorporate and fuse my own personal stories and narrative strands. But I also need to invite the stories and narrative strands of others, elements that are integral to the lives of family and friends, also people I have never met, time periods I was never part of, and places I have never lived. I arrived at a deep understanding of my 'translator's tale' through self-reflection, investigation, research and dialogue. Deep understanding involves engaging with stories.

I left Iran with my family when I was a child. Our migration occurred during a particularly turbulent period, a stretch of time lasting years with many unpredictable shifts occurring across borders. For us, migration took place

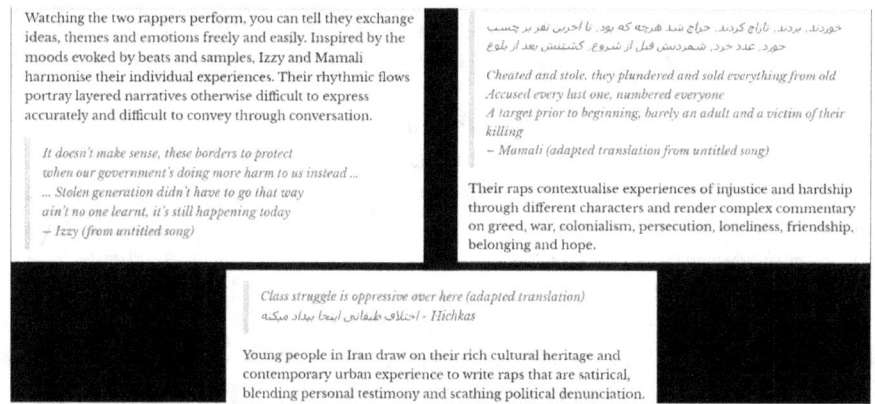

FIGURE 1.1 My early published translations embedded in Tofighian, 2014.

just before, during, and after the Iranian Revolution – different moments are marked by urgent responses, re-evaluation and replanning. Everything was fluid, changing and involved crossing borders – even moving back and forth for a time. After moving to the US on temporary visas (tourist visas), soon followed by the violent and unpredictable developments associated with the revolution in Iran, our migration suddenly became an indefinite journey until we finally arrived in Australia years later. Some dimensions were constantly fracturing, but in retrospect I view it as an incremental process that spanned years. The reasons for travelling to the US and then Australia are multiple – determined by the unsteady and wavering situation – and dependent on the specific moment within the extended migration process.

Intergenerational persecution and struggle were a reality for many families in Iran, especially those from marginalised and stigmatised groups. Even before the revolution there existed a lack of hope about the future for many excluded individuals and collectives. The various forms of systemic discrimination in Iran have deep historical roots and need to be understood based on both distinct and intersecting socio-cultural, religious, and political experiences and outlooks. Some life projects emerged in response to historical injustice, which included plans to leave the country. Many of our immediate and extended family were among the significant number of Iran's marginalized groups that were becoming more disenfranchised. This feeling had been developing over decades and influenced generations leading up to the revolution; as a result, some relatives were either planning or had already started leaving Iran (Tofighian, 2020; I also discuss some of these issues in an interview with Lucille Cutting for *The Pin*, see the appendix to this chapter). However, some extended family stayed through the 1979 revolution and the subsequent Iran-Iraq war (1980–88) before leaving, while others remained there under the Islamic Republic. The majority left after us at different times over the past forty-five years, some are currently making plans to leave, and some have decided to stay.

My experiences learning English as a child and communicating and thinking in two languages (Persian/Farsi and English) corresponded with living across and between a range of different cultures and societies (my father used three languages and shared with us his experiences and insights into using German and its relationship with Persian and English). During those early years in the US after we left Iran, and later as we started to build a life in Australia, creative exploration and interpretation of different languages – the languages we knew and those of people we got to know along the way – was a necessity for working through the unpredictability associated with the inequalities that exist in the modern globalised world. The issues pertaining to migration were only part of the bigger picture.

One narrative thread that has a meaningful place in my story and informs my journey towards translation work is the move from Iran to the US and then to Australia which I mentioned above, a move that spanned about five years. This period resists compact definitions of migration and involves many divergent experiences and encounters, different forms of transition and forced movement. This period is also hard to describe and analyse in terms of language acquisition and the development of skills that eventually contributed to my practice and philosophy of translation. Expression, interpretation and meaning-making activities emerge and are established within lived experiences and relationships, and if the socio-cultural and personal dimensions of one's life are fragmented, disrupted, disjointed and shattered it is inevitable that those same features will also characterise one's engagement with language and thought.

In an interview about my translation and collaboration in *No Friend but the Mountains* (*The Pin*, 2019 – see appendix to this chapter) – not long after winning the 2019 Victorian Prize for Literature and the Victorian Premier's Award for NonFiction – I reflect on the translation process and the fractured and volatile qualities of both the situation, the collaboration and the project itself:

The Pin: Do you think you'll ever be able to read back passages and not be able to relate them to where you were?

Different things happen every time I read the book. Sometimes I recall those times, sometimes I just go into the book itself and get lost. Sometimes I think about what's happening now or another conversation Behrouz and I had. This is important, this disruption and fragmentation. It's so important to understanding Behrouz's interpretation and critique, what he

produces and even our relationship. I think that's the best way to describe it. Everything is so unpredictable. Everything is so shattered.
(Tofighian and Cutting, see appendix to this chapter)

Another significant narrative thread from that precarious period in my migration story stands out for me. After a short trip back to Iran from the US our plans were severely altered when my father was blacklisted by Iran's new revolutionary government, and his name published in the media. The lives of many people were affected in unexpected ways when not long after the revolution the US embassy in Tehran was taken hostage – many of these individual and family stories have never been documented. As a result of becoming stigmatised in this way my father could not return to Iran after that short trip back; he could no longer manage and complete our transition and our overall plans were thwarted, our lives in indefinite limbo. We found ourselves in this situation because as we were trying to determine the next steps in our migration journey while living in the US on temporary visas and waiting for permanent residency, my father had flown back to Iran to manage our affairs there. He left Iran to join us in Los Angeles and only about an hour after he landed the authorities at the airport in New York where he was transiting suddenly began to refuse entry to Iranian travellers, a measure that was directly connected to the hostage crisis. This experience and many similar ones coincided and interlinked with people we knew.

Over time our encounters in the US and Australia, our perceptions of the experiences and events, and the way we began to tell our stories, became reframed and conditioned by the stories of others. In time our reflections on the past became compounded by new narratives – our own and others. This dynamic played a valuable role in learning and developing language and fusing different cultures. In retrospect, I came to realise that individual stories are, more accurately, composites. This realisation factored into my translation work, from my interpreting responsibilities for different people to my later role as a translator of various forms of writing. A translator's vision is not only indispensably tied up with their past, but it is also inseparably linked with the histories of others. I understand now that a translator's approach and vision emerges from their past; critically analysing how I arrived at translation practice (or retelling the stories that make up translation plans, processes and products) helps me to better understand the different histories involved and the meaning and significance that the art has for me.

Translation is a hermeneutical activity. Translation work is not limited to the interpretation and transformation of the text at hand; that is, analysis of translation cannot be limited to process and product, but must include translation plan. As Ramakrishna argues, translation choices and one's interpretative horizon involve pre-translation relationships and encounters, preparation, purpose and promotion:

> Another instance of personal choice which contributed to changing the terms of cultural transmission in India during the colonial period, toward the end of the nineteenth century and beginning of the twentieth century, is Premchand's translation of Anatole France's *Thaïs*. Premchand's choice of a French writer was not language-related but rather ideological: he was fascinated with the novel and considered the French author superior to many English writers. He selected the particular work for what he considered its special affinity to Indian values, and one which would serve as an eye-opener to another world for Indian colonial readers, his fellow writers and translators, or *rewriters*. He therefore sought to adapt the novel to the Indian cultural context with a view to making it reader-friendly… The translations by Premchand, Vidyarthi and other contemporary writers of the time would pave the way for many later translations of European works, such as those by Molière, Dumas, Maupassant and Rolland, among others. The choice of work to be translated was usually determined by the translator's "existential hermeneutics,"' by his environment and historical space.
>
> (Ramakrishna, 2000, pp. 90–91)

My work as a translator has involved interpreting the life narratives and experiences of the people I collaborate with; stories filled with the vacillating struggles and innovative visions associated with forced migration (see Bennett and Tofighian, 2020). My approach to translation involves paying close attention to those tales, how they illuminate the text (or spoken account), the individual's approach towards writing (or expressing themselves verbally), and the attitude and imagination of the writer (or speaker). Like the personal and political elements in the lives of refugees, the structure and content of the works are characterised by fragmentation, disruption, disjointedness, and shattered experiences and phenomena. The works I choose to translate, the techniques I have developed, and what I aim to achieve through translation, all reflect the same qualities (Bennett and Tofighian, 2020, p. 753). In fact, the personal and political elements, the structure and content, the style and techniques, all reciprocally reinforce each other – all share and mutually enhance the same qualities of fragmentation, disruption, disjointedness and shattered developments. This form of 'reciprocal reinforcement' empowers the message and emotion of the works in remarkable ways (I have used a similar trope in previous research related to the relationship between myth and philosophy in Platonic dialogues, see my use of 'mutual scaffolding' in Tofighian, 2016).

In a 2019 interview, after winning a number of prestigious awards and with Boochani still incarcerated in Manus Prison, I reflect on issues regarding the reciprocal way different features of the translation plan, process and product reinforce each other in the context of my edited translation of *No Friend but the Mountains*:

Louisa Luong: What was it like translating a book described as "horrific surrealism"? Did you struggle with translating and dissecting someone else's intimate trauma, especially someone you know so personally.

OT: There are many reasons we decided to use the term "horrific surrealism". My experience translating the book was totally surreal. Also, the response to the book has enhanced this surreal factor. In fact, so much about our relationship and the work we have been doing together is surreal. We collaborate closely and understand each other very well; we are close friends who speak almost daily, we support each other regularly and in multiple ways, and there are many things about our identities that connect us. It is a remarkable partnership, but it is also totally surreal because of many stark contrasts between us and our circumstances. The power differential is striking in terms of citizenship status, mobility, and so many related factors. And, of course, this surreal aspect is combined with the horrific reality of imprisonment in Manus, Australia's border regime, and the psychological and emotional dimensions of the lived experience. (Tofighian and Luong, see appendix to chapter 5)

I will address the issue of horrific surrealism later in this book, but it is important to clarify here that developing this hermeneutical schema was essential to creating cohesion between the fragmentation, disruption, disjointedness, and shattered features of the works I have been translating, editing, co-creating, and writing about (it works like a kind of aggregation function).

The structural dimensions of my edited translations are influenced by the methodology I employ in earlier scholarship, especially my book *Myth and Philosophy in Platonic Dialogues* (2016) (the comments, debates and articles by translators of Plato and other philosophers, in fact, played a significant role in developing my critical approach and arguments). The connections between different periods and perspectives in my research are significant because they add further narrative threads to the stories that inform translation plans, processes and products. In my study of Plato's myths I conduct case studies of numerous dialogues using a systematic approach that 1) analyses the opening scenes in the dialogues and the role of characters with attention to theme introduction, setting and narrative mode; 2) unpacks the main myth within the dialogue; 3) examines Plato's philosophical arguments; 4) and conducts a study of the unifying nature of myth and argument using a method I designed and refer to as *mutual scaffolding*; 5) I illustrate the importance of plot structure; and 6) I examine the significance of character selection (Tofighian, 2016, 'Introduction', pp. xi-xv). Rather than interpret different elements in the dialogues in isolation I consider them as a unified whole through the lens of mutual scaffolding which interprets myth and philosophy as interdependent and in harmony with the various intellectual, cultural and literary features that constitute this integrated unit – all diverse (and sometimes conflicting) elements reciprocally reinforce each other within this unity in place-based (according to the dialogue's *mise-en-scène* and cultural milieu) and situation-specific ways. In my edited translation work and collaboration with people subject to border violence, the hermeneutical schema I call horrific surrealism functions in similarly unifying, integrative and multiplicative ways (like an aggregation function that allows for continuous intensification) which I will explore in subsequent chapters.

Experiences of forced migration and crossing borders represent a whole range of instabilities, fissures and schisms. However, when interpreted as interdependent and parts of an intellectual and cultural whole, these same elements have the power to generate new and enriching creative, intellectual and political perspectives and representations; that is, epistemic resources and knowledge production. Engaging with real and symbolic elements pertaining to forced migration and border crossing is a lifelong relationship – an intimate encounter and a process of self-reflection and conscientisation – for those with lived experiences of displacement and exile. For me, translating narratives from Australian immigration detention requires employing many personal and critical lenses and displays individual, interconnected and intersectional histories.

Representing and translating carceral-border narratives

The experience of migrating to Australia over forty-two years ago was shaped and directed by multifaceted developments associated with border politics, particularly obstacles related to visas, citizenship, and the vicissitudes and transformations pertaining to policies and bureaucratic structures. It was late 1982 when our family arrived in Australia from the US. The Coalition government (conservative) was in power under Liberal leader Malcolm Fraser – this was just years after the White Australia policy had been officially abolished and the first government policies promoting multiculturalism established nationally. It was also months before the Bob Hawke Labor government (social democrat) came to power. When we made the transition we only had void Iranian passports since they were issued under the pre-revolution government. The Iranian Revolution was about four years old at the time and the Iran-Iraq war had already started and was continuing to intensify. As I mentioned, there were many reasons influencing us to leave the US for Australia. One important factor involved obstacles associated with our application to remain in the US permanently; we had been waiting for five years and it was still unclear how our application for a Green Card (Permanent Residency Card) was progressing. Our application was in the US Embassy in Tehran when it was taken hostage and this evidence was exploited by the revolutionaries when they decided to blacklist my father. This caused unpredictable and unprecedented setbacks that no one – including specialist lawyers – was sure how to navigate through and resolve. The information within such applications were manipulated by the hostage takers and the Iranian government in deleterious ways, forcing many people into exile. After almost five years in the US our tourist visas – issued in Iran before the revolution[1] – were close to expiring which, in addition to losing the limited rights that the visa provided, would end up causing a new set of problems. One option available for us was to apply for asylum in the US based on oppression of minorities in Iran. In the case of most of our family members and friends in the US (and around the world) this was the only option. Our situation was slightly different since we had already been residing in the US for those few years on a five-year tourist visa and my father had started establishing us economically and socially. Since there was little time left on our temporary visas, and little news about our application for residency, a close friend who had already made plans to move to Australia (but through a different category to the one we eventually applied for) advised us to make an inquiry with the Australian consulate (we were living in Los Angeles at the time). The political changes in Australia around that time, especially the recent implementation of policies promoting multiculturalism (after many decades of the White Australia policy) and my father's professional qualifications as an architect (a master's degree from an Austrian university) and his specialised work experience in Iran and the US, were no doubt influential and helped to explain the kind of enthusiasm he encountered when inquiring about migration to Australia. As I mentioned, our pre-revolution Iranian passports were void at the time which could have been a major obstacle. But, in fact, this did not prove to be a problem in any way.

It is remarkable when I think back to the way things developed and how our application was expedited; the Australian government assisted our migration process by creating special travel documents that enabled us to fly directly to Australia. No passports, no visas, no travel documents from an international organisation. The whole process – from the time we had our interview at the consulate to boarding our flight from Los Angeles for Sydney – took approximately two months and was facilitated by inquiries and offers of support by Australian consular staff. My youngest brother had just been born in Los Angeles and rather than being frowned upon as a problem, our whole family were invited to the consulate for an interview together in what seemed like an attempt to facilitate a fast and smooth transition. We all received Australian citizenship in three years.

The contrasts separating aspects of my experience with the state violence suffered by people seeking asylum over the past few decades in Australia are incredible, disturbing and a cause for anger. This is one of the reasons I use the concept of surrealism to describe the paradoxes and absurdities that appear when comparing different people's migration journeys to Australia; surrealism is an appropriate lens through which to interpret the differences between my encounters and those of the people I collaborate with – people fleeing systemic discrimination and dehumanisation; targeted persecution; harassment and intimidation; threats to their loved ones; war and other similar forms of danger; statelessness, abandonment and intolerable socio-political environments.

The complex and absurd differences in our experiences informed and challenged my critical interpretations and self-reflection about border politics; they helped shape my theorising; my method of collaborating with displaced, exiled and incarcerated peoples; and the modes of engagement.

Omid: I read your recent article ... I really admire your work.
Behrouz: That's very kind ... I just hope I wake up from this nightmare soon.

(Tofighian, 2018, p. xiii)

These translated messages are part of the initial exchanges I had with Boochani when I reached out to him while he was incarcerated in Manus Prison (they also appear at the very beginning of my translator's note for *No Friend but the Mountains*). When his boat travelling from Indonesia was intercepted in Australian waters, he was initially incarcerated in the Christmas Island detention centre (an Australian territory). After approximately one month in that carceral site he was exiled to Manus Island, part of Manus Province in Papua New Guinea (he discusses these periods and experiences in Chapter 5 of the book). The forced removal of people across international borders and between two separate sovereign states (Australia's offshore detention centres in PNG and Nauru) did not involve consultation with any of the refugees involved and was conducted without using standard procedures involving passports, visas or other official travel documents. For all refugees held onshore and offshore, the many forms of imprisonment within Australia's immigration detention industry throughout the years – including Boochani's and other collaborators – never involved any judicial process of any kind. Between 2013 and 2019 he was held in different carceral sites: first the detention centre on the Australian external territory of Christmas Island; then the Lombrum Naval Base on Manus Island (2013–2017); the East Lorengau detention centre in Manus Island (2017–2019); and finally, another form of confinement in Port Moresby (capital of PNG).

In a complex plan that involved taking up an invitation to participate in the WORD Christchurch Festival, Boochani managed to escape to Aotearoa New Zealand in November 2019 (leaving from Port Moresby airport and traveling there through Manilla in the Philippines to avoid inevitable problems with transiting through Australia, which would have resulted in his return to detention in PNG). This escape from imprisonment and uncertainty is part of the overall story of translating his writing. Supporting Boochani by translating and collaborating in his writing, which included numerous examples of journalism, speeches, film subtitles, and the multi-award-winning book *No Friend but the Mountains*, illustrates significant points regarding the political potential of translation. The translations, particularly the book, attracted the attention of festivals around the world including WORD Christchurch in New Zealand where Boochani is now a resident after being granted refugee status. Translation here was leveraged for liberation – it contributed to the beginning of a free and secure life after suffering a lifetime filled with many forms of injustice.

Notes on translation

- Throughout the English edited translation of *No Friend but the Mountains* the text switches between prose and verse. All the WhatsApp Persian text messages were written in prose; however, many of the original texts represent a poetic style of prose which opened up possibilities for translating them as poetry. Also, during the translation and editing process we decided that every chapter begin with a poem. In a couple of cases a poetic section had to be moved to the beginning and adjusted to suit the opening of the chapter.
- In the notes on translation below and at the end of subsequent chapters I compare the original text messages which I used for my edited translation. The section below is an exclusive study of the prose-verse transition.
- During the translation and editing process I changed the narrative from past tense into present tense. The 2020 Persian edition edited by Boochani with Nashr-e Cheshmeh remains in past tense.

46 Creating new languages of resistance

The examples below are English translations as they appear in the published book (with italics and poetic format). Figure 1.2 displays the original text messages for these stanzas.

Example 1 - on pp. 70–71:
For years I had pondered the mountains /
For years I had dwelt on the war involving occupiers of the Kurdish homelands /
A war against those who had divided Kurdistan between themselves /
An occupation that has devastated an ancient culture /
An invasion that has decimated what was of cultural value to the Kurds /
Destroyed what was cherished by the Kurds /
What was necessary for the preservation of Kurdish identity.

Example 2 - on p. 78:
My lot in life after thirty years /
After thirty years of trying my best in that dictatorship /
After thirty years struggling within that theocracy known as Iran /
After thirty years my lot in life was nothing /
What else could I have taken with me besides a book of poetry?

Example 3 - on pp. 114–115:
Daddy's moustache is a symbol of his strength /
The strength of a father who could protect his family /
The strength of a dad who could take his helpless little daughters under his wings /
The strength of a dad who would never let anyone harm them /
A dad who certainly didn't have any power inside that prison /
A dad who is now unable to protect his family /
A dad who is held captive /
A dad who is rendered weak /
A dad who feels ashamed in front of his family /
A dad who feels humiliated in front of his little daughters /
He is so disempowered that he feels he had made his family captives with his own hands /
He feels that perhaps he has caused his children pain and suffering /
He feels that perhaps he had spoiled the dreams of childhood /
A dad ageing rapidly with anguish.

Example 4 - on pp. 284–285.
Down below is scattered with chestnut oak forests /
Down below is flourishing with forests of wild figs /
Down below is the village I became accustomed to in every way /
Until I left it . . . only to return again /
Oh the joy, running ahead through the panorama of youth /
Through the smell of springtime /
Through the thousands upon thousands of chamomile flowers /
The season is spring, the season of youthful anticipation, the season that unleashes the smell of fresh grass /
In flight ahead atop the zenith and towards the mountainside /
Traversing over the hills /
Treading on fresh mushrooms /
Travelling past a nest of partridges /
Traipsing past a nest of sand pheasants /
Trekking past a nest of sparrows /
Touring past a nest of nightingales /
Rushing towards the river.

The poem in Example 5 is quoted by Boochani from an unknown source (the original text message embeds the poem within a prose section).

In contrast to the other four passages above, my English translation for this poem is not an instance of changing prose into verse – the Persian stanza is translated into the same genre.
Example 5 (p. 43 from *No Friend but the Mountains*):
Righteous is the one who can see /
I horrify, like a wayward sensibility /
But, my god, could I ever be a frightening being? /
I, I who was never anything more than a flimsy, stray kite /
Upon the rooftops of a misty sky . . .

All original text messages for the above examples are in Figure 1.2.

Example 1

داد. برای سال ها بود که به کوه ها فکر می کردم و به جنگ با کسانی که سرزمین کردستان را تصرف کرده بودند. جنگ با کسانی که کردستان را بین خودشان قسمت کرده بودند و در راه نابود کردن فرهنگ باستانی و همه ی ارزش هایی بودند که هر کردی با آنها هویت پیدا می کرد. می خواستم پیشمرگه شوم و زندگی ام را

Example 2

کنم. واقعا هم چیز با ارزشی نداشتم. سهم من از سی سال زندگی و دوندگی در ایران دیکتاتوری و مذهبی، هیچ چیز بود. چه چیزی می توانستم با خودم بیاورم (به) جز یک کتاب شعر. واقعیت قضیه این بود (که)

Example 3

مانوس همه مان را کلافه کرده بود و می خواست همه مان را بسوزاند. سبیل های بابای خانواده نماد قدرتش بود. قدرت یک بابا که می توانست خانواده اش را و دختران کوچک و بینوایش را زیر بال و پرش بگیرد و نگذارد کسی به آنها آسیبی برساند. بابایی که مطمئنا در داخل آن زندان هیچ قدرتی نداشت و نمی توانست از خانواده اش حمایت کند. بابایی که اسیر بود و ضعیف و همیشه از خانواده اش و دختران کوچکش خجالت می کشیده است. اینکه آنقدر ضعیف بوده که آنها را با دستان خودش زندانی کرده است و شاهد دردها و رنجها و پایمال شدن آرزوهای کودکانه شان بوده است. مطمئنا همه ی این ها او را پیر و پیر تر کرده است.

Example 4

شدم،کنار بوی کنگرها و خاک تازه،من آنجا بودم،زیر تک درخت بلوط روی قله،سگم هم آنجا بود،شاید هم لحظاتی پیش مرا به قصد شکار خرگوش ترک کرده بود،اما احساسش می کردم،پایین تر جنگل بلوط ها و انجیرهای وحشی بود و دهکده ای که همیشه عادت داشتم تا ترکش کنم و دوباره به آن برگردم.چه خوش است دویدن در فضای نوجوانی و بوی بهار و هزاران هزار گل بابونه،فصل بهار بود و دلهره ی نوجوانی و بوی چمن تازه،دویدن از روی قله به سمت دامنه ی کوه،گذشتن از تپه ها با گذاشتن روی قارچ های تازه،عبور از کنار لانه ی کبک ها،تیهوها،گنجشک ها و بلبل ها ،دویدن به سمت رودخانه پرشهایی که بیشتر پرواز بود از روی تخته سنگ ها،احساس کردن عبور باد از کنار شقیقه ها،دویدن،دویدن به سمت خروش رودخانه،دویدن به سمت نیزارها،دویدن به سمت دلهره ی عشق. "جیژوان" آنجا بود،زنی

Example 5

برای لحظاتی در زیرفشار موج ها حبس می کشیدم و با تمام ماهیچه های ام مقاومت می کردم و بعد که سرم به سطح آب می رسید دیوانه وار قایق موتوری را جستجو می کردم. و چهره ای شگفت،از آن سوی دریچه به من گفت" حق باکسی ست که می بیند،من مثل حس گمشدگی،وحشت آورم،اما خدای من آیا چگونه می شود از من ترسید؟ من،من که هیچگاه جز بادبادکی سبک و ولگرد بر پشت بام های مه آلود آسمان چیزی نبوده ام...

FIGURE 1.2 Original text messages in Persian prose appear in consecutive order to match the translations into English poetry: Example 1-5. The final passage (Example 5) is Persian poetry and was translated into the same genre.

Appendix

The following text is a 2019 interview with me published in *The Pin*, an online discussion platform created by Lucille Cutting and Nkechi Anele dedicated to addressing race, culture and identity in an Australian context. The interview was conducted by Cutting during a time when I was travelling to different cities to participate in festivals, events and activities (many involving Boochani via video link from Manus Prison) and was interviewed regularly. This interview for *The Pin* was published in June leading up to Melbourne's Emerging Writers' Festival, which Cutting was collaborating with at the time: the two events I was involved in were 'The Art of Translation' and 'Work in Progress: Telling Other People's Stories'. The interview is no longer available online and I express thanks to Cutting for providing me with the text and permission to publish here.

Omid Tofighian: Being Australian…it all comes down to chance

It's difficult to describe Dr Omid Tofighian as a translator without feeling like you're missing a big part of the picture. In 2018 stateless refugee and journalist Behrouz Boochani released *No Friend but the Mountains: Writing From Manus Prison*, a literary tour de force and first-hand account of five years in exile.

Tofighian's role in this? To translate the now 416 page book chapter by chapter from WhatsApp text messages and PDFs sent by Boochani from Manus Island on a smuggled mobile phone. A task that called upon Tofighian's areas of academic research, interest and own cultural background.

It took a team to complete the project and involved much more than translating from Farsi to English. It was a project that required a shared vision and a fearless approach to storytelling.

No Friend but the Mountains: Writing From Manus Prison has since won the Victorian Premier's Literary Award Victorian Prize for Literature 2019.

Meet Omid Tofighian.

Omid Tofighian. I grew up interpreting for my parents from a very early age. I never realised this was a skill that could develop into other skills. I owe a lot of my ability to interpret and translate to the role and responsibility I had growing up.

So much of what I have been doing with Behrouz Boochani began many years before I met him, you could even say it goes all the way back to before I was born. Both of my parents are lovers of storytelling, and pretty much all of my life growing up I listened to stories from their experience in Iran; their experience of moving to the United States, and then moving to Australia and trying to find our way here. Iranians of all backgrounds, all ethnic groups, and all social, cultural and religious backgrounds are really proud of a multiple range of poetic traditions, so poetry was also an important part of my life growing up. I was hearing stories not only of my parents experiences, but going back even further and right back into the mythological past. I think that in combination with my area of research and my interests I was in a good place to interact with Behrouz and understand what he was trying to say.

The Pin. **When you received the first of many PDF or Whatsapp messages of the book did you feel your skill sets combining as you read through and translated it?**

OT. Right at the very beginning, maybe two or three pages in, I knew it was going to be a masterpiece. I was already sensing all of these multiple layers and different dimensions to the text and felt not only the connection that Behrouz has to all of the things I am familiar with and passionate about in terms of my own research and background, but there were also elements I was not familiar with. I realised I would have to do a lot more research myself to be able to become familiar with it and to be able to get it right if I were to translate it.

I'd been translating his journalism for over six months before beginning the book project so to some extent I had an understanding of his writing style and his literary identity, but I don't think any of that really prepared me for what I was reading when I got the first chapter.

Yes because it seems like you were dealing with translating from Farsi, which has a very different structure to English, and a different style to pieces written for the *Guardian* **or the** *Saturday Paper*. **How did you adjust your mindset from a journalistic approach to a more creative yet still journalistic one?**

OT. Because so much of the work that I do with Behrouz is unpredictable and in reaction to something really distressing or horrifying we don't have a lot of planning time or know what to expect. So much of the work we do is us trying to respond in the best way we can. We don't have time to think about it much, although we can reflect on it afterwards and we often do at length. When I moved from journalism into the book, I just immersed myself and waited for the surprises. I knew how important this book would be historically and politically and I didn't want to lose that opportunity even though I was anxious about taking on such a huge project and having not being trained as a translator, but once I got into it I just developed a rhythm.

We had a lot of conversations where Behrouz would explain a lot of the philosophical ideas and his own cultural history and heritage. I was in constant consultation with Behrouz throughout the process so I could ask him things and would even make suggestions. We would even debate a couple of features every now and then. There were also two people involved, Moones Mansoubi who was his first translator and who I met with every week or fortnight and Sajad Kabgani who was a researcher from Iran specialising in education and literature. I would meet with him sometimes as well.

It was a shared philosophical activity, there was a series of people in Australia, in Iran, and even on Manus Island in conversation with each other, all committed and dedicated to this one project. All with the same kind of intention and way of thinking. Maybe you could even say the same stream of consciousness.

You did not meet Behrouz until you were 80% of the way into completing the book. How important was this meeting to finishing it? Was it an important part of telling his story?

OT. Absolutely critical. It was absolutely important that I meet Behrouz just so that I could first of all thank him, congratulate him, and show my support in person. I felt that was something I could do face-to-face that I could never do over WhatsApp. Sitting down and talking to him on a more intimate level was important because all of our conversations were until then just over voice text and through WhatsApp so we could never really talk in real time.

I also felt that at least one full read through the chapters and being 100% sure was vital. I knew from the first few pages that it was going to be one of the most important political cultural documents for decades to come so I wanted to get everything right. But more importantly, the book would provide a platform and create new networks that would enable Behrouz to become even more empowered and give him a sense of liberation. This book going out into the world is a form of freedom for him as well.

Ultimately you've taken a story that Behrouz has written in Farsi and translated it into English, and the translation will be read many times more than the Farsi version. How do you navigate being a platform to empowerment and the feeling that you're changing the original story in some way?

OT. That's an interesting point and gives me a bit more of an opportunity to talk about the collaborative process. It was a consultative process that involved deep analysis of what Behrouz had written. There were conversations we had that influenced my translating that would also influence his writing style and the direction of some of the stories. I don't think the translation would have been able to come out the way it did without Behrouz's own input.

The translation has taken on a character of its own, and has its own identity as well. There's something really unique in the English version that has gone beyond the Farsi original, but then again there are things about the Farsi original that the English translation will never be able to embody. Thinking about it as a translation I think is slightly inaccurate or insufficient in any conventional sense. It's something in between a translation and a whole new creative enterprise. I think this is what is special about the translation. Creatively it really reflects so much of the disrupted fragmented purgatory state that the writer is in himself and the situation he's talking about. It wears so much of that in the way it's written. Its style, content, structure and mode of production as well.

You've never worked as a translator before working with Behrouz, what have you learnt from the experience?

OT. It's really difficult even now to think of myself as a translator. When someone introduces me as one it feels kind of awkward. There were so many different skill sets I had to draw on in order to translate this book. I talk about literary experimentation in the translators notes of the book. I realised I had to experiment so much in the translation. Behrouz's situation, identity, the tropes he draws upon, the narrative frameworks, and diction are so unique and mix together in unprecedented ways. That experimentation and being open to new possibilities – absolute or radical openness – I think was one of the most important things. Not just for working on this project but for what I plan to do in future.

It would have been good if I had come trained as a translator but the fact that I didn't helped me even more.

It removed constraints...

OT. Yeah, it just catapulted me into these new phases or landscapes of literary, philosophical and artistic thinking.

There's something special about the book, the style, the character to Behrouz's writing. I don't want to call it a genre, but there's a particular kind of attitude in the book that I refer to it as horrific surrealism and this surrealism is very close to many Kurdish writers in different parts of Kurdistan – whether it's Syria, Turkey, Iran or Iraq. Kurdish creatives and Kurdish thinkers have this particular surrealist way of seeing the world and representing it, but there's also the horrific as well because of the political situation. Behrouz uses this really well to show the absurdity of the whole situation. It's represented in this fragmented and disrupted identity of the situation, there's all of these different stories and experiences and he has tried to put them into a whole and they never fit.

If you look at Behrouz's relationship with me, Behrouz is stuck in this disgusting place that has been created by a country that prides itself on human rights and on an island that is part of its former colony so already we are starting to get some sense, some feel for the absurdity or the surreal nature of it. He is communicating with me through WhatsApp and sending me his work and I'm translating it but I'm crossing borders at will and have very few problems when it comes to crossing borders. I was in Sydney, Cairo and Manus Island while I was translating. I was answering or asking him questions through WhatsApp text while I was preparing for my classes or I was at a coffee shop having an espresso. He'd send me a text message that he wanted to tweet something and I'd be there having breakfast and trying to translate something about an attempted suicide. The whole thing is just remarkably ironic, it's so surreal, it's disgustingly absurd and it shows something about the gross inequalities that are part of this globalised modern world.

Has it made you reflect upon your own background and cultural heritage?

OT. Absolutely. There's so much I could draw upon thinking about my own heritage and my own experiences of this place and exile but my family and I left at a time when certain things didn't work for us. We didn't manage to come to Australia immediately but did when things didn't work out for us in the United States.

Globalisation, the shifts in geopolitics, attitudes, different kinds of policy decisions, and certain people in power in some way ended up working for my family and they haven't worked for Behrouz. This all really comes down to chance, so much of this comes down to luck. That just again shows us the horrific, ever surreal nature of this whole enterprise, this whole collaboration, this whole project.

The Pin. Do you think you'll ever be able to read back passages and not be able to relate them to where you were?

Omid Tofighian. Different things happen every time I read the book. Sometimes I recall those times, sometimes I just go into the book itself and get lost. Sometimes I think about what's happening now or another conversation Behrouz and I had. This is important, this disruption and fragmentation. It's so important to understanding Behrouz's interpretation and critique, what he produces and even our relationship. I think that's the best way to describe it. Everything is so unpredictable. Everything is so shattered.

Note

1 Another important point of contrast that highlights the radically changing nature of border politics is that US authorities in Tehran before the revolution issued our US visas within 30 minutes. My mother visited the US embassy in Tehran

alone; she did not even bring her children along when acquiring the five-year tourist visas for all of us. When my father's applied earlier on the process was just as easy.

Bibliography

ABC (2014) 'Iranian-Indigenous Hip Hop Duo', *ABC Radio National, RN Drive*. www.abc.net.au/listen/programs/radionational-drive/iranian-indigenous-hip-hop-duo/5707016

Adamson, P. (2016) *Philosophy in the Islamic World: a history of philosophy without any gaps, volume 3*. Oxford: Oxford University Press.

Baker, M. (ed) (2016) *Translating Dissent: voices from and with the Egyptian revolution*. New York: Routledge.Oxon: Routledge.

Barseghian, A. (2020) 'che gooneh behrouz boochani ketab-e khod ra dar noskheh-ye nashr-e cheshmeh ((momayezi)) va ((akhteh)) kard', *hadeaghal kalanshahr*: metropolatleast.ir. https://tinyurl.com/n4kae54x

Benjamin, W. (1996) 'The Task of the Translator', in Bullock, M. and Jennings, M. W. (eds), *Walter Benjamin: selected writings*, Vol. 1., translated by Zohn, H. Cambridge and London: Belknap Press, pp. 253–263.

Bennett, S. and Tofighian, O. (2020) 'Translation as Freedom, experimentation and sharing: Omid Tofighian on translating *no Friend but the Mountains*', *Biography* 43(4): pp. 748–754. https://doi.org/10.1353/bio.2020.0076

Bielsa, E. (2023) *A translational sociology: interdisciplinary perspectives on politics and society*. London: Routledge.

Boochani, B. (2018) *No Friend but the Mountains: Writing from Manus Prison*. Translated by Tofighian, O. Sydney: Picador-Pan Macmillan.

Boochani, B. (2020) *hich doosti be joz kouhestan*. Tehran: Nashr-e Cheshmeh. www.cheshmeh.ir/Book/4565/16059/___%20_____%20__%20__%20_____

El Tarzi, S. (2016) 'Ethical Reflections on Activist Film-Making and Activist Subtitling', in Baker, M. (ed), *Translating Dissent: voices from and with the Egyptian revolution*, translated by Moger, R. Oxon: Routledge, pp. 88–96.

El-Tamami, W. (2016) 'A Wish Not to Betray: Some Thoughts on Writing and Translation Revolution', in Baker, M. (ed), *Translating Dissent: voices from and with the Egyptian revolution*. Oxon: Routledge, pp. 21–32.

Elsadda, H. (2016) 'An Archive of Hope: Translating Memories of Revolution', in Baker, M. (ed), *Translating Dissent: voices from and with the Egyptian revolution*. Oxon: Routledge, pp. 148–160.

Gaber, S. (2016) 'What Word is This Place?: Translating Urban Social Justice and Governance', in Baker, M. (ed), *Translating Dissent: voices from and with the Egyptian revolution*. Oxon: Routledge, pp. 97–106.

Grossman, E. (2010) *Why translation matters*. New Haven: Yale University Press.

Kebsi, J. (2024) 'A Decolonial Translation: Omid Tofighian's Collaborative Approach in Behrouz Boochani's No Friend but the Mountains', *Nawaat*. www.nawaat.org/2024/06/18/decolonizing-translation-omid-tofighians-collaborative-approach-in-behrouz-boochanis-no-friend-but-the-mountains/

Kebsi, J. (In press) 'The challenges of translating world prison literature: Omid Tofighian's contribution to *No Friend but the Mountains*', *Antipodes: A Global*

Journal of Australian/New Zealand Literature. https://researchers.mq.edu.au/en/publications/the-challenges-of-translating-world-prison-literature-omid-tofigh

Khalili, S. and Stavans, I. (Spring 2019) 'A Lover alone in Prison: a conversation between Ilan Stavans and Sara Khalili', *Michigan Quarterly Review* 57(6). www.sites.lsa.umich.edu/mqr/2019/04/a-lover-alone-in-prison-a-conversation-between-ilan-stavans-and-sara-khalili/

Mbuvi, A. M. (2023) *African Biblical studies: unmasking embedded racism and colonialism in Biblical studies.* London: T&T Clark.

Missaghi, P. (2018) 'Translating Iranian Fiction: An Interview with Sara Khalili', *Asymptote*. www.asymptotejournal.com/blog/2018/08/27/translating-iranian-fiction-an-interview-with-sara-khalili/

Mortada, L. (2016) 'Translation and Solidarity in Words of Women from the Egyptian Revolution', in Baker, M. (ed), *Translating Dissent: voices from and with the Egyptian revolution*. Oxon: Routledge, pp. 125–136.

Nida, E. (1964) *Toward a science of translating: with special reference to principles and procedures involved in Bible translating.* Leiden: E. J. Brill.

Ramakrishna, S. (2000) 'Cultural Transmission Through Translation: An Indian perspective', in Sherry Simon and Paul St-Pierre (eds.), *Changing the terms: translating in the postcolonial era*. Ottawa: University of Ottawa Press, pp. 87–100.

Rizk, P. and Baker, M. (2016) 'Interview with Philip Rizk', in Baker, M. (ed), *Translating Dissent: voices from and with the Egyptian revolution.* Oxon: Routledge, pp. 225–237.

Selim, S. (2016) 'Text and context: translating in a state of emergency', in Baker, M. (ed), *Translating Dissent: voices from and with the Egyptian revolution*. Oxon: Routledge, pp. 77–87.

Simon, S. (2000) 'Introduction', in Sherry Simon and Paul St-Pierre (eds.), *Changing the terms: translating in the postcolonial era.* Ottawa: University of Ottawa Press, pp. 9–30.

Tofighian, O. (2011) 'Iranians continue to be persecuted after fleeing Iran: Australia's human rights dilemma', *Literature & Aesthetics* 21 – *Fear+Hope*: pp. 20–22.

Tofighian, O. (2011a) 'Prolonged liminality and comparative examples of rioting "down under"', *Literature & Aesthetics* 21 – *Fear+Hope*: pp. 97–103.

Tofighian, O. (2014) 'Aboriginal Hip-Hop Meets Iranian Diaspora in a Cross-Border Rap', *The Conversation.* www.theconversation.com/aboriginal-hip-hop-meets-iranian-diaspora-in-a-cross-border-rap-29159

Tofighian, O. (2016) *Myth and philosophy in Platonic Dialogues*. London: Palgrave Macmillan.

Tofighian, O. (2018) 'Translator's Tale: A Window to the Mountains', in Boochani, B. (ed), *No Friend but the Mountains: Writing from Manus Prison*, translated by Tofighian, O. Sydney: Picador-Pan Macmillan, pp. xi–xxxiv.

Tofighian, O. (2020) 'Introducing Manus Prison theory: knowing border violence', *Globalizations* 17(7): pp. 1138–1156. https://doi.org/10.1080/14747731.2020.1713547

Tofighian, O. (2022) 'On representing extreme experiences in writing and translation: Omid Tofighian on translating the Manus Prison narratives', *Humanities* 11(6): p. 141. https://doi.org/10.3390/h11060141

Tymoczko, M. (2014 [2007]) *Enlarging translation, empowering translators*. London: Routledge.
Walkowitz, R. (2015) *Born translated: the contemporary novel in an age of world literature*. New York Chichester, West Sussex: Columbia University Press.
Wolfson, T. and Funke, P. N. (2016) 'The Contemporary Epoch of Struggle: Anti-Austerity Protests, the Arab Uprisings and Occupy Wall Street', in Baker, M. (ed), *Translating Dissent: voices from and with the Egyptian revolution*. Oxon: Routledge, pp. 60–73.
Zhang, D. (2016) 'Always Already Translated', *Public Books*. www.publicbooks.org/always-already-translated/

2
TRANSLATION AS PUBLIC PHILOSOPHY

Creating new knowledges

Creative resistance from inside the prison camps: the role of collaborators and translators

I use the term creative resistance to describe the collaborative activism I have engaged in with people targeted by the border-industrial complex. Maria Tymoczko questions the metaphorical significance of the term 'resistance' as a mode of activism (she prefers the term 'engagement'), critiquing the use of the term in the translation scholarship of Lawrence Venuti (Tymoczko, 2014 [2007], p. 210). I understand and acknowledge the problems she highlights in her critique concerning agency and the vague contexts in which the term is used; however, my use of 'creative resistance' is always applied within the parameters of specific examples of border violence and attempts to foreground the collaborative and experimental nature of the collective activism. Therefore, in the context of the collaborative and experimental artistic, intellectual and political projects I discuss, I feel it is appropriate to interpret translation and writing as unique forms of creative resistance.

The use of translation, however, as a descriptor for the collective work I have been involved in can be misleading since for most people the concept conjures up images of a basic mechanical process of language transfer or a search for language equivalence (Bielsa, 2023, p. 52). The multifaceted dimensions associated with my activism represent something extremely different. Translation coincides and is interlinked with so many other vital activities that mutually reinforce and blend into one other. The effort and skillset involved in producing a translation can be described through numerous narrative threads within a multidimensional and multilayered story – the use of language skills is only one part of the equation.

Every one of my translation projects has been different – including each translation task for the same person regardless of how similar the separate examples of writing. This is because of the diverse, compounded and fluid conditions imposed by the border-industrial complex. Considering the nuances associated with different contexts is important because every individual and every example of their writing manifest stages consisting of accumulating moments of border violence. One way to interpret the vastly different instances of translation plan, process and product under the one category of translation is through Tymoczko's notion of translation as a cluster concept (pp. 83–90). Drawing on the philosophy of Wittgenstein, she argues that we should move beyond looking for necessary and sufficient conditions to categorise translation and instead perceive (look for) diverse examples of translation through family resemblances (she draws on Wittgenstein's study of games). This approach is essential for understanding a concept that represents significantly different instances across cultures and time. It is *practice* and *usage* that determine membership within a cluster category rather than logic. This view renders an understanding of translation plan, process and product available only to empirical analysis rather than *a priori* stipulation or definition. Therefore, the extremely different and unique translation projects I am describing in this book – which include intralingual, interlingual and intersemiotic translation – are analysed as interdependent with political practices; their use in activist strategies and tactics; personal, stylistic and structural features; cultural nuances; and the mechanics associated with specific periods of border violence. Therefore, I have started using the term 'edited translation' as an attempt to reflect a sense of this complexity, fluidity and co-creation – my reference to editing here must not be reduced to practices such as copy editing, proofreading, proof editing, or structural editing; many edited translation projects also go beyond practices such as developmental editing and line and sentence-level editing. When addressing the complexities associated with each individual edited translation or writing project I explain how and why it was different and what the general notion of edited translation means in each instance.

My edited translation projects also coincide with a range of scholarly activities related to border violence and other forms of structural discrimination and oppression. While engaged in translation and editing, I have also been committed to my own multi-genre forms of writing and simultaneously supporting the creation of works of art (often involving intersemiotic translation). There are many examples of activism, scholarship, art and translation working together in remarkably productive and transformative ways. In relation to texts, the translation and editing of different genres (many of the texts I refer to as anti-genre) function in complex and interdependent relationships with mentoring and advising, co-writing, rewriting, experimental revision, and other forms of politically focused and research-inspired creative collaboration. This diverse work has been aimed at exposing the systematic torture designed and conducted within Australia's detention industry and the wider border-industrial complex.

One important example that reflects the intersection of community engagement, critical and cultural border studies research, philosophy and teaching is my contribution to the making (through consultation and creating subtitles), promotion (particularly at film festivals), interpretation and study (through scholarship and media) of an important film about Australian border violence. In the context of teaching and talks about the indefinite offshore imprisonment of refugees and the creative resistance from inside detention centres, I regularly use the film *Chauka, Please Tell Us the Time* by Behrouz Boochani and Arash Kamali Sarvestani (2017; the film includes my translated subtitles). My collaboration in this film and relationship with the filmmakers resulted in co-editing a special issue of *Alphaville: Journal of Film and Screen Media* on refugee filmmaking (2019). Within this volume I curated a special dossier dedicated to the film and its socio-political and cultural-artistic importance (I mention this special issue and the other editors as an upcoming project in my 2019 interview with SBS Persian, see appendix 1 following Chapter 3). In addition to my own article about the film in the main section of the issue – which draws on theories such as accented cinema, Bakhtin's notion of the chronotope, and epistemic injustice (Tofighian, 2019a) – the dossier features diverse studies about the project, including my edited translation of articles by each of the filmmakers (and I published a photo essay about the film in the dossier [Tofighian, 2019b] which also includes contributions by Galbraith [2019], Elphick [2019], and my introduction to the dossier [Tofighian, 2019c]). The contribution by Boochani (2019) was written via WhatsApp text messaging while he was still incarcerated in offshore immigration detention, and Kamali Sarvestani (2020) submitted his contribution to me for translation and editing by reading his handwritten draft paper and sending via voice texts from the Netherlands. In many ways, the mode of production for the writing, translation and editing of the journal articles reflects and reinforces the critical and cultural border studies themes and topics addressed in the content and through the lived experiences. The film itself, our participation at numerous film festivals to discuss the film, and our research and media contributions about the film, all contribute to a unique knowledge ecosystem that has benefited students, scholars, activists and the general public. In similar ways, I am now collaborating on projects dedicated to critical and cultural border studies with other filmmakers and producers. Notable examples include journalist, architect, artist and activist Elahe Zivardar (originally from Iran and now based in the US) who was incarcerated in Nauru for six years and is making a film based on her never-before-seen archive of footage/images/interviews/art/documents from the detention centre (upcoming film titled *Architect*), and an exhibition at the

UTS Data Arena (*Weapons of Slow Destruction,* developed with the UTS Data Arena team and co-curated by Zivardar and myself). Zivardar created a 3D interactive model of the detention centre (and a short video tour of the 3D model) which features in both her upcoming film and the exhibition. She has also created a series of paintings called *Border-Industrial Complex* (see Zivardar and Tofighian, 2021; Tofighian, Boochani, Mira and Zivardar, 2022; Tofighian and Zivardar, 2024; Ramrath, 2024; Zivardar and Tofighian, forthcoming; for discussion regarding the significance of her archive in relation to other earlier refugee archives from Nauru see Whitlock, 2024).

When I began collaborating with people in immigration detention, we realised early in our work that the language and format of journalism are insufficient and potentially misleading when it comes to communicating the brutal realities of indefinite detention. This is especially the case in relation to the psychological, emotional and cultural dimensions of systematic torture; the colonial dimensions of border violence; the interlocking nature of the oppressive structures; and the connections between immigration detention centres and Australian society (and further beyond through the global border-industrial complex).

One of the articles I translated and edited for Erfan Dana (aka Shams Hussaini), a refugee from Afghanistan who was held in Australian-funded detention centres in Indonesia, reflects the complexity and pervasiveness of the structural oppression that refugees face. The reciprocal relationship between his message and my edited translation approach is represented in many arguments throughout the piece and emphasised in my decisions regarding word choice, phrasing and format (converting the source text into the appropriate format for the target text was part of the editing process conducted while translating).

> At the moment Indonesia has approximately 14,000 refugees and asylum seekers from many different countries. In the last few years the number has increased rapidly, reaching the highest figures to date. This is due to factors such as Australia blocking entry by sea, and that countries that have traditionally welcomed refugees have reduced their settlement quotas regarding refugees from Indonesia.
>
> Indonesia has never been a country known for welcoming refugees; it is not a signatory to the UN Refugee Convention. However, the location functions as a transit route for refugees. At this point in time, this transit country has been treating refugees with resentment. Refugee claims receive little attention and processing their dossiers is slow. In addition to the oppressive feeling of resentment, refugees also experience additional strain from Indonesian institutions set up to deal with immigration issues…
>
> But beyond all these issues, there is a broader concern that is extremely important and receives little attention. That issue is the incapacity and

inability of the United Nations High Commissioner for Refugees (UNHCR) and IOM to manage the situation....

In reality, both of these organisations are powerless and have huge problems trying to manage the situation.

These organisational regimes are in the midst of an extremely important and pivotal period, one may interpret it as a 'management crisis.' This crisis indicates the difficulties caused by the increasing numbers of refugees that is unprecedented in Indonesia. If they were able to implement a reasonable, logical and calculated approach they could resolve this crisis. However, these two organisations have not yet admitted this is a critical situation.

In reality, both organisations have only implemented a system of surveillance in their management program, and for this reason the managers approach the predicament of the refugees without any urgency.

The role of managers here, in fact, seems to be to actually disobey the objectives of the institution or organisation that they are employed by. They do not fulfil their duties, and even when they do act responsibly it is more in terms of practicing formalities – looking after refugees is all about enacting a performance.

At the same time, these two organisations do not actually supervise the actions and behaviour of their own employees, most of whom are Indonesian citizens. Corruption is pervasive and increasing regardless of attempts to stop it.

And these two organisations are not held accountable in the international scene moderated by the United Nations. Complaints filed by refugees are not attended to properly. And whenever anyone files a complaint they just receive a cold and indifferent response, they tell refugees: 'No one forced to you to come here.'

(Dana, 2018, pp. 28–29)

Like a number of other people I have worked with over the years, Dana already had a strong command of English when we began working together and was regularly writing in Persian and English (the passage above was originally written in Persian). In situations involving multilingual people who produce writing in English, our working relationships open up fascinating new possibilities that complicate traditional and common definitions of translation. In these instances, when we approach written and artistic works we first engage in detailed analysis and planning in Persian/Farsi even though the writing is produced in English. In some cases rough drafts are already completed, and other times texts are still in the process of being written or in the planning phase when we begin collaborating. In all practices, however, conversations occur in Persian usually using WhatsApp communication technology (in some random instances we use Zoom video meetings).

I incorporate some of the results from these discussions by translating them into English and interweaving them into the English drafts that have already been written or are being prepared to submit later. There have also been instances where another language has been involved and, therefore, a third individual facilitates by interpreting and translating when necessary. Whether translation, editing, rewriting or co-writing, the different practices are conducted simultaneously. At times additions and changes are sent to me via WhatsApp voice text in Persian. For some co-authored projects I combined my own writing with 1) examples of writing from the collaborator/s involved; 2) examples of speech from videos or recordings; 3) comments conveyed to me over WhatsApp text and voice messages; and 4) fragments from other places, to construct the piece.

I translated an article by Boochani about the fathers imprisoned with him in offshore detention for which he interviewed a multilingual man from Sudan in English (with some Arabic-Persian-English interpreting assistance by a friend also held in Manus Prison). This interview was transcribed by Boochani in Persian as he wrote the piece for me to then translate and edit into English. In this article he also describes the inability of journalism to portray the plight of people indefinitely detained in Manus Prison. When translating this piece I aim to reinforce the meaning of his arguments through literary techniques, word choice and format while conveying something of the paradoxical qualities of the intersectional violence.

> Many people try to construct an accurate picture of the situation for refugees on Manus Island and Nauru using statistics: such as "five years in detention" or "2,000 individuals". I must say that applying this statistical approach cannot penetrate the depth of the issue.
>
> The central concern is the opportunity to live life well. Only through a profound engagement with the lived experiences of refugees can one realise the extent of the human disaster, only by listening to the life stories of the prisoners can one understand the torture they have had to endure.
>
> The core problem is that one cannot arrive at an accurate picture of the lives of these men by searching between the layers upon layers of newspapers, or within the arguments made by politicians and human rights activists. Perhaps this is the reason that until now Australian politicians have avoided coming to this island, perhaps this is the reason why they do not want to see these men up close. Perhaps this is the reason why they do not want to hear their life stories. They are afraid to look into the eyes of these refugees.
>
> (Boochani, 2018; republished in Boochani, 2023, p. 144)

As we all worked together as collaborators our realisation and analytical perspectives regarding the extent of the structural problems throughout different sectors (the border regime, media, UN, general public, and more) expanded, as well as the rationale we developed to explain it. We became more creative as we continued to collaborate and develop the works in more comprehensive and radical ways. These insights were shared by all the people I have worked with or interacted with in different capacities; the innumerable, absurd and deleterious experiences of border violence directed us even more towards forms of creative resistance such as literature, art and film (Boochani, 2017, p. 20; reprinted in Boochani, 2023, p. 69).

There are numerous reasons that justify this logic. Many of them have to do with the organizational networks supporting and disseminating journalism. We realised that the structure of the media, organisations and individual actors often do not share our vision or are limited in the extent to which they can help. A radical intervention was necessary to make significant changes that would challenge and transform the many existing silencing strategies and enable new voices and styles from within the carceral sites to contribute meaningfully to the discourse and engage with major actors. In many cases individuals in the media lacked the willingness to challenge and change the system the way we were envisioning and practicing. Essentially, they could not – and often did not want to – change the way information was reported and framed. Mona Baker's collection of essays about translation during the Egyptian revolution contains contributions that reinforce the critique of these structural factors in addition to other themes and topics related to translation in extreme circumstances: issues pertaining to the translation of lived experience; aesthetic interventions; the connection between the local and the global; the role of subtitling, translating new concepts; constructing narratives through selective translation; perspectives on 'profession' and 'objectivity' while translating in a state of emergency; and more (Baker, 2016, p. 14; see El-Tamami, 2016; Wolfson and Funke, 2016; Selim, 2016; El Tarzi, 2016; Gaber, 2016; Mortada, 2016; Elsadda, 2016; Rizk and Baker, 2016).

We were motivated to persevere despite these obstacles because we believed that so many things could be achieved with the right approaches and when the right opportunities arise. We imagined new and creative forms of transformation, but we realised that these changes would not materialise immediately, or maybe even within the near future. Building on approaches to translation by Venuti and Berman, which identify the violence associated with replacing linguistic and cultural differences within a foreign text and the dangers of ethnocentric translations that erase the foreignness of the original, Bielsa warns against demands of intelligibility to suit the target audience. She asks: "are we really willing to be confronted with opaque translations that offer not a presumably transparent access to otherness (to an other who can readily be recognised and assimilated into our cultural patterns) but rather make visible the difficulty of understanding others in their strangeness?" (Bielsa, 2023, pp. 69–70).

This observation reminds me of one of my collaborations with Mohamed Adam, a former refugee from Sudan who was incarcerated in Manus Island. During the several years we worked together he published the first chapter of his autobiography in a special issue of the journal *Southerly*, which I co-edited. The piece is titled "The Autobiography of Mohamed Adam" (Chapter One) (translated from Arabic by Noman Ahmed Ashraf) and the journal special issue is called *Writing Through Fences: Archipelago of Letters*, edited by me, Janet Galbraith, Hani Abdile, and Behrouz Boochani (see Figure 2.1). In his contribution Adam, who was born in a refugee camp in Darfur, reflects on his life in Sudan with a beautiful sense of strangeness. One of his memories describes playing with his siblings and friends as a child and he recollects the smells, colours, stories, and more. He also talks about the *taste of hair*. Upon reading this I questioned it, I wondered: Is that correct? An editor I was working with asked to change it to 'taste of air', but I had a feeling it was meant to be 'taste of hair'. I confirmed this with both Mohamed and the translator (I was reading a translation from Arabic by Noman Ahmed Ashraf – a former student of the American University in Cairo, originally from Yemen and now based in the US after being accepted as a refugee). "Indeed, our lives were beautiful before the war. Life was something full of joy and fun … the love of colors, the taste of hair, the beautiful stories and the wonderful legends." (Adam, 2021, p. 124) His experiences growing up with his siblings and his friends were intimate in special ways and this was manifested in his memories about the taste of hair.

In another passage he describes the dangerous boat journey to Australia from Indonesia by drawing on folktales and childhood stories to evoke the same sense of foreignness. An element that the translator and I (as editor) preserved and tried to emphasise.

> It was nothing like what we had thought, the only thing we heard was that we will get what we asked for later. We proceeded with caution and cruised through the whole day and night. Everyone was asking questions while waves hit us like a storm and large fish hovered around the boat. A pod of dolphins swam like the swarms of a revolution. I stared at the sea, it vomited everything it had. All the sea snails came to the surface. We did not know whether it was the joy of our arrival or a reckoning by an enemy who had insulted the sea. We raised our white flags to tell them that we were just passing by. I knew that there were sea shells among the sea snails; and I have known them since a very long time ago, when I used to talk to them as a child. The sea shells could talk to the sea snails in the ocean telling them that we were not worshippers of war and fire. We are travelers who were visited by displeasure and resistance; full silence and

complete tranquility prevailed in all. Everyone hoped for good and asked themselves whether they were among the dead or among the survivors.
(Adam, 2021, p. 128)

I interpret these and similar elements as introducing alternative ways of knowing, possibilities for engaging with new knowledges; epistemic gateways that have the potential to empower by forming rich and equitable imaginaries in which refugees are perceived as knowledge producers, creatives and authorities.

It has always been a priority to enable certain critical perspectives and to hear and understand the situation from people inside indefinite detention (or those recently released). The writing and other forms of resistance by refugees, and collaborations involving refugees in equitable ways, represent original and distinct markers of their positionality. These projects help expose the nuanced injustices within pervasive structures of intersectional violence. Moving beyond traditional and established modes and formats, in our work we aim to express a different creative imagination and a radical moral imagination – we realise how necessary it is to penetrate and transform

FIGURE 2.1 Special issue of *Southerly* 79(2) *Writing Through Fences: Archipelago of Letters*, Galbraith, J., Abdile, H., Tofighian, O. and Boochani, B (eds). Cover art: 'Concealed Borders' by Elahe Zivardar.

the damaging narratives underlying and driving border politics by employing new languages of resistance. We understand that this requires the formation of unique platforms, spaces, collaborations and counter-discourses dedicated to involving imprisoned writers and artists in meaningful ways. Amplifying the voices of the displaced, exiled and incarcerated involves a strategy that ensures they are heard, understood and supported.

Damaging narratives, damaging tropes/new narratives, new languages

As imprisoned non-citizens, refugees targeted by border regimes experience many forms of suppression, and one of the first and most violent obstacles they encounter is the manipulation of language as a bordering technology. In this sense, language operates in conjunction with other mechanisms of control, exclusion and punishment. Considering how language is used for the purposes of bordering, the media and literary landscape can be reimagined as a hostile environment. In many instances, mainstream media and literary actors and organisations lack the sufficient experience, vision and ability to support people who are suffering, or who have suffered, in detention. Considering the intricacies of positionality and the intellectual and cultural histories carried by incarcerated refugees, the contributions by people with lived experience of indefinite detention can help us arrive at multilayered understandings. Their accounts introduce us to exclusive perspectives which include complex insights into *how* they perceive, critique and act using different modes and frames of reference: linguistic, philosophical, artistic, stylistic, cultural, political, etc. (Tofighian, 2018c, 2019d).

In the reflection essay that accompanies my edited translation of *No Friend but the Mountains* I suggest how the border-industrial complex engulfs all citizens, thus rendering everyone complicit to different degrees – in the introduction to this book I expand on the notion of the pro-refugee/anti-refugee disposition. By employing common tropes that circulate in the media, in literature and the arts, in the discourses associated with liberal humanitarianism, and in political debates, individuals and groups become complicit in the reduction of refugee identities to one-dimensional narratives that distort and erase their experiences and capacities. Based on a deficit/surplus dichotomy that distinguishes non-citizens from citizens, further distinctions and divisions are reinforced and (re)applied to damage and derail the struggle of displaced and exiled peoples, and further promote the superiority associated with citizen privilege. The list of tropes I discuss in the introduction are not exhaustive and in many instances they are combined; to reiterate:

- Caged person – escape to the West
- Desperate supplicant

- Struggling overcomer – the battler
- Tragic and miserable victim
- Broken human being
- Mystic sage – quirky and mysterious, a trickster.

"[E]ach trope has the potential to reduce refugees to essentialist, voyeuristic, patronising and disempowering narratives."

(Tofighian, 2018b, pp. 365–366)

Clearly, there is a widely accepted constellation of selective and reductive terms and stereotypical themes about refugees determined mainly by the state and a range of liberal institutions. They are disseminated by journalists who replicate, reinforce and multiply the power, control and violence characteristic of methods used at the border. The creation of new languages of resistance – which includes collaboratively produced counter-discourses involving people with lived experience of border violence – consists of radical critiques of terminology. Naming is a political and creative act; the creation and designation of terms is embedded within dominant social imaginaries and has epistemic weight, and the repercussions of naming for knowledge creation about border regimes cannot be underestimated (Tofighian, August 2019).

Tymoczko argues that rather than simply transposing linguistic codes translators have the potential to communicate cultural difference; she describes this as a power that can never be replaced by machines. Translators exercise agency when they adjudicate between cultural disparities and asymmetries, and the epistemological problems they can cause. Through the work of translators we benefit from the emergence of new ideas, from expanded possibilities for experiencing other cultures and ways of being, and from richer intellectual encounters (Tymocsko, 2014 [2007], p. 231).

Translators have the potential to challenge injustice in ways unavailable to other activists (however, they also have the power to enact violence in ways that other oppressors are unable to). Successful resistance against the border-industrial complex and the development of transformative social imaginaries begin with the rejection of the borders constructed and empowered by language: the language of oppression, exclusion, control and submission, or kyriocentric language.

By suggesting radical changes to specific areas in biblical studies, Schüssler Fiorenza encourages a new emancipatory paradigm. One of the important shifts that must occur in this new model, she suggests, pertains to biblical language. She argues that the grammar of the bible is androcentric and kyriocentric (lord/master) and that women are always forced to question and analyse whether they are represented and respected when reading and engaging. Many important spiritual and moral teachings, principles and promises centre men, and women are either implicitly or explicitly represented as subordinate. As part of her intersectional feminist critique of the Western andro-kyriocentric language system she indicates that feminist scholars from cultures whose language systems do not reflect the same gender discrimination have the potential to "break the power of biblical male-centred language", and those who have been raised and trained in these different language systems have the potential to introduce new perspectives and expertise to feminist emancipatory translation, thought and theology (Schüssler Fiorenza, 2020, p. 15).

Throughout my work on border violence I have incorporated aspects of Schüssler Fiorenza's work. Her notion of kyriarchy plays a central role in my translations, activism and critique of the border-industrial complex. In this section I will explain my creation and application of the term 'kyriarchal system'. This concept emerged out of the translation process and is heavily influenced by my different research interests including philosophy, religious studies, critical and cultural border studies, coloniality and decoloniality. The kyriarchal system is a term I constructed while I was translating *No Friend but the Mountains* and grappling with Boochani's notion of *system-e hākem*, a concept that brings a place-based, situation-specific, intersectional and decolonial interpretation to the violence within the detention centre and the wider border-industrial complex.

'Kyriarchy' was first introduced in 1992 by radical feminist theologian Schüssler Fiorenza in her work *But She Said: Feminist Practices of Biblical Interpretation* (1992). As I explained in more detail in the introduction, the concept was intended to move beyond patriarchy to describe gender oppression in a way that emphasises interlocking systems of oppression, domination and submission. Schüssler Fiorenza applies an intersectional approach in her radical biblical hermeneutics to illustrate how a range of diverse and violent social systems reinforce each other and mutually increase powers. In addition to gender, she factors in other forms of systemic oppression and control such as race, ethnicity, class, disability, sexuality, colonialism and militarism. It is important to note that Schüssler Fiorenza's analysis has always been in conversation with Black Feminists, Mujeristas, Chicana Feminists, feminist theologians from different parts of Africa, and others.

It helps to understand the kyriarchal system in relation to intersectionality theory and matrix of domination (See Collins' arguments comparing intersectionality with matrix of domination in *Black Feminist Thought*, 2009 [2000]). It involves a series of intersecting and mutually reinforcing structures. It is also important to extend this description by adding that it is bent on domination, oppression and submission. The drive behind this intersectional form of oppression is an insatiable and marauding desire to reproduce, reinforce and expand. Boochani created the Persian term to introduce what he refers to as the 'soul of the system' and describes it in the book metaphorically as a being with agency.

> The health and medical service contracted for the prison is International Health and Medical Services or IHMS. A twisted and convoluted system that takes pleasure in observing sick human beings. When someone falls ill, the doctors and nurses have the perfect opportunity to unleash their power complexes. A prisoner is reduced to a useless piece of meat to be destroyed. Would The Kyriarchal System want it any other way? To see a defenceless piece of meat and then destroy it by subjecting it to a predetermined system, subjecting it to the system until swallowed up by it, subjecting it to the system until what is left is thrown away, back to the country or homeland from which the refugee fled.
> (Boochani, 2018a, p. 303)

> The place was a cockfighting stadium. The only thing on the minds of the prisoners was to damage the organism that is The Kyriarchal System; to inflict a blow on those who had imprisoned them.
> (Boochani, 2018a, p. 342)

- See notes on translation in relation to these passages at the end of this chapter which compare the English translation with the original Persian text messages.

The term helped him understand and analyse his experiences; he drew on his educational, cultural and political background to develop and apply the term while incarcerated in Manus Prison. Boochani's neologism in Persian has roots in the persecution and struggle of Kurds and the socio-economic and cultural environment pertaining to his rural upbringing in Ilam Province (Tofighian, 2018d). When investigating Kurdish history and intellectual culture, folklore and resistance, I discovered more topics and themes that helped me understand the wide-ranging associations with Boochani's Persian term (In particular, the connections I saw between jineology in the work of Abdullah Öcalan and Schüssler Fiorenza's radical feminist hermeneutics; for examples of Öcalan's scholarship see 2015, 2017a, 2017b. Also, consider the Kurdish political slogan *jin, jiyān, āzādi* or Woman, Life, Freedom and its connection to the Kurdish women's movement, Kurdish resistance in Rojava, Öcalan's political philosophy, the Persian translation *zan, zendegi, āzādi* and its recent development and application by protesters from diverse backgrounds across Iran and in diaspora).

As a translation of *system-e hākem*, the notion of the kyriarchal system takes some of Boochani's original elements further by incorporating new layers associated with my experiences and research vision. My plans involved using the theoretical and political aspects of the kyriarchal system for building new philosophical frameworks which would support public philosophy activities and cultural engagement, as well as specialised academic endeavours (this has occurred, for instance, with Manus Prison Theory and Nauru Prison Theory). My aim was to continue expanding on the notion through philosophical engagement with diverse audiences and to imagine ways of incorporating it within various forms of political action. My vision for the kyriarchal system included exchanges with both academics and the general public. This resulted in events, activities and projects that represented different ways of doing philosophy; in particular, I was interested in possibilities for expanding and invigorating the shared philosophical activity.

My translation of Boochani's *system-e hākem* into the broader notion of the kyriarchal system attempts to communicate the extreme situations, personal encounters and struggles of all the refugees I have worked with over the years. The kyriarchal system represents their accounts of prison life, the complex realities of indefinite detention, their analyses and dialogues with others, their life after release, and also how I situate these perspectives within transnational philosophical discourses and cultures of resistance. That is, the kyriarchal system is a term that introduces a multidimensional, relational and dialectical understanding of the neocolonial regime refugees are subjected to. The translation and theorising of the term involved engaging with Boochani's work in combination with my own, also a profound awareness of and interaction with people in other locations around the globe in similar situations. This required communication with the different actors involved in our collaborations, people we have encountered and learned from in the past, and the ongoing resistance from within Australia's carceral-border archipelago.

The confrontation between incarcerated refugees and Australian authorities on the maritime border and in carceral-border sites must be understood as warzones; therefore, the interpretations and thinking that have emerged to challenge border politics are theories of war, and the strategies and tactics to dismantle the border-industrial complex make up a manual for self-defence and resistance against warmongers. From the time of his confinement in Christmas Island to his exile to Manus Island, from the different periods of incarceration in Port Moresby to his escape to Aotearoa New Zealand and struggle to obtain permanent residency, Boochani and I were continuously adding new dimensions to this thinking in collaboration with a small group of people. All through our working relationship the dialogues and strategising shifted with the multifarious dynamics of the situation, and with that the theorising evolved. We became committed to rethinking the nature and meaning of interlocking forms of oppression in more rigorous, interdisciplinary and transdisciplinary ways. Our collaborations also involved finding the most sustainable and effective methods for combating border violence. These elements were key to our joint projects – one of the results being Manus Prison Theory, which is also a way to unite relevant positionalities and approaches with different philosophies of resistance; and then document their development. These principles and practices make up the foundations for unique examples of public philosophy.

It was difficult finding an accurate translation for *system-e hākem*, an original idea with various cross-cultural and interdisciplinary and transdisciplinary roots. After several attempts I felt I had found the perfect translation by introducing a new term in English and creating a new way of thinking about border violence in European languages. Translation can be a decolonial act when it involves a reading that is inspired and infused by decolonial ways of thinking and doing (Kebsi, 2024, and In press; Tofighian, Boochani, Mira and Zivardar, 2021, pp. 126, 128 and 130; Tofighian, 2018a, pp. xxv-xxvi, 2018b, 367 n. 21). Nuances from various critical perspectives characterise my edited translation in ways that illuminate the colonial foundations of the detention industry and the wider border-industrial complex. To make this clear, and emphasise the central role of the kyriarchal system, I had to incorporate some technical terms into the literary work using multiple synonyms and other techniques. In the supplementary essays ('Translator's Tale' [2018a] and 'Translator's Reflections' [2018b]) accompanying *No Friend but the Mountains* I explain the issue of genre and how literary approaches are fused with political commentary and language from different scholarly discourses. In my edited translation I highlight the nature of the prison as a neo-colonial experiment to create a literary translation that exposes this – my purpose was always to make a decolonial intervention.

In many cases I chose academic terminology and concepts for my edited translation to help communicate the co-creation between author and translator, and to represent the mix of influences in the book. Our critical analysis of colonialism drew on our education, research interests and lived experiences. It was important to convey an anti-colonial critique which focuses on histories, philosophies and insights into incarceration (with Boochani and others they also drew on their visceral experiences).

The ideological substrata of the border-industrial complex are constituent parts of the kyriarchal system. Thinking about the situation through kyriarchy helps to describe, expose and attack the ideology and mechanisms governing the prison. As mentioned, it is meant to depict the 'spirit' ruling the detention centre and the border-industrial complex. If the correct term could not be found I was actually considering the possibility of leaving *system-e hākem* untranslated and explaining the meaning and its untranslatability using a footnote. Some vocabulary options available to me for translation were 'oppressive system', 'repressive system', 'dominating system', 'domineering system', 'ruling system', 'controlling system', 'merciless system', 'punitive system', 'tyrannical system', 'system of governmentality' (I use 'governmentality' in other places in the book in relation to applications of the system) or 'sovereign system'. I found these terms to be limited or inaccurate for many reasons. Kyriarchy was the only term that represented the intensification of intersectional forms of violence, its global and systemic nature, its colonial legacy, the physical-psychological-emotional-spiritual nexus of the systematic torture, and the omnipresence of torture and dehuminisation in the detention centres. It also helps explain the multiplicative and multiplying qualities of the interlocking violence. Another example of using experimental and philosophical approaches to translate words or phrases (or in some cases whole passages) relate to the Persian word *dard* which is commonly translated as 'pain'. In *No Friend but the Mountains* Boochani uses this word in many passages, all depicting extremely different situations, dynamics and themes. To translate that one word in Persian with only one word in English (pain) would have limited opportunities to elevate the literary and philosophical meaning and message. Like in many other examples, I explored the creative use of synonym: I translated *dard* differently in different places to convey so many diverse levels and complexities: pain, suffering, anguish, agony, sorrow, torment, hurt, injury, affliction, and more (for an example see the opening poem of Chapter 10; *dard* is almost always translated as 'affliction' throughout this chapter rather than the more commonly translated term 'pain' to help convey a philosophical meditation on pain that I try to communicate through the edited translation).

Subverting language is concomitant with challenging domineering and violent systems, their ideologies, and the underlying narratives. The creation of new terminology, which we produced in collaboration, facilitates resistance and is infused with a multilayered theoretical apparatus. It also has an aesthetic basis. From this framework and foundation emerges a transcultural and decolonial symbolic system (Alimardanian, 2020; Tofighian, August 2019; Boochani, 2017). Describing the need for a multipronged approach that factors in epistemic and symbolic dimensions in addition to the social imaginary pertaining to displaced and exiled peoples, I highlight the importance of structural approaches that address material, narratological and philosophical issues.

> This is why challenging and dismantling border regimes must focus on the *epistemic* conditions that characterize and help shape the material conditions. It is necessary to transform the symbolic aesthetic underlying the social imaginary, particularly in relation to beliefs, attitudes and stereotypes about displaced and exiled peoples. Of course, these elements are reflected in policies and different forms of anti-refugee behavior and systems. And this social imaginary is represented in many examples of racist sentiment. But this social imaginary that I refer to is so pervasive that it also exists within activist communities and in pro-refugee behavior and systems.

Problems associated with knowledge production, narratives, images, and symbols exist among all of us, including people who want to make change and transform the system. Addressing these problems is key for revising practical political strategies. Changing the social imaginary is critical when developing and choosing the right tactics and engaging with and advocating for displaced and exiled peoples. A combination of methods linking material, epistemic, and aesthetic factors is fundamental when thinking through exactly what needs to happen in order to make positive and sustainable transformation. If the political economy of the detention industry and the political and legal machine that governs it is to be disrupted and radically transformed, this must be done in combination with challenging and changing the disempowering and damaging tropes, images and narratives constructed to represent refugees among people with citizen privilege.

Abolishing Australia's border regime requires structural changes in multiple spheres.

(Zivardar and Tofighian, forthcoming, emphasis added for last line)

Within our networks of struggle – the diverse people I have collaborated with inside and outside detention – we always agreed that it is necessary to move beyond traditional discourses and genres associated with journalism, scholarship, literature and art; or at least redefine their parameters and features. We want to convey the lived experience of systematic torture. We want to form a new transnational and transcultural discourse derived from diverse cultures and histories of resistance to render a nuanced interpretation of the experience of border violence and the wider global systems of oppression that create and reinforce it. Our critique of discourses and genres involves searching for and devising unique methods of communication, analysis, representation, and translation methods; new forms of creative resistance that explore, question, reinterpret and expand artforms such as literature, poetry, painting, photography and cinema.

In relation to areas such as journalism, academia and literary publishing, the contemporary obstacles and problems we have faced have deep colonial roots. The lack of openness, the restrictions and cultures of exclusion, all pertain to limitations and biases in terminology, discourses, narratives and representations. News publishing and broadcasting, scholarly publishing and literary publishing exhibit barriers that are inseparable from the structural problems that exist in Australian history and contemporary society (also globally). To unpack, critically assess and change structural discrimination and oppression – Australia's border regime being just one example – it is necessary to identify the way different structures are linked through their constituent industries and ingrained exclusionary ideologies.

I saw first-hand the struggles associated with writing and publishing by collaborating with and translating for people imprisoned within the detention industry (or recently released). For instance, a major obstacle created by the media and publishers was their policies and organisational culture; people in managerial roles either refused or made it impossible for refugees to pursue writing and other forms of communication, leaving them limited in their ability to contribute to discourse (unless they had a very influential patron). The structural and cultural issues condition many decision makers in the media and publishing so that they are unable to compromise or change, and in cases where there were possibilities the repercussions were too inconvenient or considered potentially problematic for organisations. In some cases, people in positions of (relative) power could not even imagine a situation in which supporting and publishing writing or other forms of expression from inside the detention centres was even possible, or how deep and meaningful dialogue with detained refugees could be productive and of interest to audiences. These issues are complicated further by the fact that some of the perceptions and decisions made within media and publishing fluctuate or completely shift randomly, so much so that decision makers at different moments could be identified as a supporter, detractor or antagonist. This point highlights the idea that within the border-industrial complex we all occupy a pro-refugee/anti-refugee disposition – the differences between us is the degrees to which we practice one side over the other.

The difficulties I have described here are not exclusive to journalism, the media and publishing. We have faced similar issues in academia, art institutions, art and community projects, and more. I will address different aspects relating to these other spaces but it is significant to reiterate that the problem is structural and can be interpreted within what Charles Mills calls 'an epistemology of ignorance' (2020 [1997], pp. 18, 93, 96–97, 132–133); or under what Gaile Pohlhaus Jr. calls 'willful hermeneutical ignorance' (Fall 2012; 2017, pp. 17 and 20) and Kristie Dotson calls 'contributory injustice' (2012). In other words, individuals recognise the nature and extent of the oppression and exclusion but ignore, deny, minimise, or just proceed anyway as though it were business as usual. The pro-refugee/anti-refugee disposition illuminates this critique further, it relates to situations where barriers are constructed by people who in most cases generally try to make individual or concerted attempts to help. Zivardar reminds us of what is at stake when such imbalances of power and issues of epistemic injustice are left unaddressed:

> [O]ur work should communicate to create epistemological shifts. Just "spreading awareness" as some activists describe it is not enough. After

my experiences incarcerated in the border-industrial complex, I am more critical of support networks – we have to address gender discrimination in activist spaces. I think one of the reasons that I was being denied a lot of support and exposure when I was incarcerated in Nauru was because I did not play the familiar role of a victim. I do not know why, but a lot of activists are more interested when we talk about displaced and exiled peoples as being in poverty or in different positions of weakness and need. They seem to respond better to narratives and depictions of people who need food or clothing, or similar kinds of things. Of course, those things are important, but some pro-refugee entities do not seem to be open to the image of the refugee that empowers and humanizes refugees.

I have encountered a lot of supportive people, but I have also often encountered activists who have discriminated against me based on gender and race.

(Zivardar and Tofighian, forthcoming)

Notes on translation

The first passage in this chapter quoted from *No Friend but the Mountains* (Boochani, 2018a, p. 303):

- The passage is highlighted within the section from the Persian text messages represented below (Figure 2.2).

آی اچ ام اس سیستم پزشکی زندان بود،سیستمی پیچیده که عاشق دیدن انسان های IHMS.ایجاد می کرد مریض بود،وقتی کسی ناخوش می شد بهترین فرصت برای نمایی قدرت دکترها و پرستارها بود و زندانی شبیه به تکه گوشتی بی مصرف می شد که باید له می شد.مگر سیستم حاکم بر زندان چه چیزی غیر از این می خواست؟دیدن یک تکه گوشت بی دفاع و آنگاه کشیدنش به داخل سیستمی که از پیش آماده بود تا او را قورت دهد و تفاله اش را به آشغال دانی پرت کند،منظور از آشغال دانی همان کشور یا سرزمینی بود که یک پناهنده از آنجا آمده بود.آنقدر زندانی مریض را اذیت می کردند و به او قرص می دادند تا روزی دستانش را به علامت تسلیم بالا ببرد.درمانگاه مجموعه ی چند کانتینر بود که در انتهای زندان و چسبیده به اسکار برپا شده بود،محیطی کثیف و پر از قوانین ریز و درشت و دست و پاگیر،محیطی که آدم وقتی گذرش به آنجا می افتاد هر نوع اتفاق عجیبی ممکن بود برایش بیفتد.مثلا کسی که قلبش تیر می کشید ممکن بود دکتر به او توصیه کند که "پسر آب زیاد بخور،پسر یادت نره همیشه باید آب زیاد بخوری" یا مثلا کسی مثل حمید ممکن بود چپ و راست به بدنش سرم وصل کنند و گاهی اوقات پرستاری با چشمانی جدی داخل سرمش آمپول تزریق کند و بعد بگوید"پسرم همینجا ساکت دراز بکش تا خوب خوب بشی،نگران هیچ چیز هم نباش،خوب خوب میشی،فقط ساکت باش".مردان و زنانی با روپوش هایی سفید،همیشه خندان با چشمانی که در کار

FIGURE 2.2 Excerpt from Boochani's text messages which were compiled into PDFs by Moones Mansoubi and sent to me. The translation of the highlighted passage corresponds to the passage that follows in English.

76 Creating new languages of resistance

- Due to difficulties with transferring WhatsApp text messages to PDFs some sentences became fragmented in confusing ways which I worked out as I was trying to translate and edit. The end of the first highlighted sentence shows IHMS in English script amongst Persian script. IHMS should have been at the beginning of the sentence which would have then been followed by the Persian transliteration of the acronym. Another misplaced fragment (which is not highlighted) appears after the first highlighted section and is a continuation of the sentence immediately before the highlighted passage begins (and where the English acronym IHMS should have placed). The errors appear as a result of the complexities associated with transferring Persian text messages into a PDF. As part of the edited translation process I needed to unravel these puzzles which occur in random places and for different reasons; it was necessary to work out what and where misplaced fragments should have been.
- The first sentence after the highlighted passage was moved. When dividing the long text message into paragraphs the highlighted passage becomes one paragraph and the removed sentence was reinserted to appear at the end of the subsequent paragraph. This was done for the purposes of coherence, style, meaning and narrative fluidity.
- Persian source text is in past tense, English edited translation is in present tense.

The health and medical service contracted for the prison is International Health and Medical Services or IHMS. A twisted and convoluted system that takes pleasure in observing sick human beings. When someone falls ill, the doctors and nurses have the perfect opportunity to unleash their power complexes. A prisoner is reduced to a useless piece of meat to be destroyed. Would The Kyriarchal System want it any other way? To see a defenceless piece of meat and then destroy it by subjecting it to a predetermined system, subjecting it to the system until swallowed up by it, subjecting it to the system until what is left is thrown away, back to the country or homeland from which the refugee fled.

The second passage quoted in this chapter from *No Friend but the Mountains* (Boochani, 2018a, p. 342):

- The passage is highlighted within the section from the Persian text messages represented below (see Figure 2.3).
- I have also highlighted another section under it to help illustrate how Persian prose was translated and edited into English verse (appears on p. 343 in English edition).
- The names of the people in this whole section were changed during the translation process; an Arabic name 'Saddam' was changed to

ده ها زندانی در انتهای میدان جنگ و پشت کریدورها موزاییک ها را خورد کردند و تکه هایش را به سمت جاده ی خاکی و افیسرها و پاپوها پرت می کردند. آن طرف تر پاپوها اما قدرتمندتر ظاهر می شدند و سنگ های بزرگ تری با شدت بیشتری به سمت زندانی ها پرتاب می کردند. در این بین چند نفر هم زخمی شدند, هر چند خیلی در هیاهوی جنگ کسی به فکر این نیست که چه کسانی زخمی شده اند و یا در چه شرایطی هستند.

آنجا میدان خروس های جنگی بود که به تنها چیزی که فکر می کردند وارد کردن ضربه ای بر پیکر سیستم حاکم و کسانی بود که آن ها را زندانی کرده بودند. همچنان صدای هیاهو در زندان ها دلتا و اسکار می آمد, شبیه صدای جهنم بود و این طرف زندان مایک در زیر رگباری از سنگ ها بود, اما زندانی ها در فضای ترسناک جنگ احساس آزادی می کردند و زندان و قدرت زندان در زیر قدم های آن ها حقیر و کوچک احساس می شد, این اولین بار بود که قدرت فنس ها احساس نمی شد و قوانین هیچ بودند, حسی از برادری در حرکات خشمگین زندانی ها احساس می شد و نمود پیدا کرده بود. این هم از شگفتی های جنگ است, در زیر لایه های خشن جنگ این احساس برادرانه که زندانی ها به برادر زندانی شان داشتند غریب بود اما احساسی واقعی بود. زندانی ها حالا کاملا کنترل زندان را به دست آورده بودند و حتی دیگر این فرصت را به دست آورده بودند که به نشانه ی پیروزی به همدیگر لبخند بزنند و به قوانینی که دیگر حالا کاملا غیب شده بودند.انگار جنگ به یکباره تمام شد, سنگ ها دیگر پرت نشدند و زندان ساکت شد, آشکارا فضا وارد یک مرحله ی دیگر شد, پاپوهای روی جاده غیب شدند و آفیسر های استرالیایی تعدادشان کمتر شد," صدام" می خندید و سیگار می کشید در حالی که به یک میله ی فلزی تکیه زده بود, بیشتر شبیه یک بازیگر در فیلمی کمدی بود و در همان حالت به جمعیت نگاه می کرد, " کله پوک" بیش از هر زمان دیگری احساس قدرت می کرد و طوری چشمانش را به اطراف می چرخاند که انگار پادشاهی ست که کشور دیگری را تصرف کرده است, از یک زاویه ای احساسش واقعی بود چون مایک و فوکس یکی شده بودند و فنس های بین دو زندان و تمام قانون ها نابود شده بودند. او طوری لبخند می زد که یک فرمانده ی انقلاب است که در اوج پیروزی ست, راست هم می گفت, شب های زیادی گلوی خودش را پاره کرده بود تا زندانی ها را بر علیه سیستم حاکم و قوانینش بشوراند. جنگ هم پدیده ی عجیبی ست, غیر قابل پیش بینی ست, ناگهان شروع می شود و ناگهان تمام می شود, اما این سکوتی ترسناک بود, شبیه آرامش قبل از طوفان و شبیه لحظات قبل از مرگ, حتی خود زندانی ها که هنوز هم خونشان گرم بود و رگ های پیشانی شان داغ و پر از خون جوشان بود احساس این سکوت را امری عجیب و غریب می پنداشتند و احساس می کردند. این وضعیت خیلی طولی نکشید و به یکباره گروهی از نیروهای ضد شورش در جلوی گیت زندان پدیدار شدند, گروهی شاید دوازده نفره که بیشتر شبیه مردانی آهنی بودند با کلاه خودهایی آهنی, و لباس هایی فلزی و البته سپرهایی در دست. شبیه گروهی از حیوانات بودند که با هم به شکار می رفتند, دست هایشان کاملا در هم قفل شده بود و سپرها را به شکلی آماده در روبه روی خودشان گرفته بودند, چند قدم برداشتند و بعد ایستادند,

FIGURE 2.3 Excerpt from Boochani's text messages which were compiled into PDFs by Moones Mansoubi and sent to me. The edited translation of the highlighted passages correspond to the passages above in English.

'The Comedian'; and a derisive and satirical moniker in Persian '*kaleh pouk*' – literally 'empty head', meaning 'stupid', 'airhead' or 'half-wit' – was changed to a very different moniker in English: 'The Hero'.
- Before the translation of prose into poetry a line in Persian was omitted to avoid repetition and confusion. A reference to Mike and Fox was

removed. After the quoted passage at the beginning there is a reference to Delta, Mike and Oscar, and it was not clear how to relate and explain the later mention of Mike and Fox which appeared just after the line 'status of a conqueror'. The omitted line also repeats earlier references to the removal of fences and rules and regulations.
- Persian source text is in past tense, English edited translation is in present tense.

Highlighted passage 1:

The place was a cockfighting stadium. The only thing on the minds of the prisoners was to damage the organism that is The Kyriarchal System; to inflict a blow on those who had imprisoned them.

Highlighted passage 2:

> *War is such an extraordinary phenomenon /*
> *Unpredictable /*
> *It erupts unexpectedly /*
> *It ceases unexpectedly /*
> *There is a terrifying silence /*
> *Like the calm before the storm /*
> *Like the moment prior to death /*
> *Even the prisoners found this silence peculiar /*
> *Their blood still hot with excitement /*
> *Their veins still rippling /*
> *Their foreheads still streaming with boiling blood.*

Appendix

The dialogue in this appendix is from 2020; an interview with me recorded for *ABC RN*'s *The Philosopher's Zone,* presented by David Rutledge. The interview explores the philosophical dimensions of my translation, activism and collaborations with displaced, exiled and incarcerated peoples. We also discuss barriers in professional philosophy and the issue of epistemic injustice. At the time of the interview I had already presented as a speaker in numerous public events, conducted seminars and given conference papers at numerous international universities about my translation and collaboration work. My contribution begins with the thought experiment I created and published in the philosophical essay 'Translator's Reflections' which accompanied my edited translation of *No Friend but the Mountains.* The thought experiment addresses Australia's carceral-border regime and raises questions and concerns regarding border violence, colonialism, incarceration, epistemic injustice and knowledge production. The recording of the interview is available online and I express thanks to Rutledge and the ABC for granting me permission to publish the transcript here.

Border patrol

Interview with ABC's The Philosopher's Zone
https://www.abc.net.au/radionational/programs/philosopherszone/omid-tofighian/12182884
https://www.abc.net.au/radionational/programs/philosopherszone/border-patrol/121827982a)

- Interview with David Rutledge (*ABC, The Philosopher's Zone*)

26 April 2020

DR: A conversation this week about borders and the question of epistemic injustice. Who gets to determine the things that are worth knowing, and what kind of knowledge counts as belonging to us, the citizens of Australia?

OT: *There is an island isolated in a silent ocean where people are held prisoner. The people cannot experience the world beyond the island. They cannot see the immediate society outside the prison and they certainly do not learn about what takes place in other parts of the world. They only see each other and hear the stories they tell one another. This is their reality; they are frustrated by their isolation and incarceration, but they have also been taught to accept their predicament.*

News somehow enters the prison about another island where the mind is free to know and create. The prisoners are given a sense of what life is like on the other island but they do not have the capacity or experience to understand fully. The people on the other island have special insight: they see things that the prisoners cannot, they create things that the prisoners cannot, and they certainly know things that the prisoners cannot. Some of the prisoners resent the people on the other island. Some simply do not understand the people there or try to undermine them. Some are indifferent to the other society. Some prisoners feel pity for them because they are confident that their own situation is changing for the better and will eventually provide greater freedoms.

The two islands are polar opposites. One island kills vision, creativity and knowledge – it imprisons thought. The other island fosters vision, creativity and knowledge – it is a land where the mind is free.

> *The first island is the settler-colonial state called Australia, and the prisoners are the settlers.*
>
> *The second island contains Manus Prison, and knowledge resides there with the incarcerated refugees.*

DR: If you've read the extraordinary account of life in immigration detention on Manus Island that was written by the Kurdish Iranian journalist Behrouz Boochani then you'll know that the book includes two essays written by the translator Omid Tofighian. What you hear there was an excerpt from one of those essays read by Omid, who is my guest this week. Omid is an adjunct lecturer at the University of New South Wales in the School of the Arts and Media. He's also attached to the Department of Philosophy at the University of Sydney. And until recently he worked in philosophy at the American University in Cairo. So a solid academic philosophical background, which makes it interesting that Omid considers himself a counter philosopher.

OT: Since I began studying philosophy and engaging in discussions and debates on philosophical topics I always saw myself as introducing or concerned with things that maybe weren't necessarily a priority for many of the philosophers that I was interacting with. In fact, I think about counter philosophy as a way of maybe reclaiming philosophy for myself and for people like me who are passionate about philosophical inquiry and also community, and many other things that maybe don't traditionally fit together very well. So, for instance recognizing and engaging with systems of thought and forms of reasoning and particular topics and issues that maybe philosophy, particularly in recent times, has sort of relegated to other disciplines.

DR: I read a nice quote recently from Arundhati Roy. She was talking about the way in which a lot of what happens in the world happens outside the realm of common human understanding. And she says that it's the writers, the poets, the artists, the singers, the filmmakers who can make connections, who can find ways of bringing it into the realm of common understanding. I read that and I thought, well, what about the philosophers? Because it seems as though, on paper at least, that is what philosophy is supposed to do. Sort of forge new understandings, new ways of thinking about the world, and then bring those into the realm of common human understanding. But then I wonder sometimes about the extent to which the academy really allows for that. What are your thoughts on that?

OT: I really like that quote. In fact, it reminds me of why I became interested in themes and topics related to popular culture and also the nature of knowledge production. I think professional philosophy is particularly characterized by certain bordering practices. The way that philosophy takes shape in different contexts, especially within institutions, academic institutions, I think that it reinforces some of those bordering practices rather than transform them. So essentially, I think yes, professional philosophy can say something significant to the common understanding, but I think that it needs to take new directions. I think that a certain kind of disruption needs to take place, especially in terms of pedagogy and organizational culture. For me, when I think about borders, and I think about debordering, I consider borders to be material and symbolic, but also epistemic. In fact, this kind of debordering practice, this kind of disruption, is essentially what philosophy has always aimed to do. How philosophy has always seen itself or characterized itself. I don't see myself as doing something completely distinct or counter to what philosophy has always done through different periods and in different places. I see myself as carrying on a long tradition or working within a tradition that has given philosophy its reputation all over the world.

DR: This leads nicely into the work that you've done with Behrouz Boochani. You've described his writing, and in fact his entire way of being, as part of a debordering practice. He's had a very interesting influence on your understanding of philosophy, your philosophical work. We'll get to that in a minute, but first of all, I'd like to talk about his work, which you describe as an anti-genre. In what sense is Behrouz Boochani's work an anti-genre?

OT: When I first started translating for Behrouz, I started with his journalism. I noticed that he was using different techniques and styles and approaches, something that I wasn't familiar with in terms of journalism. And he was transgressing a lot of the conventions and expectations when it came to journalism. So for me, it was something fresh, unique, and also something really inspiring and admirable, particularly since it was coming from within the prison. In fact, I saw what he was doing as not just a way of conveying information about what he was going through and what the people around him were going through, but it was also a new way of knowledge production. It was a critique of the very medium. Once I started translating his book I noticed that it was taken to a whole new level. I started reading the first chapter and started translating the first chapter and I knew from the first few pages that this was going be a masterpiece. Now, what struck me was the way that he was fusing philosophical meditation with psychoanalytic examination, with political commentary, and on top of that, with other styles and other forms. In particular, what

I was impressed with was the way he was working in myth and epic and folklore into his writing.

DR: That's very interesting. Not something that you expect to find in philosophy, right? But you've said that the translation work you did together was a form of 'shared philosophical activity'. And in what sense was that the case?

OT: Well, it's interesting. I was thinking about this notion of anti-genre and when I started to look into it a little bit further I noticed that writers such as Dostoyevsky were interpreted in terms of an anti-genre, Nietzsche work is also referred to as anti-genre in some cases. Myself, I consider even Plato and his dialogues to be anti-genre in some sense, as well. The fusion of myth and philosophy, and maybe some other styles and frameworks. I think anti-genre maybe hasn't been appreciated enough in terms of the philosophical tradition. So that's something I'd like to explore further in the future. But in terms of creating or working with Behrouz on *No Friend but the Mountains*, I thought about the interactions that I was having and the collaborations I was engaged in with other colleagues, with other friends. And I started to think about the way that this book was taking shape, the way that it was being produced. To give you a rough outline, Behrouz was writing text messages on his phone, sending them out through WhatsApp. And these messages, he had started even before I'd met him. He'd started sending the messages to another translator, his first translator Moones Mansoubi who lives in Sydney. Based on his instructions Moones would compile these text messages into chapters. And when I came onto the project, Behrouz had written about 30% of the book in draft form, and Moones had compiled the earlier messages into chapters. She emailed them to me once she put them into PDFs. So when I received the first few chapters I was basically looking at every chapter as one long text message. Every week or two I'd meet with Moones or another friend, Sajad Kabgani. We'd meet and we'd discuss my translation. They were, you could say, my translation consultants. There was this really interesting and complex and dynamic relationship going on between translators and confidants and friends. Behrouz was also sending the original Farsi sometimes to friends of his in Iran for feedback.

I thought to myself, some of us don't even know each other. Some of us haven't even had any contact but we're all working towards the same goal. There's something interesting happening here. And we would talk to Behrouz about the collaboration that we were engaged in. And it was amazing. It was remarkable that we both had the same experience. Sometimes I would make a suggestion to Behrouz and he would say 'I was actually thinking about this exact same thing'. He would make suggestions to me and I would maybe a day earlier, or two days earlier, or even the same day, I would be thinking exactly the same thing.

So there was something remarkable taking place here, and I thought about this in relation to some work done in philosophy in the area of metaphysics, personal identity. You know, the idea that there is one body, multiple identities. Maybe what's happening here is a particular way of thinking, a particular way of knowing, or a way of identifying that involves multiple bodies but one mind. I noticed that there's a whole area in philosophy that looks at joint commitments, collective intentionality, shared agency, collective purpose, joint beliefs. I really felt that there was a particular kind of force or purpose that resonates with philosophical debates and discussions. And I think also there's an ethical dimension to it as well, which makes it even more interesting. The way that we all felt this certain kind of duty towards history, towards challenging the injustices that were taking place. We all felt the urgency when it came to this book coming out into the world. So it's remarkably ripe for philosophical investigation. Not only the book itself, but also the process, the mode of production.

DR: We're talking about refugees, often spoken and written about as victims. People who inhabit the far side of a boundary, separating them from all the things that we citizens know and love about our homeland. But what if the refugee actually knows things about our country that we don't, things that maybe we should know in the interest of our own security and freedom?

OT: One of the reasons I felt so driven to work on this project with him, the book project, and then continue afterwards, is the fact that sustainable long-term transformation needs to address the underlying narrative or ideology that gives rise to these kinds of sites, these forms of violence. And I think what Behrouz was doing was creating a new narrative about how to think about refugees. He was breaking down this idea, this notion of refugees as weak, needy supplicants, as broken people, as the unknown, as the Other. And maybe this is something that's a factor in communities, in groups, in individuals right across the political spectrum. The idea that there is this dichotomy between the non-citizen and the citizen, between the displaced and exiled person and the person with citizen privilege. And I think what Behrouz was doing, and what he continues to do, was to really disrupt that narrative.

It's the narrative that drives so much of border politics that we see now and has been a part of Australia's experience with migrants, and of engaging with migrants. And it goes all the way back to invasion. It's part of the way

Australia was set up as a penal colony. And it features in so many of the other aspects of Australia's history, the way that prisons have multiplied, the way that they've been replicated, not just detention centers and prison camps, but even we could consider missions and reserves and cattle stations where Aboriginal and Torres Strait Islander peoples were contained. And then we go right through the history of Australia and we see this story continuing and taking new forms and developing, and the technologies improving as a result of these experiences.

So what Behrouz has been trying to do with his work is to say that the data, the reports, the journalism, everything that has been produced to try to explain what happens in these sites, the situations that are the outcome of this particular narrative, will never quite penetrate and will never quite disrupt the underlying ideology, the driving force behind these particular policies, these particular actions. In order to really transform the situation, in order to really move forward, requires us to basically challenge, or first of all acknowledge and identify that narrative, and then challenge it with a new narrative. And I think that's what's important about Behrouz's work, he's replacing that narrative with something new. And in this case, suddenly the incarcerated refugee is no longer a weak, needy supplicant, no longer broken, no longer other or outsider. The incarcerated refugee is showing us a side of Australia that we may not have seen before, showing us something we didn't think the state was capable of. The incarcerated refugee knows more about Australia than the settler does.

And, in fact, Behrouz is indicating that there is some very close connection between what's happening on the small island, on Manus, and the big island, in Australia. It's possible that the kind of technologies of domination, control, subjugation, are somehow seeping into our own political culture, into our own society. And so in this case, the incarcerated refugee becomes a knowledge producer, becomes someone who's empowered, someone who has liberated themselves and is basically engaging with us on their terms.

DR: Well, I'd like to finish up by talking a little about your work. I know that you're writing a book at the moment about displacement and exile as philosophical positions. That sounds really interesting. Can you give me just a brief thumbnail sketch of the terrain that that book is going to be covering, and if it may be draws on your own experiences of displacement and exile in Iranian society and in Australian society that I know you've talked about before?

OT: Yeah, thank you for raising this. It gives me an opportunity to reflect on some of my own philosophical work away from the translation or the shared philosophical activity that I'm engaged in with Behrouz and other activists. One factor that really facilitated my interaction with Behrouz was the fact that we both come from marginalized groups in Iranian society. So, Behrouz being a Kurd and also from a rural area in Iran, and my family were discriminated against in Iran based on socio-religious status. So that's one thing that really connected me with Behrouz. The other thing was the fact that my family left Iran around the time of the revolution and were planning to migrate to the United States, and that was disrupted as a result of the hostage crisis in Tehran at the US Embassy. And so after a number of years, four or five years in the United States, we weren't able to stay there. It's a very complicated story, but we weren't able to gain citizenship and remain in the United States but at that time an opportunity came up to come to Australia. So, it's very interesting that when we came to Australia it was less than 10 years after the White Australia Policy was officially abolished. And the way that the state engaged with us at that time was in complete contrast with what refugees from Iran are experiencing now. So the Australian consulate made special documents for us to be able to travel to Australia, and the whole process took less than two months to finalize. In fact, my father originally wasn't very interested in coming to Australia and missed his first interview. The Australian consulate actually called him to ask him why he didn't turn up and was really keen in terms of offering him another interview.

I mean, there're just so many details there that show how fluid and ever-changing and also unfair border politics, and politics related to migration, can be. I think these particular stories, and the stories that I heard growing up of family members and friends, really informed my way of thinking, my way of engaging, the kind of questions I asked, the concerns that I had, the insights that I brought to the table when it came to interacting and collaborating.

The book project, the academic book that I'm thinking about, brings together my interests in popular culture, displacement and exile, particularly a lot of important work done in critical border studies, critical philosophy of race, social epistemology. I build on some work that has been done by philosophers such as Miranda Fricker, Elizabeth Anderson, Kristie Dotson, Charles Mills, José Medina.

My argument essentially is that when it comes to people who are displaced and exiled, that the NGOs, advocates, campaigns, organizations can do so much in these spaces. So much can be contributed in terms of supporting refugees. But if certain kinds of issues, certain points, aren't addressed, if they're not integral to the campaigns, to the support networks, then it's highly likely that that particular narrative that I was discussing earlier, that ideology, the underlying ideology related to displaced and exile peoples, can continue. And so here I'm thinking about not just systemic change, but also changing the social imaginary. And for that to take place I think something more than just philosophical arguments are necessary, something more than just critical inquiry is needed. And here, I think, popular culture, literature and storytelling are pivotal. I think they can inform us or allow us to enter new spaces where the imbalances that characterize the relationships between citizen and non-citizen can be broken down and new collaborations, new forms of solidarity can take place.

DR: Okay, so this is where the issue of pride comes in, doesn't it? Because I know you've been thinking about how a certain notion of pride can be instrumental in making these changes within the social imaginary, to shift the popular understanding of refugees and migrants as weak and helpless and a drain on the resources and the goodwill of the state. So tell me about that pride.

OT: There's some important work done by Elizabeth Barnes. She wrote a very good book called *The Minority Body* about epistemic injustice and disability. And there she raises the importance of pride movements. She argues that in terms of its emotive support, pride has a way of combating shame, creating solidarity, and collectively building self-esteem and also building agency. But she goes beyond that to argue that pride also has an epistemic value and it helps us to know things that otherwise cannot be known. This is in the context of disability. She argues that it's politically important in that it cultivates new knowledges. So I was inspired by this and thought that maybe we can start thinking about displacement and exile in the same way. People who have had experiences of displacement and exile can help us to know things that cannot otherwise be known. And also the fact that new knowledges are created if the right kind of infrastructure, if the right kind of settings, are devised and developed.

DR: Well, this talk of pride makes me think of Anzac Day, which has just passed. Not this year, but traditionally it provides an occasion for a certain kind of celebration, right? Busting out the flag and taking pride in being Australian. But in recent years, we've seen that pride become a little like the pride associated with January 26th. It's also an occasion for the extreme right and other exclusionary elements to make their voices heard. What are your thoughts on that?

OT: There's a lot to say about this topic, especially when it comes to the earlier discussion that we had about narrative and the influence of narrative on a social, political and also epistemic level. But I think one thing I should clarify is that when I talk about pride I don't mean hubris or arrogance. In fact, pride here in relation to displaced and exiled peoples, and also the way that Elizabeth Barnes uses it in relation to disability, is about inviting other groups in, other knowers into the conversation. It's about relationality. It's about not excluding or bordering. What this particular approach tries to emphasize is the relationship between pride and knowledge in a way that is not a foolish kind of pride or a destructive kind of overconfidence.

It's a kind of bottom-up approach, rather than a top-down approach. It's about allowing communities the space, the freedom, to be able to empower themselves, to create new platforms for thinking, for engaging, and also to share that with other communities and bring other communities in so that there are new conversations taking place, new forms of solidarity, new kinds of action. And this, itself, this kind of intersection between different communities who are acknowledged as being different kinds of knowledge producers suddenly gives us opportunities to create new knowledges. So all of the negative aspects that I'm contrasting with this particular kind of pride that I'm proposing or suggesting, clearly you can see the connections with the kind of ugly nationalism that exploits historical events, exploits politics and creates a kind of narrative that is based on new forms of bordering, new kinds of exclusion, new forms of othering.

In the case that I'm talking about, in the kind of pride that I'm suggesting here, you suddenly see the epistemic consequences, combined with development of virtue. And this kind of new fusion or this new relationship, I think, is a fair justification of certain pride movements. There's a very specific use of pride in this context. We can think about pride movements such as Indigenous sovereignty movements, we could think about Black Lives Matter, we could consider gay pride, for instance. All of these different kinds of pride movements, I think, are distinctly different to something like white supremacist movements or ugly, destructive forms of nationalism. So, a really serious philosophical analysis of pride here can be fruitful, particularly when understanding the situation of displaced and exiled people. Particularly because so many experiences of displacement and exile are seen in terms of that kind of weak, needy, deficit model rather than as people who could contribute something intellectually, culturally, politically to our social landscape.

Bibliography

Adam, M. (2021) 'The autobiography of Mohamed Adam (Chapter One)', translated by Ashraf, N. A. Southerly – Writing Through Fences: Archipelago of Letters 79(2): pp. 124–133. www.southerlylitmag.com.au/shop/writing-through-fences-archipelago-of-letters/

Alimardanian, M. (2020) 'Ethnography of a nightmare: public anthropology, indefinite detention and innovative writing', *American Ethnologist* 47(1): pp. 86–89. www.anthrosource.onlinelibrary.wiley.com/doi/abs/10.1111/amet.12870

Baker, M. (2016) 'Beyond the Spectacle: Translation and Solidarity in Contemporary Protest Movements', in Baker, M. (ed), *Translating Dissent: voices from and with the Egyptian revolution*. London: Routledge, pp. 1–18.

Bielsa, E. (2023) *A translational sociology: interdisciplinary perspectives on politics and society*. London: Routledge.

Boochani, B. (2017) 'A kyriarchal system: new colonial experiments/new decolonial resistance'. Translated by O. Tofighain. *Maroon Conference Magazine, Charles Town*. Jamaica: Charles Town Maroon Council, pp. 20–22. www.maroons-jamaica.com/conference-festival-2017/

Boochani, B. and Kamali Sarvestani, A. (directors) (2017) *Chauka Please Tell Us the Time* [film]. Sarvin Productions. www.vimeo.com/ondemand/chauka

Boochani, B. (2018) 'Mohamed's Life Story is a Tragedy. But it's typical for Father's Held on Manus', *The Gaurdian*. www.theguardian.com/commentisfree/2018/mar/27/mohameds-life-story-is-a-tragedy-but-its-typical-for-fathers-held-on-manus

Boochani, B. (2018a) *No Friend but the Mountains: Writing from Manus Prison*. Translated by Tofighian, O. Sydney: Picador-Pan Macmillan.

Boochani, B. (2019) 'Film as Folklore'. Translated by Tofighian, O. *Alphaville: Journal of Film and Screen Media* 18: pp. 185–187. https://doi.org/10.33178/alpha.18.15

Boochani, B. (2023) 'A Kyriarchal System: New Colonial Experiments/New Decolonial Resistance', in Boochani, B. (ed), *Freedom, only Freedom: the prison writing of Behrouz Boochani*, translated and edited by Tofighian, O. and Mansoubi, M. London: Bloomsbury Academic, pp. 69–71.

Boochani, B. (2023) 'Mohamed's Life Story is a Tragedy. But It's Typical for Father's Held on Manus', in Boochani, B. (ed), *Freedom, only Freedom: the prison writing of Behrouz Boochani*, translated and edited by Tofighian, O. and Mansoubi, M. London: Bloomsbury Academic, pp. 141–145.

Collins, P. (2009 [2000]) *Black feminist thought: knowledge, consciousness, and the politics of empowerment*. New York: Routledge.

Dana, E. (2018) 'Indefinite detention: caring for refugees in Indonesia as performance'. Translated by Tofighian, O. *Charles Town Maroon International Conference Magazine*, pp. 28–30. www.maroons-jamaica.com/wp-content/uploads/flipbook/6/files/basic-html/page29.html

Dotson, K. (2012) 'A cautionary tale: on limiting epistemic oppression', *Frontiers: A Journal of Women Studies* 33(1): pp. 24–47. https://doi.org/10.5250/fronjwomestud.33.1.0024

Elsadda, H. (2016) 'An Archive of Hope: Translating Memories of Revolution', in Baker, M. (ed), *Translating Dissent: voices from and with the Egyptian revolution*. Oxon: Routledge, pp. 148–160.

El Tarzi, S. (2016) 'Ethical Reflections on Activist Film-Making and Activist Subtitling', translated by Moger, R., in Baker, M. (ed), *Translating Dissent: voices from and with the Egyptian revolution*. Oxon: Routledge, pp. 88–96.

Elphick, J. (2019) 'Cinematic poetics and reclaiming history: *Chauka, please tell us the time* as legacy', *Alphaville: Journal of Film and Screen Media* 18: pp. 199–204. https://doi.org/10.33178/alpha.18.18

El-Tamami, W. (2016) 'A Wish Not to Betray: Some Thoughts on Writing and Translation Revolution', in Baker, M. (ed), *Translating Dissent: voices from and with the Egyptian revolution*. Oxon: Routledge, pp. 21–32.

Gaber, S. (2016) 'What Word is This Place?: Translating Urban Social Justice and Governance', in Baker, M. (ed), *Translating Dissent: voices from and with the Egyptian revolution*. Oxon: Routledge, pp. 97–106.

Galbraith, J. (2019) 'A reflection on *Chauka, Please tell us the time*', *Alphaville: Journal of Film and Screen Media* 18: pp. 193–198. https://doi.org/10.33178/alpha.18.17

Kamali Sarvestani, A. (directors) (2020) *Tall Fences, Taller Trees* [film]. Sarvin Productions. https://moviesthatmatter.nl/en/film/tall-fences-taller-trees/ https://watch.eventive.org/tallfences/play/5f6473742c821700ac16d37d

Kamali Sarvestani, A. (2019) 'Looking for Chauka', translated by Tofighian, O. *Alphaville: Journal of Film and Screen Media* 18: pp. 188–192. https://doi.org/10.33178/alpha

Kebsi, J. (2024) 'A Decolonial Translation: Omid Tofighian's Collaborative Approach in Behrouz Boochani's No Friend but the Mountains', *Nawaat*. www.nawaat.org/2024/06/18/decolonizing-translation-omid-tofighians-collaborative-approach-in-behrouz-boochanis-no-friend-but-the-mountains/

Kebsi, J. (In press) 'The challenges of translating world prison literature: Omid Tofighian's contribution to *No Friend but the Mountains*', *Antipodes: A Global Journal of Australian/New Zealand Literature*. https://researchers.mq.edu.au/en/publications/the-challenges-of-translating-world-prison-literature-omid-tofigh

Mills, C. (2020 [1997]). *The racial contract*. Ithaca: Cornell University Press.

Mortada, L. (2016) 'Translation and Solidarity in Words of Women from the Egyptian Revolution', in Baker, M. (ed), *Translating Dissent: voices from and with the Egyptian revolution*. Oxon: Routledge, pp. 125–136.

Öcalan, A. (2015) *Manifesto for a democratic civilization, Volume I: civilization, the age of masked Gods and disguised kings*. Porsgrunn: New Compass Press.

Öcalan, A. (2017a) *The political thought of Abdullah Öcalan: Kurdistan, woman's revolution and democratic confederalism*. London: Pluto Press.

Öcalan, A. (2017b) *Manifesto for a democratic civilization, Volume II: capitalism, the age of unmasked Gods and naked kings*. Porsgrunn: New Compass Press.

Pohlhaus, G. (Fall 2012) "Relational knowing and epistemic injustice: Toward a theory of willful hermeneutical ignorance." *Hypatia: A Journal of Feminist Philosophy* 27(4): pp. 715–735. doi:10.1111/j.1527-2001.2011.01222.x

Pohlhaus, G. (2017) 'Varieties of Epistemic Injustice', in Kidd, I. J., Medina, J. and Pohlhaus Jr., G. (eds), *The Routledge Handbook of Epistemic Injustice*. New York: Routledge: pp. 13–26.

Ramrath, R. (Spring 2024) 'Beautiful Colours, Bitter Paintings: gendered violence in Australian immigration detention', *The Philosopher* 112(1): pp. 32–37.

Rizk, P. and Baker, M. (2016) 'Interview with Philip Rizk', in Baker, M. (ed), *Translating Dissent: voices from and with the Egyptian revolution*. Oxon: Routledge, pp. 225–237.

Schüssler Fiorenza, E. (2020) 'Biblical Interpretation and Kyriarchal Globalization', in Scholz, S. (ed), *The Oxford Handbook of feminist approaches to the Hebrew Bible*. Oxford: Oxford University Press.

Selim, S. (2016) 'Text and context: translating in a state of emergency'.in Baker, M. (ed), *Translating Dissent: Voices from and with the Egyptian revolution*. Oxon: Routledge, pp. 77–87.

Tofighian, O. (2018a) 'Translator's Tale: A Window to the Mountains', in Boochani, B. (ed), *No Friend but the Mountains: Writing from Manus Prison*. Translated by Tofighian, O. Sydney: Picador: Pan Macmillan: pp. xiii–xxxvi.

Tofighian, O. (2018b) 'Translator's Reflections', in Boochani, B., *No Friend but the Mountains: Writing from Manus Prison*. Translated by Tofighian, O. Sydney: Picador: Pan Macmillan, pp. 359–374.

Tofighian, O. (2018c) 'Behrouz Boochani and the Manus Prison narratives: merging translation with philosophical reading', *Continuum: Journal of Media and Cultural Studies* 32(3): pp. 532–540. https://doi.org/10.1080/10304 312.2018.1494942

Tofighian, O. (2018d) 'Sanctions, Refugees and the Marginalised: Iran Uprisings are Australia's Concern Too', *ABC News*. www.abc.net.au/news/2018-01-06/iran-uprising-australia-manus-island-political-refugees-islamic/9305756

Tofighian, O. (2019a) 'Displacement, Exile and Incarceration Commuted into Cinematic Vision', *Alphaville: Journal of Film and Screen Media* 18: pp. 91–106. https://doi.org/10.33178/alpha.18.07

Tofighian, O. (2019b) 'Chauka Calls – a Photo Essay', *Alphaville: Journal of Film and Screen Media* 18: pp. 205–2017. https://doi.org/10.33178/alpha.18.19.

Tofighian, O. (2019c) 'Carceral-border Cinema: a film from Manus Prison', *Alphaville: Journal of Film and Screen Media* 18: pp. 183–184. https://doi.org/10.33178/alpha.18.14

Tofighian, O. (August 2019) 'Behrouz Boochani and the politics of naming', *Australian Book Review* 423. www.australianbookreview.com.au/abr-online/archive/2019/371-august-2019-no-413/5688-behrouz-boochani-and-the-politics-of-naming-by-omid-tofighian

Tofighian, O. (2019d) 'Disregard, dismissal and divestment: Behrouz Boochani, academia and the media'. *PEN International.* www.englishpen.org/posts/campai gns/world-refugee-day-take-action-for-behrouz-boochani/

Tofighian, O., Boochani, B., Mira and Zivardar, E. (2022) 'Narratives of Resistance from Indefinite Detention: Manus Prison Theory and Nauru Imprisoned Exiles Collective', in J. Gordon (ed), *The big anxiety: taking care of mental health in times of crisis*. London: Bloomsbury Academic, pp. 125–138.

Tofighian, O. and Zivardar, E. (Spring 2024) 'Nauru prison theory as public philosophy', *The Philosopher* 112(1): pp. 23–31.

Tymoczko, M. (2014 [2007]) *Enlarging translation, empowering translators*. London: Routledge.

Whitlock, G. (2024) *Refugee lives in the archives: a Pacific imaginary*. London: Bloomsbury Academic.

Wolfson, T. and Funke, P. N. (2016) 'The Contemporary Epoch of Struggle: Anti-Austerity Protests, the Arab Uprisings and Occupy Wall Street', in Baker, M. (ed), *Translating Dissent: voices from and with the Egyptian revolution*. Oxon: Routledge, pp. 60–73.

Zivardar, E. and Tofighian, O. (2021) 'The Torture of Australia's Offshore Immigration Detention Sydney', *OpenDemocracy*. www.opendemocracy.net/en/beyond-traffick ing-and-slavery/the-torture-of-australias-offshore-immigration-detention-system/

Zivardar, E and Tofighian, O. (forthcoming) 'Foundations for Nauru Prison Theory: Elahe Zivardar and Omid Tofighian on Australian Border Violence, Art and Knowledge Production', in Hawas, M. and Robbins, B. (eds), *Teaching politically*. New York: Fordham University Press.

3
COLLABORATION, ACTIVISM, TRANSLATION AND STORYTELLING

Revisiting the 23-day siege on Manus Prison

Collective knowledge and resisting border violence

In the previous chapters I discussed the relationship between collaboration, activism, translation and the stories that both connect and constitute these elements. I explained how these factors interweave and give shape to the collective planning, processes and products of translation work. In this chapter I will give detailed examples to explain how the intricacies of collaborative working relationships and shared intellectual, cultural and political visions operate – relationships and shared projects which centre engaged cultural partnerships, creative resistance and storytelling in the context of Australia's border regime. I also use the examples to show how the confluence of collaboration, activism, translation and storytelling apply to the production of knowledge. When collectivity, political action, translation and narrative dynamics combine in organic and subversive ways they have the potential to generate distinct epistemic resources and create the necessary conditions for building theoretical frameworks that engage specifically with the destructive and absurdly cruel nature of contemporary Australian border violence. By extension, producing more appropriate and empowering epistemic resources and conditions lead to imagining and motivating even more meaningful and impactful creative and intellectual projects. Developing essential epistemic resources and strong intellectual foundations for the creation of new languages of resistance are indispensable parts of these multidimensional collaborative and creative projects. This involves devising counter discourses and terminology; creating a new symbolic aesthetic; merging genres in experimental ways; and finding radically open and unconventional ways to facilitate philosophical discovery.

DOI: 10.4324/9781003455493-4

Collaborative work with people targeted by the detention industry requires forming place-based and situation-specific intellectual, artistic and political approaches and ways of thinking, and modes of production that honour and galvanise them. These approaches are dedicated to issues pertaining to the Australian carceral-border, while also acknowledging the global connections that condition and complicate the many entangled discourses, symbols, structures, circumstances, processes and locations related to bordering. Therefore, the selected frameworks, focus points and relationships addressed in our collaborative approaches are always open to reselection, rearrangement, re-manoeuvring and redirection. These factors are important because they account for the pernicious fluidity, unpredictability and absurdity of border regimes. They also enable the continual readjustment and reapplication of approaches to accommodate themes, topics and experiences that come into our purview from a whole range of interconnected transnational and transhistorical spheres.

Global and historical factors characterise Australia's border regime and our experimental interdisciplinary, transdisciplinary and situated methods aim to illuminate the profound relationships between various forms of injustice from other spaces and time periods. Our trajectories involve close consideration of the interconnections between divergent oppressive institutions; the different forms of violence used against diverse groups; and the numerous interlocking structures that constitute transnational and transhistorical examples of colonial oppression, domination and subjugation.

Challenging authority and the practices and processes of violence in the context of indefinite detention (even once people have been released) means that in almost every instance the situation is urgent and intense to such an extent that commonly practiced ways of planning and contemplation – steady and calculated forms of organising and deliberation – are impossible. Our planning, processes and products are characterised by the conditions, experiences and identities of the people involved and socio-political and cultural environments: all features and factors are fragmented, disrupted, disjointed and shattered. However, these features also enhance both the quality of the projects and the knowledge produced in uncanny ways. Fragmentation, disruption, disjointedness and shattered aspects characterise the stories integral to the work; through storytelling these elements pervade the collaboration, activism and translation work. These aspects operate creatively and productively in our responses to border violence; they help foster new languages of resistance since they function as powerful tools for meaning making, contribute to the aesthetic vision and provide philosophical stimulus.

Penetrating the mainstream media, socio-cultural and intellectual organisations and networks, and educational institutions, through standard practices and established channels has seemed impossible. Breaking through the barriers that limit our collective work has been hard; there are too many obvious and unacknowledged systemic silencing strategies to overcome. It was clear from early on that to make a meaningful and sustainable impact on the discourse regarding Australian border politics a special kind of collective approach was required that is conditioned by and led by the circumstances and people involved. This approach is planned, produced and presented in close collaboration and consultation with people targeted by the border regime.

Carving our own spaces and using our own language to achieve goals has always involved the serious risks of being further marginalised, suppressed, ignored and/or misunderstood. However, some of the advantages of the fragmented, disrupted, disjointed and shattered nature of our experiences and projects relate to the potential they have for making 'cracks' within the standard practices and established channels. The potential for creative and political intervention appears when traditionally excluded voices imagine new radical possibilities and organise collectively and innovatively, interrupting dominant spaces and causing ruptures. In addition to the creative and political cracks or interventions that this approach has caused, our collaborative projects have made breaks and ruptures that opened possibilities for epistemic justice – they have caused renegade moments which demand radically different ways of knowing.

Working in extreme situations and with limited resources and support, unique opportunities often arise when several important and unexpected factors align. In the past, new opportunities have presented themselves during some of the most brutal and intense periods of border violence. It was in these situations that we began witnessing some valuable outcomes of the shared philosophical activity and creative experimentation (I also use the term literary experimentation in relation to writing projects such as *No Friend but the Mountains*).

In 2017 a major shift occurred in our planning, process and production with several significant developments. Towards the end of that year the translations of Boochani's journalism, other writing and continuous collective acts of resistance from inside the prison, attracted unprecedented international attention. The main reason for the increase in focus was due to the events around the 23-day siege at the Manus Island detention centre (Boochani and Tofighian, Summer 2018; Boochani, 2017a, 2017b, 2017c, 2017d, 2017e, 2017f, 2017g, 2017h, 2017i, 2017j, 2017k, 2017l, 2017m).

On 26 April, 2016 the PNG Supreme Court ruled that the Manus Island detention centre located at the Lombrum Naval Base was illegal and unconstitutional and ordered its closure (Doherty, Davidson and Karp, 2016). On 31 October, 2017 the Australian government officially closed the carceral site (Davidson, 2017; Davidson and Wahlquist, 2017). Notice had been given about the closure months in advance and three other detention centres had been built in the main town of Lorengau: officially named East Lorengau Regional Transit Centre, West Lorengau Haus and Hillside Haus (see UNHCR, 2018). PNG authorities were ordered to transfer the incarcerated refugees to the new detention facilities from the original prison camp. However, the majority of the detainees refused to move. They demanded freedom.

Shifting to another prison camp was a continuation of the systematic torture; another form of displacement, exile and incarceration; and an unacceptable and cynical tactic on the part of the Australian government. Refugees argued that this was a step towards forcing them to resettle in PNG. A plan was in place to evict everyone who defied authorities and remained in the Lombrum prison camp in protest. For 23 days, starting on the date of closure, the site was under siege. Water and electricity were shut off and food, medicine and other services were discontinued. Guards and other staff were removed leaving refugees vulnerable in many ways. At one point authorities employed extreme tactics to pressure refugees to leave; they entered the camp to destroy drinking water tanks, which refugees had arranged with little resources and hardship, and they also removed shelters.

I collaborated with Shaminda Kanapathi on different examples of his writing and sometimes assisted to find publishers for him while he was incarcerated in Manus Prison, a collaboration we continued after he was released (see Kanapathi, 2021; Hassaballa, Abdul, Boochani, Adam, Zazai and Kanapathi, 2021). For instance, we worked together to prepare his contribution to the co-translated/co-edited collection *Freedom, Only Freedom: The Prison Writings of Behrouz Boochani* (Kanapathi, 2023). The book has a whole chapter dedicated to the disastrous period in 2017 which includes a selection of the articles I translated for Boochani (also including one diary report translated by Mansoubi) and pieces by Kanapathi and Erik Jenson, founding editor of *The Saturday Paper* and the person who commissioned the iconic 'A Letter from Manus Island' (2017) which closes the series about the siege. As one of the protestors inside the prison camp, Kanapathi offers special insights regarding the ruthless treatment by authorities throughout the 23 days:

> We were left in extreme tropical heat without any basic facilities such as food, water, power and medicines, but were sustained by our resilience and the strong bond of brotherhood built up over many long years. We had to organize our water supply by saving rainwater in garbage bins and digging wells, source and prepare our own food, keep the camp clean and generally maintain sanitary conditions. This was a huge responsibility and challenge, but every person who remained was very courageous and we worked hard to maintain our resistance.

Obtaining food and other essentials for the 450 camp people from what was effectively a small town was a major challenge. Each night at around midnight, we would use a small boat to smuggle the food and supplies from the town and sneak the things into the prison camp. Some local people who lived near the camp and local staff who worked in the camp felt really sorry about our miserable situation. They had compassion for us and took the risk of helping us, despite being fired at by the authorities while doing so. This secret operation was necessary as the PNG Navy was stationed next to the camp and was patrolling day and night to prevent supplies getting into the camp. Both the Australian and PNG governments were aiming to starve us into leaving and moving us to Lorengau, the main town on the island, where there were supposedly newly built facilities; in actual fact these were still under construction and, as we were to discover, not fit for purpose.

(Kanapathi, 2023, pp. 124–5)

To support PNG immigration officials, the PNG police and military forces (including the military police, navy and PNG's notorious paramilitary Mobile Squad) were directly involved throughout the siege. Eventually, severe violence was used to move all the refugees.

As Kanapathi indicates, a series of remarkable, spontaneous (but extraordinarily well-coordinated) and collective acts of resistance took place during this period involving various forms of collaboration between refugees protesting inside the prison, refugees in Manus Island but located outside the prison, and activists and supporters in Australia and beyond. I translated and co-authored an article with Boochani in which we discuss the role of one particular refugee in Manus Island, Helal Uddin also known as Spicy, who was outside the prison during the siege and was organising with those inside the prison camp:

The first person to bring food for the protesting refugees was Spicy. He received a call from the leaders of the resistance and travelled from Lorengau at 10 pm with food supplies. PNG Navy officers were still around the camp, so Spicy waited in the mosquito-infested waters for seven hours so that his companions could have food.

This act of solidarity and friendship started a wave of other shipments by local people over the coming weeks. On that first night, Spicy returned to Lorengau early in the morning only to transport a stranded Australian journalist to the prison camp. Roads were closed and private fishing boats were the only mode of transportation.

(Boochani and Tofighian, 2021; a slightly modified version was also published a week later in PEN – Transmissions, see Tofighian and Boochani, 2021)

The vital and complex role of refugees who acted as interpreters and translators within Manus Prison, or within other examples of Australia's carceral-border archipelago, has yet to be examined in detail. One interpreter/translator and the widely recognised main leader from inside Manus Prison who I have collaborated with is Benham Satah (also spelled Behnam Satah). His role in different aspects of the creative resistance inside Manus Prison has been invaluable – he began his work from the time he was in Indonesia, then Christmas Island, Manus Island, Port Moresby, and has also continued this work since being released and resettled in France. Translation and interpreting have been vital to the strategic struggles within Australia's detention estate, and it is fundamental for this study to recognise the role of translators and interpreters such as Benham Satah and Mardin Arvin in Manus Island and Port Moresby, Elahe Zivardar in Nauru, Erfan Dana in Indonesia (all already mentioned in previous chapters), and also Homaira Zamiri (2021a, 2021b, 2021c,2022) and Sadiqa Sarwari (translation of Zamiri, 2021a) in Indonesia. I will provide details below regarding how Satah's contributions and leadership have impacted the writing and translation work discussed in this chapter and beyond (I continue to collaborate with Satah on different projects at the time of writing).

From the time he was in Indonesia and planning to seek asylum in Australia, through to his imprisonment in Christmas Island, Manus Island and other carceral sites across PNG, Satah was not only widely recognised as the main leader amongst the other refugees, but he also undertook many crucial tasks to support numerous refugees and supporters which included translation and interpreting.[1]

According to Satah, the organising involved during the siege was just one series of many important protests that began months before the notorious and internationally reported 23 days. When a few other main leaders were selected from amongst the refugees (listed below) during this period he worked closely with them to prepare and action strategic acts of resistance in the prison. He also communicated regularly with people outside the prison (sometimes leaving the detention centre himself to complete necessary tasks and engage in meetings) and with people in Australia and other countries using a number of languages: English, Persian, Kurdish and Tok Pisin (and other languages such as Arabic and Urdu through his fellow refugee interpreters).

It is important to acknowledge that during this period collaboration, activism, translation and storytelling combined in innumerable ways and within multiples spheres. The nexus of these factors involved a diverse range of actors, drew on a wide range of skills and knowledge, required spontaneous yet meticulous *planning*, involved dangerous *processes*, and *produced* creative resistance of many kinds. Everything about the narratives that Satah shared with me regarding the plight of refugees throughout the

Collaboration, activism, translation and storytelling   **97**

years he was detained and the collective organising and work he did to stand up to the oppressors reflect the fragmented, disrupted, disjointed and shattered qualities I have been examining in relation to the collaborative work described throughout this book.

Satah's accounts regarding the 23-day siege, and the months before and after it, expand the dimensions and details about the period known through activists and journalists, including descriptions and critiques by refugees such as Boochani. Satah's oral history, his stories and analyses also function as a frame narrative that requires further interpretation in order to better understand the realities of the events and related issues, especially the role of interpreting and translation in the creative resistance. I will return to discuss the work of Satah as interpreter and translator in other parts of this book and connect his activities to his position as one of the main leaders in the prison camp during the siege (and widely recognised as the main leader throughout the whole plight).

Translating interweaving narratives, combining diverse creations

The combination of collaboration, activism, translation and storytelling is crucial for understanding Boochani's series of publications that documented daily events leading up to, during, and after the 23-day siege. Using WhatsApp, he typed the reports into his phone and sent them to me for translation (one daily report was also translated by Mansoubi [Boochani, 2017c]). At the time I was in Cairo and during the ominous weeks before the intense 23 days I flew back to Sydney – while traveling back to Australia I was continuously communicating with Boochani, rushing to translate, and anxiously following the news. I recall at another point I was translating on the plane back to Cairo while everything was building up to the beginning of the siege. I needed to deliver the English text to Boochani as soon as I landed in Egypt so that he could then pass it on to his contact at the *Guardian* for immediate publication.

> 20 October 2017: "I'm going back to Egypt tomorrow and my time is really constrained. I can probably translate all the recent diary entries on the flight. Look after yourself, keep me updated."
>
> 24 October 2017: "I'll try and get the article done tonight. I was held back a bit by some internet problems and all the travelling. But I can focus now."
>
> *(Boochani and Tofighian, Summer 2018)*

At that point in time – October/November/December 2017 – I had translated the whole manuscript for what became *No Friend but the*

Mountains except for the final chapter which Boochani was struggling to complete due to the dangerous, stressful and unpredictable situation. It is significant that Boochani had started writing the final chapter just before the siege and had made attempts to complete it during the 23 days – the content of the final chapter relates to the riot/uprising of 2014 when 23-year-old Kurdish Iranian refugee Reza Barati was murdered by an Australian guard, a New Zealand guard, and PNG guards. Satah was Barati's roommate and the key witness of his murder and had his life threatened as a result of pursuing justice. He pressured PNG police and made claims through the courts: the legal documents he helped prepare, his translations of various accounts from the fatal incident and during the legal process, and his interpreting work in different spaces and with different people, all constitute a complex multidimensional narrative of struggle against systemic violence. This nexus presents its own language of resistance. Satah's fight to hold the killers and authorities accountable has been a fragmented, disrupted, disjointed and shattered process (see note one for reports covering Satah's struggle and risks in the context of Barati's death and other situations).

Although his writing was disrupted by the standoff Boochani returned to the last chapter after I translated the final article about the siege ('A Letter from Manus Island', [2017a]). The last chapter of the book was sent to me in completed draft form as one text message in the weeks after the end of the siege. This is the only chapter that was not written and translated in the same manner as previous chapters: that is, until then text messages of different lengths were sent to Mansoubi over a length of time, arranged by her into a PDF, then the PDF chapter was emailed to me for translation and editing, which then involved random messages sent to me for additions/changes, and was followed by subsequent stages of reviews and final editing.

In the case of the last chapter, the whole piece of writing was sent to me directly as a single WhatsApp message, after which I translated and edited it to become Chapter 12: 'In Twilight/The Colours of War'. The first draft translation of the chapter – and with that the draft of the whole book – was completed right at the end of 2017 (I began the book project in December 2016, the first draft translation took exactly one year).

Just after the 2018 release of *No Friend but the Mountains* I translated and constructed a unique and experimental article for the literary journal *Meanjin*, entitled 'The Last Days of Manus Prison' (Boochani and Tofighian, summer 2018). This piece brings together WhatsApp text messages and voice texts between Boochani and myself from October/November 2017, and excerpts from articles written and translated during the same months (with references at the end to the December 2017 publications). This work represents an epitext for both the siege articles and *No Friend but the Mountains*. It exemplifies the special kind of creative, intellectual and political outcomes made possible through the interweaving of collaboration, activism, translation and storytelling. This mix of translated text messages and reportage also manifests the fragmented, disrupted, disjointed and shattered qualities indicative of 1) the identities, 2) the political landscapes, 3) all aspects of the production process, and 4) literary dimensions.

In the extended version of my interview with *Vertigo* magazine (see appendix to Chapter 5; this version contains numerous responses published here for the first time) I provide some of the details and qualities relevant to horrific surrealism. My discussion of fragmentation, disruption, disjointedness and shattered phenomena in relation to the four points mentioned above corresponds directly with issues of planning, process and product. It has been helpful for me to interpret these four points as they manifest in all examples of collaborative work with refugees, especially the siege series of articles, *No Friend but the Mountains,* and 'Last Days'.

> Horrific surrealism is a scheme – a form of epistemic and aesthetic framework – that helps understand 1) the identity of the author and his experiences of oppression and domination; 2) it is important for examining Australia's political situation in the context of global border politics; 3) it is central in explaining the mode of production in the making of the book and Behrouz's other projects; and 4) it opens up appropriate and heuristic spaces for interpreting the style, content, structure and tropes used in the book. One of the great strengths of the book is the fact that all four of these factors reflect horrific surrealism. In this way they mutually reinforce each other. Therefore, a deep reading of the text requires consideration of the interconnectedness of these dimensions in the framework of horrific surrealism. This matrix includes features such as fragmentation, disjointedness disruption; absurdity; the role of the subconscious; psychological horror; dreams visions; satire and irony; assemblages of objects and symbols from the built environment and natural environment; personification and anthropomorphism; a critical form of figuration; and exploring the possibilities of anti-genre. These interpretations are the result of collaborative intellectual and creative work and involved deep consultation on all levels. This relationship and method helped with translating all the personal and traumatic aspects. (appendix to Chapter 5; also see appendix 1 to this chapter)

The translated articles pertaining to the 23-day siege document the events and experiences during one of the most ruthless and disastrous periods in the history of offshore detention (and Australia's history of migration). But they also function as forerunners or preludes to *No Friend but the Mountains* in several pivotal ways (in addition to some scholarly and non-academic publications I produced or co-authored with Boochani). For instance, they document the increasing influence of horrific surrealism – which is fundamental to all aspects of the book – on the writing and translation of the journalism pieces (which already manifested horrific surrealism but to a lesser extent in comparison to the book and several artistic projects such as the film *Chauka, Please Tell Us the Time*). 'A Letter' published just after the forced evictions is the best example of horrific surrealism in the series (and the final article in the siege series) in terms of structure, style, content, writing process and translation; and the letter can be seen as a direct bridge to the book. In addition, the 2018 co-authored article 'Last Days' operates in multidimensional ways: as an epitext for the siege series of articles from the previous year; a frame narrative for the 23-day siege; a frame narrative for the final chapter of *No Friend but the Mountains* (and for the whole work if one considers the numerous references to the rest of the book, its preparation for publication, and the poetic and symbolic interplay between the titles I devised for the first and final chapters ['Under Moonlight/The Colour of Anxiety' and 'In Twilight/The Colours of War']); and as a window into the chaotic and intense collaborative encounters related to our planning, processes and products.

Gillian Whitlock conducts an insightful and complex reading of the connections between text and epitext in this situation which I will draw on to further support my arguments about the combination between collaboration, activism, translation and storytelling. She explores 'Last Days' as a comprehensive example of how hierarchies of authorship, translation and reception are upended by the material, discursive and aesthetic impact of the border and the specific carceral-site in question, i.e. Manus Prison (Whitlock, 2020, p. 712). After engaging with Whitlock's deft analysis of the relationship between the text and epitext I will expand on certain points pertaining to epistemic injustice.

In the articles written and translated during October/November/December of 2017 (also including one article published in July, 2017 about the impending closure of the Lombrum facility), collaboration, activism, translation and multi-directional narrative threads combined in uncanny and productive ways. These connections produced a series of interweaving literary products, all created simultaneously: the articles addressing the 23-day siege; the final chapter of *No Friend but the Mountains*; and the text messages which were later coupled with excerpts from the articles to produce 'Last Days'. Whitlocks emphasises the collaborative dimensions involved in the writing and translation while giving attention to the influence of other vital factors: interaction with media contacts/editors, communication technology and the role of audience responses. Highlighting the links between multiple co-creative writing/translation projects during the siege she states: "An intense and collaborative process of translation and collaboration across languages, platforms, and media occurred at a critical moment in the development of the final chapter of *No Friend*: "In Twilight/The Colours of War." (Whitlock, 2020, p. 712)

The production of the last chapter of *No Friend but the Mountains* and a series of diary-style journalism articles for the *Guardian* ('The Diary of Disaster'), as Whitlock discusses, occurred simultaneously and are interrelated in multifaceted ways. I will add that, in addition to 'The Diary of Disaster' pieces she refers to, my translations of Boochani's writing from this time include one article for the *Huffington Post* (which features in 'Last Days'). There is also a *Guardian* compilation article published on 4 December with an introduction by deputy editor Will Woodward reflecting on the chronicles (Boochani, 2017c, only the 1 December report at the end of this publication is previously unpublished). This piece by itself functions like an epitext for 'Diary of Disaster'. Woodward refers to the forthcoming book (the title had not yet been confirmed), a journalism award Boochani won at the time, and my role as translator in 'Diary'. In addition, the articles from the siege series end with the poetic manifesto about the 23 days written and translated for *The Saturday Paper* – 'A Letter'. A piece that has been forgotten when addressing this nexus of collaborative writing and translation (even by myself before writing this book) is a July 2017 article by Boochani which I translated for *The Saturday Paper*. In this early article he discusses the situation in the prison camp once the closure of the Lombrum facility had been announced and the preparations for removal of refugees had begun. The situation in this piece corresponds with some of the oral history from Satah describing the way refugees (especially the other main leaders from the time of the siege listed below) were standing up to any attempts to intimidate, remove or attack them.

It is crucial to consider the narratives Satah has shared with me (mainly through WhatsApp voice texts in Persian) about the creative forms of protest during the months leading up to the siege (starting before Boochani's July 2017 article was written and translated), during the 23 days, and the consequences afterwards. The oral history depicting the resistance against moves by authorities to force refugees to leave are preambles to the October/November siege, they are reflections and analysis about the protests, and they provide valuable interpretations of the way those events transformed the realities and futures of the refugees involved. These examples of oral history deserve to be acknowledged and examined for so many important reasons, including the way they highlight the role of imprisoned refugees operating as interpreters and translators in the resistance.

Personal communication and reception within the siege narrative

18 October 2017:

Behrouz: Hi Omid, how are you? All good? I was just in Lorengau and on my way back now. Look, the *Guardian* got in touch, they're saying they want to publish diary entries for the two weeks leading up to the closure of the prison. Each entry will only need to be about 300–400 words. I know you're really busy, but is it possible to work on this together ... do you have the time and energy?

Omid: How interesting! The project sounds fascinating! There's a lot going on at the moment and I'm also worried about the writing and translation of the book. But I think about 300 words a day is doable.

As mentioned above, Whitlock also draws attention to the pivotal role of other actors such as our contacts in the media (including editors) and audiences in Australia and internationally (she uses the term 'witnessing publics'; 2020, p. 712). As we indicate in the text message exchanges that feature in 'Last Days', the *Guardian* commissioned the diary collection. I emphasise again that the planning, processes and products are affected by fragmentation, disruption, disjointedness and shattered qualities – fundamental features of horrific surrealism – which also coincide with the identities of the people involved; the socio-political dimensions; the mode of production and issues such as structure, style, the assemblage of content and literary techniques. In Whitlock's analysis, the role of the external actors determined many significant features pertaining to format, length, timing, arrangement and the paratexts that help present the translated works (in particular, see 'Last Days' and the *Guardian* article in which Woodward, the deputy editor, introduces a collection from 'The Diary of Disaster'). The audience and the media actors become part of the horrific surrealism. By interpreting all these elements associated with the translation of the siege series of works through the lens of horrific surrealism new understandings emerge about the planning, processes and products.

From among all the online media publications during this October/November/December period 'A Letter' is closest to *No Friend but the Mountains* in terms of the literary style of horrific surrealism and its concomitant translation approach (when I refer to the siege series I include all of these publications, including 'Last Days' and the one article from July I mentioned above). But this extensive and more complete account also illuminates how new knowledges are produced through collaboration, activism, translation and the stories that connect and constitute them.

Consider the selection of dialogues between Boochani and myself below which reflect how we worked to write and translate during the high-pressure

Collaboration, activism, translation and storytelling

and ominous period leading up to the siege. The WhatsApp voice/text messages communicate the furious anticipation and various acts of resistance leading up to the closure and the articles written and translated with urgency during that period. These selected passages from 'Last Days' also provide evidence for the essential role that external actors played in the writing and resistance. Throughout the process we considered requests and feedback from media contacts and editors, the levels of interest among audiences, and even the dynamics of WhatsApp communication, the availability of Mansoubi and myself as translators, our ambitions regarding the unfinished book and the book publisher who was anticipating the manuscript. All of these elements function to condition the planning, process and product. They also create new epistemic resources and contribute to the conditions that produce new knowledges.

25 October 2017:

Behrouz: It's really interesting ... The *Guardian* has asked for the diary entries again. I've gone and integrated the diary entries so they make up a complete article. But they want short daily reports about every-day things. Can we do that together? I really don't want to take up your time. Moones Mansoubi can help as well. It's just for a few days.

I'll send you the first diary entry tonight. It'll be short. But it's hard to express what happens here during a whole day in a succinct article.

26 October 2017:

Behrouz: The *Guardian* loved the first entry, they really want to know what life is like for the refugees inside the prison camp. Based on this response imagine the reaction to the book.
Omid: You see, I translated the diary entries in the same way I translated the book—it has a special literary quality to it. It's like a narrative, it's gripping in that way, I use literary techniques to translate the account ... I think that's why they liked it. It's like the article about Duck Man. This is the story about 'The last days in Manus prison'.

31 October 2017 (first day of the siege [my addition]):

Behrouz: The whole thing is critical. The authorities have gone and left us alone here. We're stuck here in the prison camp and no-one is around.

Hey Omid, the *Guardian* has got in touch ... they're asking me to keep writing. Do you have time to translate something short?

Omid: For sure, send it.

1 November 2017:

Behrouz: The first article was fantastic. It had such a great response. Richard Flanagan got in touch with me to express his support. It's significant that the article was shared continuously on Twitter. You know what that means? A lot of people are reading about what is going on here. It's pretty extraordinary. Even when a president posts on Twitter it usually doesn't get this many retweets. There are a lot of readers. The *Guardian* loved it as well... So much interest and outrage over the atrocities happening here.

Omid: I'm so pleased to hear it.

Behrouz: Hi Omid, I wanted to share some good news with you ... you'll be happy to hear that I've won the Amnesty International award for journalism. Two articles were sent through with my nomination: the one we published about Faysal Ishak Ahmed and the one that Moones Mansoubi translated about the island I used to visit off Manus. I wanted to let you know, thanks for everything.

Omid: Congratulations, Behrouz! I'm so happy to hear this. It's wonderful news. You should be given awards from everywhere. You're doing such important work. And it's really special that the Faysal article was acknowledged together with Moones' piece. We're a good team ... we're always with you. It's fantastic news. There's more to come.

Behrouz: I'll write something tonight for publication tomorrow. It'll just be like this for a few days. I just want to say that what we're doing is like a new style of literature. These are the beginnings of some important literary projects that we need to work on in the future. It's not simply journalism ... it's part of our bigger project.

Omid: You're absolutely right. These articles are now part of a legacy. They're part of history ... they'll be here forever. For years people will be referring to these articles.

Behrouz: I'll send you another article in three to four hours.

2 November 2017:

Behrouz: The nights are horrible here. The mosquitoes are torturing us. It's not just starvation and thirst. We're fighting off the mosquitoes all the time.

Thanks for the translation, I'm going to put the title as you suggested: 'Manus is a landscape of horrific surrealism'.

You know ... people on the outside don't know. It's really horrific in here. It's really tough. We need to talk about it later ... I just woke up and received some bizarre messages.

The *Guardian* wants to publish something every day this week.

Omid: Send them! I'm here.
Behrouz: I'll send another one to you tonight.

2 November 2017:

Behrouz: ... The *Guardian* got in touch and says that three of the top five shared articles today are mine.
Omid: A journalist from AJ+ got in touch and wants to contact you in order to create a video.
Behrouz: Hi Omid, are you all right? It's 5 am here. I just sent you the article. I swear I'm so tired. I hope you can translate it quickly.

I wrote it using a literary voice ... something like the book.

7 November 2017:

Behrouz: I notified the *Guardian* and told them I haven't eaten a thing and I'm starving, so I simply can't write today.
The *Huffington Post* is going to publish the last article.
(Boochani and Tofighian, Summer 2018)

Epistolic networks and legacies: writing and translating letters about a tragedy

I think it was sometime after the publication of the *Guardian* diary entries and the *Huffington Post* article, and while I was still translating the retrospective piece 'I write from Manus as a Duty to History' (published 6 December) Boochani received a request from Erik Jensen, editor of *The Saturday Paper*, who had already published many of Boochani's translated articles (including the article from July 2017 related to the announcement of the closure of the Lombrum facility – the first publication in the siege series). Boochani was asked to write something new about the tragedy, the ruthlessness of the events that had unfolded, and the inspiring resistance in Manus Island over the past two months. Sitting outside his sleeping quarters soon after being manhandled, evicted, arrested for hours, intimidated and threatened, and finally taken to a new carceral site in Lorengau, Boochani wrote something that blended epistolary, manifesto and a kind of literary prose which I translated and edited as poetry (an excellent example of the term anti-genre which I use to refer to his works and those of other imprisoned/recently released refugees; see appendix 1 to this chapter). I translated the work in the same way as most of the diary entries, an approach very close to the way I translated *No Friend but the Mountains.* This involved translating Persian prose into poetry in English – something I had already been developing at the time while translating the text messages that ended up becoming the book, a practice I felt was perfect for this closing piece about the siege (in relation to Chapter 12 of the book see notes on translation at the end of this chapter).

The translation of 'A Letter' received an extraordinary reception which included several artistic and scholarly responses. These performances and publications amplified the importance of the message, the depiction of events, and the literary style of 'A Letter'. Also, by extension, they created a unique multidimensional and interconnected legacy for the catastrophic 23-day siege. The scholarly responses must also be considered epitexts and frame narratives for the siege chronicles and articles (published in *The Saturday Paper, Guardian* and *Huffington Post*); they also function in the same way, albeit indirectly, for the final chapter of the book, and they are linked intertextually with 'Last Days' (for example, see Whitlock, 2020).

In one example of performance, *The Saturday Paper* arranged for writer Maxine Beneba Clarke to read the genre-defying letter in the courtyard at the Malthouse Theatre in Melbourne on the day of publication. Also, in an extremely important example of scholarly writing about 'A Letter', academic Anne Surma wrote her own letter in response to Boochani which was later published in *Continuum: Journal of Media and Cultural Studies* as "In a Different Voice: 'A Letter from Manus Island' as Poetic Manifesto" (2018). Before its publication, Surma's letter itself elicited its own response from her addressee when the managing editor of the journal requested that I contact Boochani (still held in Manus Island at the time) to arrange a response letter to Surma's own response letter. My translation of Boochani's reply was later published alongside her piece as "Manus Prison Poetics/Our Voice: Revisiting 'A Letter from Manus Island', a Reply to Anne Surma" (2018c).

The translation of Boochani's response letter further emphasises the important confluence of collaboration, activism, translation and storytelling in the construction of these forms of creative resistance and knowledge production. A close analysis of these factors is vital for illustrating how these collective initiatives achieve epistemic justice. Like the other projects, the writing and translation of Boochani's response letter manifests the fragmented, disrupted, disjointed and shattered qualities indicative of the identities involved, political environment, mode of production and literary dimensions. After receiving the request from the journal's managing editor

I discussed the opportunity with Boochani; as soon as he accepted we devised a strategy to produce the response. We had limited time; there were many divergent pressures related to the detention industry; we both had other responsibilities and projects; and we had our own personal concerns and commitments. Therefore, I proposed that I summarise and translate Surma's letter in a series of WhatsApp voice messages. Producing a written Persian translation of Surma's academic paper for Boochani to engage with would have been an enormous task – something that would have been extremely difficult to complete for publication considering the timeframe, conditions, level of complexity, and other factors. Boochani listened to the voice texts repeatedly and asked me some questions by text and voice message. Eventually, he wrote his response letter (to Surma's response letter) on his phone, sent it to me by WhatsApp text message, and I translated and edited it in time to meet the deadline. I also wrote my own academic article for the journal (a more traditional scholarly piece in which I incorporate translated personal correspondence with Boochani from the preceding years): all three papers are published in *Continuum* (2018) in the following order:

Anne Surma (2018) – "In a Different Voice: 'A Letter from Manus Island' as Poetic Manifesto"; Behrouz Boochani (2018c) – "Manus Prison Poetics/Our Voice: Revisiting 'A Letter from Manus Island', a reply to Anne Surma", translated by Omid Tofighian; and Omid Tofighian (2018c) – "Behrouz Boochani and the Manus Prison Narratives: Merging Translation with Philosophical Reading."

The journal issue was reproduced as a book in 2021 by the issue editors and the journal's managing editor (Timothy Laurie) who contacted me with the original request for Boochani: *Unsettled Voices: Beyond Free Speech in the Late Liberal Era*. I was also invited to contribute to writing the afterword for the book: Tanja Dreher, Michael Griffiths, Timothy Laurie and Omid Tofighian, 'Afterword: Reconstructing Voices and Situated Listening' (2021).

In 2023 Moones Mansoubi and I edited *Freedom, Only Freedom: the prison writings of Behrouz Boochani*; the translation of Boochani's second book (2023). This publication consists of short pieces which Mansoubi and I translated and edited over many years and helped to publish in different forums. We also invited many collaborators from over the years to write reflections on some of the pieces. Surma (2023) contributed a piece to this collection about Boochani's writing and expands on themes from her 2018 response to 'A Letter'. Titled "Boochani's 'Political Poetics': subverting and reimagining the fiction of politics", her piece also discusses an example of a co-authored piece by Boochani and myself which was originally published in 2020 and republished in the new 2023 collection (Boochani and Tofighian, 2023 [2020]). Surma also assisted us with editing several other contributions.

The articles in *Freedom, Only Freedom* are arranged chronologically with one whole chapter dedicated to the 23-day siege. As I mentioned, Kanapathi (2023) wrote a piece about his experience resisting during the siege alongside Boochani and the rest of the men. He also explains how Boochani advised him regarding the development of his own writing and media work. Erik Jensen (2023), the managing editor of *The Saturday Paper*, wrote about the importance of writing and publishing during this period and commissioning 'A Letter'. The afterlife of 'A Letter' manifests in multiple ways, as does the other translation products from the time of the siege. As an example of 'born-translated literature' (Bielsa 2023, pp. 23–24; Walkowitz, 2015; Zhang, 2016) 'A Letter' – like all other works by Boochani apart from *No Friend but the Mountains* which was published in Persian in Iran [2020] after the English edited translation [see Barseghian, 2020] – was not published in the source language (and most likely will never be published). Actually, there was never a plan to publish *No Friend but the Mountains* in Persian but Boochani decided to release the Persian edition after the success of the English edited translation. These points invite interesting reflections regarding Benjamin's notion of translation as the afterlife of a work; in the cases I describe the boundaries between translation and original are blurred. The works warrant discussion about hierarchies, definitions and practices of authorship, translation and co-creation, and non-linear production processes.

In another extremely significant example of co-created writing that emerged from the siege, six imprisoned refugees involved in the protests contributed their social media reportage from the October/November 2017 period to help produce a riveting and edifying article. The article was completed in 2018 and published several years later in the special issue of the journal *Southerly* 79(2) – *Writing Through Fences: Archipelago of Letters* (2021) – as mentioned earlier, I was one of the guest editors with Janet Galbraith, Hani Abdile and Behrouz Boochani. The co-authored piece consists of an introduction written by the journal guest editors and many social media posts (mainly Twitter) written by Hass Hassaballa, Samad Abdul, Behrouz Boochani, Mohamed Adam, Walid Zazai and Shaminda Kanapathi (2021); the curators of the posts are Janet Galbraith and Mohamed Adam (who was still held in Manus Prison in 2018 while he was collaborating with Galbraith to curate the article). The special issue, which I have already explained, is dedicated to writing and art by people (women, men and children) who were held in Australia's carceral-border archipelago or were recently released while writing; the archipelago refers to carceral sites in Manus Island/Port Moresby in PNG, the Republic of Nauru, Christmas Island and the Australian mainland, and Australian-run facilities in Indonesia.

'Siege' is an assemblage of writing posted on social media in the form of urgent reports, curated by one of the imprisoned refugees (Adam) together with a refugee rights activist in Australia (Galbraith). Adam is himself a writer who published the first chapter of his autobiography in the same issue (2021; translated from Arabic by Noman Ahmed Ashraf, a former student of the American University in Cairo, originally from Yemen and now based in the US after being accepted as a refugee). I also worked with Adam to publish a piece about the siege in *Transition: the magazine of Africa and the diaspora* (2018; a special issue about Bla(c)kness in Australia [edited by Sujatha Fernandes and Jared Thomas] and which also includes a contribution by Hassaballa, 2018 [another contributor to the 'Siege' article], poetry by Abdile, 2018, and a scholarly article by myself, 2018b). Galbraith is also a writer who founded the Writing Through Fences collective (and maintains it in collaboration with Abdile) from which the majority of the contributions to the special issue come from. As I discuss in my translator's note to *No Friend but the Mountains* (Tofighian, 2018d, pp. xix-xx), she was instrumental in Boochani's writing, media presence and resistance; the book is dedicated to her. These examples offer yet further connections between Boochani's writing from the siege, the writing and other acts of resistance by all refugees involved in the siege, and my translation of Boochani's book and other writing. Last, but not least, in her reflection piece on the special issue of *Southerly*, writer Melissa Lucashenko writes about and quotes from 'Siege':

> These words from the innocent are unforgettable. Which is precisely why Australian governments have tried so hard to close their voices down, and prevent any free press access to them. There is no freedom of expression about refugee lives offshore, because free expression is a powerful and moving thing that will ultimately force change.
>
> *Mosquitoes kindly don't bite us tonight ...*
> *we are already tortured by horrible people.*
>
> It's my deep hope that one day every non-refugee seeking Australian citizenship will have to read and study and analyse Siege, rather than some bullshit weasel words from governments about freedom of the press being a core Australian value, when it transparently is not.
>
> *6 days since AUS GOV cut FOOD, WATER, POWER on*
> *#Manus refugees camp but we've humanity-siblings in AUS.*
> *Thank you 4 standing, supporting us,*
> *love you.*
>
> This is what literature can be. Should be.
>
> *Dear moon thank you for your companionship.*

This is speaking truth to power in the simplest, most significant way imaginable. If you don't read anything else this year—read *Siege*. And then act. Nobody is illegal on stolen Aboriginal land.

(Lucashenko, 2021, p.23)

The co-authored article 'Siege' epitomises the notion of horrific surrealism. In particular, consider the power of the first tweet in the collection, and possibly the first social media post about the siege, written by Hassaballa:

'—Hass Hassaballa. First Response
Shout out with us #WorldPeople.
WE DON'T WANT TO BE MOVED TO ANOTHER DETENTION
WE WANT THE #FREEDOM' (p. 267).

Like the earlier examples, these details about 'Siege' emphasise the important confluence of collaboration, activism, translation and storytelling in projects of creative resistance and knowledge production. By including messages written in real time by people inside the prison during the October/November siege period, the article is an extremely pivotal intellectual and political resource and can be leveraged to arrive at epistemic justice. Elements such as fragmentation, disruption, disjointedness and shattered qualities are clear in all aspects of the work: the identities involved, political context, mode of production and literary properties.

After the siege was over, the final article 'A Letter' was translated and published, and the draft version of the final chapter of *No Friend* was translated and partly edited (both works completed in December 2017). From that point the complete first draft of the book began to move in new and important directions leading up to publication on 31 July, 2018. From December 2017 forward, with the full text completely translated, Boochani's role shifted. In the last six months before publication I simply clarified my editing decisions with him (decisions made in collaboration with the copyeditor at the publisher; for examples of the development see notes on translation at the end of this chapter), most of which he agreed with. At the end of 2017 all the translated chapters were still rough drafts and I needed to do some comprehensive editing work, conduct more research about many points and issues, fact check, make stylistic and structural adjustments, finalise chapter titles, format the text, and so much more – I dedicated another six months to completing the English text once the first draft of the full manuscript was translated.

The attacks on detained refugees ignited multiple acts of coordinated resistance from within the prison and involved collaboration with supporters outside – people on Manus Island, Australia, and around the world. The acts of defiance that took place during this period became the basis for many important productions and continue to inspire further examples of creative resistance. A unique shift was created, one that was necessary for reaching broader global audiences. The events of this period, the efforts of the people inside Manus Prison, and the international media attention, meant that the creative resistance was no longer relegated to the fringes of international conversations about border violence – Australia's border regime became a regular global talking point and many prominent individuals involved in international political debates and issues related to refugees made public statements demanding a response from Australian authorities.

The final visit to Manus Prison

In January 2019 I travelled to Manus Island for a third and last visit. Around that time we were informed that the translation of *No Friend but the Mountains* had won the award for non-fiction at the 2019 Victorian Premier's Literary Awards. It was due to be announced at a ceremony in Melbourne at the end of January, just a short time after I was due to return to Australia. The timing was perfect, I was able to attend the Melbourne ceremony in person. At that point we were not aware that we also won the 2019 Victorian Prize for Literature (we received that information just a short time before it was announced, toward the end of the ceremony). One of my tasks during my visit was to assist Boochani in preparing and filming his acceptance speech. After I edited and helped develop his notes, he read the speech while the ABC cameraman recorded. During that trip we were involved in extensive collaboration with the ABC, mainly to film footage for the two-part *Australian Story* documentary program about Boochani (ABC, 2019 and 2020).

During my third visit I developed ideas and plans with refugees who had been analysing their predicament in new ways and writing about diverse aspects of their experience using original approaches. I had important conversations with Kanapathi who had already been publishing his writing in English at that point and had a strong online presence. After our discussions in Manus Island I worked with him to produce a number of articles (Kanapathi, 2021), including his contribution to *Freedom, Only Freedom* (2023). During that trip I met Mardin Arvin who is a Kurdish Iranian man and friend of Boochani. He was the influence behind one of the characters from Boochani's account of the disastrous first boat journey from Indonesia in *No Friend but the Mountains*: The Friend of the Blue Eyed Boy (see chapter 2: 'Mountains and Waves/Chestnuts and Death/That River… This Sea'). After the PNG Supreme Court ruling Arvin spent most of his time outside the detention centre after he was welcomed to stay with a Manusian family. He became fluent in Tok Pisin and developed a strong understanding of the social, cultural and economic dynamics on the island. He was well known as a mediator and coordinator and would be called upon to facilitate visits to Manus Island. As with Satah, Arvin's interpreting and translating skills were important in many instances. He explained to me that when he met Manusian locals after first arranging a meeting by phone, upon seeing that he was a foreigner they often did not believe it was the same person whom they had spoken to by phone because his Tok Pisin language skills and knowledge of socio-cultural dynamics during the phone conversation were so advanced. Arvin assisted many refugees with different things over the years; in fact, Arvin explained to me that he helped Boochani smuggle his first mobile phone into the prison camp.

During my January 2019 trip to the island Arvin worked with the ABC crew to arrange almost everything that was necessary for travelling to the locations where they planned to film. Spending time together between our activities, he explained that he had been writing a short story using an approach that blended fiction and nonfiction and he wanted me to translate and edit for him. We remained in contact through WhatsApp and that year he was transferred to Australia for urgent medical treatment made possible by the Medevac Bill (Reilly, 2019). However, like all the other refugees transferred to Australia under Medevac, Arvin never received the medical treatment he needed and was instead imprisoned in two different Melbourne hotels for over a year (also known as Alternative Places of Detention or APODs). The piece he was writing when I met him, which he finished while detained in an Australian hotel, is a fictional story that incorporates aspects of his real-life experiences in Manus Prison and the boat journey to reach Australia. I finished translating the story 'Close the Eyes of Your Conscious' in 2020 and it was published by the literary journal *Meanjin* (Spring 2020). Using a very compelling and original approach, it is written from the narrative voice of a woman psychologist working in Manus Island. After this piece I translated opinion pieces and helped Arvin publish them in the *Guardian* (2020a, 2020c, 2020d), *Overland* (2020b) and *Critical Legal Thinking* (2021).

An extensive non-fiction narrative of his experience living with a Manusian family is published in the special issue of *Southerly* (excerpt printed in hardcopy [2021], full story published online in Long Paddock [2021]): 'Pokun the Little Black King'. I suggested the eponymous title which refers to the young boy from the family. I translated the story but at one point I suggested that Arvin, who is also a translator, provide me with selected words in Tok Pisin to include within the narrative. This added a unique quality to the text and drew attention to the embedded nature of his experience and writing. I translated the story and Arvin's translated terms contributed to the final product.

Before my January 2019 trip to Manus Island I was contacted by presenter and comedian Dan Ilic who was commissioned by Doha Debates to create videos about the situation in Manus Island. He asked me to assist which I did by introducing him to people, providing advice for planning the visit, and acting as a consultant. We had long conversations about many aspects of the intellectual, creative and political work I had been doing in collaboration with refugees over the years. Boochani and I are credited as writers for one of his videos which features Boochani and refers to my translation of text messages. The video also shows footage from the time of the siege (Doha Debates, 2020a). In another video (Doha Debates, 2020b) Ilic was influenced by the arguments in my article 'Black Bodies for Political Profit' (2018b) which I sent him to read before his visit (the contents of which we discussed at length) together with the writings of Hassaballa (2018) and Adam (2018) whose articles I helped produce and publish in the same issue of *Transition*. The three pieces were published in 2018 together with poetry by Abdile (2018). Ilic also collaborated closely with other refugees to critique Australia's border regime by producing forms of political satire (he made the second 2020 video with Shaminda Kanapathi, Abdul Aziz Muhamat, Amin Abofotila and Omar Jack; see Jeffreys, 2019).

I started working with Adam after I saw one of his online posts which included a photo of him during the 23 days of protests – the sign he was holding referred to their situation as a new form of slavery. Inspired and curious about his message, I asked Boochani to introduce us and we soon began collaborating. His protest image and our conversations about his perspective influenced my article for *Transition* and guided us as we worked together to produce his contribution and the piece by Hassaballa. These works in turn helped shape the dialogue in Ilic's video (for details of Ilic's visit to Manus Island see Piotrowski, 2019). Adam introduced me to Hassaballa who immediately expressed interest in collaborating to create his article (to create the pieces by Adam and Hassaballa I assembled and interweaved fragments of their protest slogans, social media posts, WhatsApp messages, short biographies and new writing).

The video influenced by the *Transition* pieces features Kanapathi, Omar Jack and Abdul Aziz Muhamat who won a prestigious human rights prize in 2019 – the Martin Ennals award – for the work he did on *The Messenger* podcast (co-produced by Behind the Wire and published by the *Guardian* in 2017). Muhamat became known internationally during the siege for his leadership role in the prison camp and his collaboration with the Australian and international media. He was invited to Geneva, Switzerland to receive the award. After traveling there for the ceremony he was granted asylum (Guardian 2019; HRLC 2019).

Finally, like my previous trips I met with Satah a number of times during my final visit to Manus Prison. He was always busy working in support of other detained refugees which often involved interpreting and translating. While Boochani and Muhamat were widely known internationally as the main voices for people held in Manus Island, Satah was acknowledged as one of the most active and influential amongst the various communities within the prison and throughout the island: refugees, local staff, Australian staff, international staff, UNHCR, and others. His imprisonment lasted long after I last saw him in 2019 (he departed from Port Moresby in 2020), and after most had left PNG. Over the years we have maintained our relationship over WhatsApp and communicate regularly now that he has been resettled in France. Satah continues to advocate for people forgotten and stranded in Port Moresby, and people who were held in Manus Island and Nauru and are experiencing hardship after being transferred to Australia or resettled in a third country. He even maintains his role as interpreter and translator by phone, messaging app or email because of the insufficient support provided in most cases. We have also begun discussing collaborative projects to document, represent and analyse the atrocities that have taken place and continue to damage people's lives.

During one of our recent discussions and planning sessions Satah sent me recordings of speeches he and other refugees made during the 23 days. The connections between these forms of oral history and the published works from the siege are remarkable and worthy of further study. During these speeches made by Satah and others they announce to a large gathering for the first time that the protesters must make their demands clear since they were concerned about the way their resistance was being portrayed in the media. They shared information about agreements made in earlier meetings between the main leaders selected during the siege period. Their conclusions, established principles and proposals for the best way forward culminated in a series of statements made at various times during the siege which can be interpreted as part of a manifesto.

One of the main points they communicated to the entire group present at the gathering – which was recorded using a mobile phone – was the fact that they were demanding nothing but *freedom*. The protests had nothing to do with food, water, electricity, medicine, or other services. *Only freedom*. They were protesting at this crucial time for *freedom from indefinite detention*, and nothing else. In the audio recordings Satah and other organisers spoke English and engaged in a call and response exchange with everyone in attendance to confirm the principles from this aspect of their manifesto. Those in attendance who functioned as interpreters shared this information with others within their communities.

The many diverse examples of political organising, chains of interpreting and translation work involving many languages and dialects, the work of the main leaders during the siege, and the cumulative presentations through speeches and meetings in the months leading up to, during and after the siege constitute a special form of manifesto. The assemblage of some of these elements are represented in Boochani's 'A Letter', which has itself been referred to as a poetic manifesto. In 'A Letter' Boochani pays tribute by referring to the pivotal role played by leaders representing various communities during the siege; these individuals were Benham Satah (Kurdish Iranian), Yasir Hussain (Pakistani), Bashir Osman (Sudanese) and Abdul Aziz Muhamat (Sudanese).

> When the police chief stood in front of the community of half-naked refugees and named the leaders over the loudspeaker, asking them to surrender themselves, everyone called out:
>
> 'I'm A …!'
> 'I'm Y …!'
> 'I'm B …!'
> This was the scene that emerged in Manus prison.
>
> *(Boochani, 2017a)*

Other features of the collective manifesto that I referred to above correspond with Boochani's writings and the projects initiated by others. The speeches presented by Satah and his fellow organisers are reflected in Boochani's important article from the siege period. He writes:

> The issue is plain and simple. We did not come to Australia to live in a prison. The peaceful protest by refugees is not because we want to remain in this prison. We are resisting because we want freedom in a safe environment. The core concern is *freedom … only freedom*. The rest of what you hear are just peripheral issues.
>
> *(Boochani 2017f, emphasis added)*

The collective organising and discussions, speeches by Satah and other organisers/protesters, and other aspects of the resistance are mutually reinforcing elements within a unique knowledge ecosystem which continue to have multiple afterlives. The above statement published in the translated article reflects Satah and his fellow organisers' clarification regarding the priority of freedom from indefinite detention (and nothing else). The phrase 'freedom, only freedom' was written on placards at protests in Australia, and later became the title of the co-translated/co-edited book *Freedom, Only Freedom*.

Notes on translation

- The highlighted passages from Chapter 12 of *No Friend but the Mountains* were incorporated into a musical adaptation (part 12) – see appendix 2 below.

116   Creating new languages of resistance

- The first pages are from the initial draft translation with the corresponding source text in Persian. Both of these were competed during the 23-day siege (see Figures 3.1 and 3.2).
- The highlighted parts in the draft correspond to the subsequent excerpts from the published English edition. Also, past tense in the draft was translated into present tense for publication.

Chauka was chanting. The melody wandered through.

Chauka was screaming. Then it sang once again.

Screaming.

Chanting.

Screaming and chanting had now fused into one within the voice of the bird.

Silence for a moment.

Chauka screamed once again.

Screaming.

And screaming.

A harmony linked by screams.

A chain of screaming extending out into the furthest depths of the jungle, down into its darkest cavern.

Screaming.

Screams reverberated out of the throats of all the birds on Manus Island.

The screams of all the birds on Manus in symphony.

A ritual of screams.

All of them reached their climax within the voice of the Chauka.

چوکا آواز می خواند، صدایش می آمد، جیغ می کشید و دوباره آواز می خواند، جیغ و آواز در گلوی پرنده حالا یکی شده بود، برای لحظه ای ساکت شد و دوباره جیغ کشید، جیغ کشید و جیغ کشید، زنجیره ای از جیغ ها که تا اعماق

جنگل تاریک پیش می رفت، جیغ هایی که از گلوی تمام پرنده های جزیره در گلویش جمع شده بود.

We could hear the voice of The Hero. His voice echoed in the distance.

He was wailing. Lamentations of a man.

The sorrow of a man. His grief pouring over the prison, pounding down onto the prison.

Chauka was frightened.

Chuaka fell silent.

We could only hear the voice of The Hero.

The entire tent descended into silent.

All the men inside there became silent for a moment.

No one was around him.

The Hero was alone.

Lamenting.

Wailing.

Chauka flew down from the summit of the tallest coconut tree in the prison in order to come and unite with The Hero. Chauka descended from the highest peak.

Chauka lamented.

The Hero lamented.

The chant of a bird and the chant of a man.

Both chants blended into one.

This lament…of nature…this lamentation of nature.

This lament… of the human being… this lamentation of the human being.

The message arrived.

They killed The Gentle Giant.

صدای" قهرمان" می آمد، از دور می آمد، ناله می کرد، ناله هایی مردانه که بر سر زندان می کوبید، چوکا ترسید، چوکا ساکت شد، دیگر فقط صدای " قهرمان" می آمد، چادر و تمام مردانش برای لحظه ای ساکت شده بود، هیچ کس آنجا نبود، تنها و تنها ناله ی" قهرمان" بود، چوکا از روی بلندترین نقطه ی بلندترین درخت نارگیل زندان به سویش پرواز کرد، چوکا می نالید، " قهرمان" می نالید، صدای پرنده و صدای مرد با هم یکی شده بود، ناله ی طبیعت، ناله ی انسان، خبر این بود " غول مهربان" را کشتند.

FIGURE 3.1 and 3.2   Excerpt from Boochani's text messages which I transferred to a word doc, broke up into passages/sentences, and used to complete my English edited translation. The translation of the highlighted passages of the Persian source text and the first draft English translation correspond to the passages that follow from the English publication.

- All highlighted parts in Persian were written in prose; all excerpts from the published English edition were translated from prose into verse. The first draft of the translation had not been formatted completely as poetry yet, although it was translated in a poetic style. In particular, punctuation was a key factor when translating prose to verse and representing the poetic qualities of the target text.

Chauka is chanting. The melody wandered through /
Chauka is screaming /
Screaming /
Chanting /
Screaming and chanting fused in the voice of the bird /
Silence for a moment /
Chauka screams once more /
A harmony linked by screams /
A chain extending into the furthest depths of the jungle /
Down into its darkest cavern /
Screams reverberate from the throats of all the birds on Manus Island /
All of the birds on Manus are in symphony /
All reach their climax in the voice of the Chauka.
(Boochani, 2018a, pp. 354–355)

...
The chant of a bird and the chant of a man /
Both chants blends into one /
This lament ... of nature ... this lamentation of nature /
This lament ... of a human ... this lamentation of the human being.
(Boochani, 2018a, p. 356)

Appendix 1

This chapter includes two appendixes derived from interviews. The first appendix is from 2019 and is a translation of an interview with Fatemeh Hashemi from SBS Persian. The interview was conducted in Persian/Farsi and I translated by listening to the Persian audio and transcribing into English text – an approach I have used with many diverse collaborations. This is the first interview I conducted in Persian after the release of *No Friend but the Mountains* and winning the 2019 Victorian Prize for Literature. We discuss many issues pertaining to philosophy in relation to displacement and exile, systematic torture, colonialism, the 2017 co-directed film *Chauka, Please Tell Us the Time*, translating the term kyriarchal system, and anti-genre.

"Boochani's Book is Anti-Genre"

Interview with Omid Tofighian by Fatemeh Hashemi (SBS Radio Persian – Sydney, Australia): 28 May, 2019

- Translated by Omid Tofighian

© SBS – Omid Tofighian was interviewed by Fatemeh Hashemi for the SBS Persian podcast https://www.sbs.com.au/language/persian/fa/podcast-episode/dr-tofighian-boochanis-book-is-anti-genre/q3j7yhmlr

FH: Omid Tofighian is a researcher, translator and assistant professor of philosophy focusing on religious studies, popular culture and discrimination from a transnational perspective, and migration and displacement of people. He is affiliated with the American University in Cairo and the University of Sydney. His central research concerns and the topics of most of his work and publications involve narrative and philosophy in relation to displacement. In connection with this field of research he has also been engaged in a wide range of activism supporting refugees and migrants. Tofighian is also the translator of Behrouz Boochani's critically acclaimed book *No Friend but the Mountains* which won Australia's most important literary award last year. At the moment he lives in Cairo and during a brief visit to Australia last week I, Fatemeh Hashemi, had the opportunity to have a short conversation with him. During our dialogue I asked him about the role of literature and philosophy in illuminating the issue of displaced peoples, the achievements and hopes for Boochani's book in relation to the situation of people seeking asylum in Australia and other parts of the world.
Dr Omid Tofighian, thank you for accepting our invitation to talk to SBS Radio Persian.

OT: Thanks, Thank you very much for your invitation.

FH: At the recent 2019 Sydney Writers' Festival you participated in two events: a panel called Taking Flight: Stories of Expulsion and Migration, also a special event for the critically acclaimed book *No Friend but the Mountains*. Both of these pertain to stories of migration and displacement which is the subject of your research and many publications over the past years. I wanted to ask about the role of philosophy and literature for illuminating this difficulty associated with today's globalised world.

OT: This is a very interesting and important question. Actually, one of my concerns has been to ask why this issue of displacement and exile has not been central within discourses, with the history and methods of philosophy, particularly Western philosophy. I am interested in why these issues have not been pivotal, why these concerns have not been urgent or very important for most philosophers. I mean, they may have analysed or discussed these subjects but the topics themselves were not considered as forms of knowledge, an epistemology, or as concepts that could be considered philosophical. Why have they not been considered to a large extent, or focused on very much, in the history of philosophy? What I aim to do is combine my research and my perspective on epistemology, particularly social epistemology; combine the issue of displacement and exile with narrative and identity in this way to see the philosophical outcomes, in response to global issues, issues pertaining to identity, especially in contemporary society which is so tied up with issues of mobility, migration, borders and nationalism. What can we learn philosophically if we concentrate more on this matter, if we combine these different topics?

FH: There was also a special event at the Sydney Writer's Festival on the critically acclaimed book by Boochani for which you produced an extremely creative translation into English. I wanted to ask what central issues were expressed and what did the debates relate to?

OT: In my view, the most important topics in this book are, firstly, the issue of systematic torture. For years Behrouz wrote journalistic accounts, which I translated – Moones Mansoubi, who also had a very important role, also translated many of them. Behrouz would write these and people would become aware of the situation in Manus and Nauru, but we came to the conclusion that after reading these articles people still could not understand the kind of torture experienced by refugees in these prisons. Behrouz even co-directed a film from inside the prison using his phone, communicating through WhatsApp with Arash Kamali Sarvestani in the Netherlands. They made this film and it was screened in some of the biggest international film festivals like London and Sydney, and other places. However, after producing all these works he realised that people still have not understood exactly what has been taking place. He was convinced that the only way to introduce this message to people, this argument, this analysis, was by using literary methods. This is the first point: systematic torture and how other methods and frameworks are too weak, and how literature is the only way to reach people.

Secondly, there is something we translated into English as the kyriarchal system. The term that Behrouz constructed in Persian for this concept is *system-e hākem*. Now it is interesting that *system-e hākem* can be translated in numerous ways, in my opinion it is a really original and profound concept. *System-e hākem* is the soul, or ideology or thinking that created this prison, it also has roots in Australian society and history. It can be translated a number of ways into English 'governmental system' or 'system of governmentality', 'controlling system', 'dominating system', 'oppressive system', 'ruling system' – there are different words that could be used. However, none of them quite get at the soul, feeling or sentiment behind this concept. Luckily, I work on a theory by a feminist theologian who teaches and works at Harvard University named Elisabeth Schüssler Fiorenza. She coined a new term which has roots in [ancient] Greek but was not a term used in ancient Greece – the term she constructed is completely new: 'kyriarchy'. It can be described as an intersectional theory, it connects these systems and structures of power, discrimination and violence. Schüssler Fiorenza's argument is that if one really wants to understand violence in the contemporary world, in fact right through history, one cannot just consider racism or misogyny, or discrimination based on social or economic status. One must address the intersections between all of them. This is very important and very interesting. So I saw what Behrouz was doing through his use of *system-e hākem* was just this – he is showing how this prison is about violence or suppression related to militarism, its is about colonialism, it is about racism, even misogyny or the violence associated with homophobia, the violence or discrimination against someone's socio-economic status. One needs to consider all of these together to truly see the soul or aim of this system. As a result, I adapted this term kyriarchy to make 'the kyriarchal system'; I mean, I gave new shape to *system-e hākem* by using a term from feminist philosophy and so created a new concept in English – because what Behrouz was doing is completely original and unprecedented.

Thirdly, the colonial logic. What we are trying to do with this book is consider the roots of the things that are happening in this prison which are found within European colonialism in Australia. What has occurred in relation to the Indigenous peoples of Australia – Aboriginal and Torres Strait Islander peoples – and what is still occurring, the discrimination they face, their marginalisation, or even a form of genocide, I argue that this same system, methods and techniques are being applied in these prisons. This is really horrific and frightening. We can see how these policies, debates, discourses and theories have a lot in common. There is a lot to say about this. But the logic at work here in administering this prison can be connected directly to the logic of colonialism.

The final point is about how this book is an anti-genre. One cannot say this book is just a memoir, or an autobiography, or a philosophical treatise, it is even difficult to label it a novel. This book is really an anti-genre. There is philosophy, psychoanalysis, myth, epic, personal views and feelings, and poetry – he mixes and fuses all these together to bring about this book. The only thing I could think of to describe this book is that it's approach or attitude is 'horrific surrealism'.

FH: What do you think are the achievements of this book for communities of people seeking asylum in Australia and around the world? What do you hope it will achieve?

OT: So I have spoken a lot about this with Behrouz. Actually, we are not very hopeful regarding this generation, unfortunately. People have been so active, there have been so many different campaigns – things have not progressed, they have regressed. One of the things we expect is for people to be self-critical. After considering this book and all the things that have happened in the prison, thinking of everything together, it is really important that the work that people have been engaged in, the phenomenon of refugee activism, really has to develop into something new. We need to build foundations for the next generation.

FH: You mean we need a change of perspective, is that right?

OT: Exactly. Actually, we need to change the way we see displacement, seeking asylum, migration, and the concept of the refugee. With this book Behrouz has shown that a refugee has the ability to write the best book for these times – someone who came by boat, someone who in the media and in social discourse, unfortunately in the opinions of the majority of Australians, has always been a weak, a worthless person, a criminal, someone we should not allow into this country, someone who does not deserve rights. There is a form of knowledge manifest in the existence of this person that is unprecedented, not in anyone else. Not even me who translated his book, it still represents something that is so vast.

Therefore, one of our objectives was this – to change people's strategies, people's activism, people's methods. Also, change people's thinking, people's perspectives – their views about people in these situations really has to transform.

FH: I had another question, you are currently teaching at a university in Cairo?

OT: Yes, I was at the University of Sydney until 2017 when an opportunity appeared for me to go to Cairo. I am now teaching at the American University in Cairo, I teach philosophy and I am conducting research. Actually, it was a really good opportunity, I benefitted a lot. I have met some very interesting people. The issues and questions about refugees, borders and nationalism are also discussed a lot. Many are working on this subject, in fact there is a very large centre there with important experts [Centre for Migration and Refugee Studies]. It is interesting that in Australia I was working with Behrouz for nearly four years and found it hard to explain the significance of this work we are doing to many of my colleagues in the university, it was difficult to convey why the work of this writer was so vital and why he should be supported, and open up spaces for him. It took a long time and things progressed slowly. It is interesting that in Cairo it took no longer than two minutes before people understood and offered support and opened up spaces for this kind of work. In my view, this was a very interesting contrast.

FH: Do you have a new project or book now being prepared for publication?

OT: Yes, I recently co-edited a journal special issue with Stephanie Hemelryk Donald (University of Lincoln in UK, formerly at UNSW), Lucia Sorbera (Department of Arabic Languages and Cultures, University of Sydney) [and Kaya Davies Hayon (University of Lincoln, UK)]. Actually, Stephanie is working hard to promote our book and Behrouz's work there. This special issue is about filmmaking or cinema and refugees. I mean, films about refugees or films made by refugees. This special issue is being published and I am curating a dossier about Behrouz's co-directed film *Chauka, Please Tell Us the Time* (2017). Behrouz also has an article in this issue which I translated into English. Arash Kamali Sarvestani also has an article, along with a few others [Janet Galbraith and Jeremy Elphick]. I also have two articles in this issue. I think it will be published in October.

I have another project that might take about one or two years. It relates to the work I do in the area of social epistemology in connection with issues around seeking asylum, migration, borders and related debates [referring to the present book].

Appendix 2

The second appendix is a transcript of an audio interview with me by Roza Germian from SBS Kurdish and conducted in English. The interview is about the musical adaptation of *No Friend but the Mountains* by composer Luke Styles: *No Friend but the Mountains: A Symphonic Song Cycle* (2020). The work was completed in 2020 and first performed on 21 March, 2021 (Sidney Myer Music Bowl, Melbourne). The work is made up of twelve songs performed by a bass baritone soloist (Adrian Tamborini) together with the Melbourne Bach Choir, with the music performed by the Zelman Symphony Orchestra. The words for the twelve songs in the composition come directly from selected parts of *No Friend but the Mountains* and are made up of the poetic sections in the text. This includes an important part from the final chapter written around the time of the 23-day siege about the riot/uprising in the prison and the murder of Reza Barati: Chapter 12, "In Twilight/The Colours of War". Boochani is credited as libretto to acknowledge the use of words from the book. However, as I have explained in many publications, presentations, interviews and talks, the poetic parts of *No Friend but the Mountains* represent a more radical form of experimental rewriting; that is, the edited translation of Persian prose into English verse. While the edited translation of the whole book employs unconventional experimental methods, and the mode of production is heavily influenced by collaboration, the poetic sections in English reflect the experimental dimensions in more extreme ways. The musical adaptation of the book raises interesting questions about the relationship between authorship and translation.

The writing and translation of the book, musical adaptation, the premiere of the performance, and the two-part documentary series about the making of the composition and premiere (*No Friend but the Mountains: A Journey Through Song*, 2021), can all be interpreted as celebrations of creative resistance that evoke joy and pride, emotions that inspire and motivate further acts of creative resistance. Through collaborative projects aimed at challenging and transforming border regimes – and the multifarious forms of reception they attract – practices such as creativity, translation and celebration become political acts. Germian and I discuss these issues in addition to addressing the role of music in creative resistance, and we make connections between the marginalisation and oppression of different groups around the world, including Kurds and other peoples who experience forced migration.

Germian is also one of the contributors to *Freedom, Only Freedom* (2023): 'Kurdish Identity and Journalism: reporting to record history.' Her piece includes her own translation of a poem by the late Kurdish writer and journalist Sherko Bekas, who is known for his work on Kurdish identity, homeland and resistance by depicting dream visions and using other surrealist tropes, and incorporating existential themes throughout his work. Bekas is also a heavy influence on Boochani.

"In order to resist people also need a cause for celebration"

Interview with Omid Tofighian by Roza Germian (SBS Kurdish – Sydney, Australia): 25 February, 2021

© SBS. Interview originally published at https://www.sbs.com.au/language/kurdish/en/podcast-episode/dr-tofighian-in-order-to-resist-people-also-need-a-cause-for-celebration/pa1x5lcjv)

RG: Music has always been a powerful form of expression, whether be it emotional and personal, or as a means of resistance and conveying a much more important and larger cause. Now, the book by Kurdish author and journalist Behrouz Boochani *No Friends but the Mountains: Writing from Manus Prison* is being translated once again, this time into a musical symphony. With us today is Dr Omid Tofighian, the translator of Behrouz Boochani's book, *No Friend but the Mountains: Writing from Manus Prison*. Omid, welcome to SBS Kurdish again.

OT: Thank You for having me.

RG: It was through your amazing work of translation that the English speaking world, generally speaking, got to read Behrouz's writing. How do you feel about this musical production?

OT: Well, to be honest I had the view that this would happen one day, and I'm really excited about it. I think this is basically only one of many more adaptations and interpretations of this work.

RG: The success of the book in itself has been huge globally, but particularly in Australia. What does this mean to you?

OT: The most important thing for me and for Behrouz was to communicate what systematic torture means. This is a story about oppression. It's about domination. It's about subjugation of all marginalized, oppressed, excluded groups. Not just in the Australian context, but globally. And particularly in relation to Kurdistan. So for me, this is really important because it actually brings in different audiences, people with different, interests, different sensibilities, different ways of communicating, people who speak different languages. It introduces them to these particular themes and invites them into the debate. So hopefully with new communicators, new people to interact with, we can actually expand this conversation and bring people into the collective movement.

RG: You have been involved quite heavily in this question and this cause for refugees, particularly in Australia and the situation for asylum seekers in the recent years. Do you believe music has become a powerful method of survival and resistance for the refugees and asylum seekers in Australian detention?

OT: It's an excellent question. Certainly, for people who are held in indefinite detention, people who are subject to Australia's border regime, there's very little opportunity to resist. And people are looking for almost anything they can to fight against the system and to survive this system. So something like music is important for many different reasons. One, it connects people with their cultural heritage. It reminds them of who they are, what their character involves, what they're passionate about. And it maintains their identity because this system is designed to break people and to strip them of their identity. It's important in that respect. But also in terms of resistance. So, music, poetry, storytelling, art are always used by people in order to challenge the system in order to expose the system.

What's really interesting is that in a place like Manus Island people who were detained there would connect with different sounds, not just with music. They would connect with nature, they would connect with the stories and the culture of the local people on Manus Island. They would connect with people in other parts of the world through platforms like WhatsApp, for instance, or Facebook. And these would always involve rhythm and melody. I think this is really important because in order to resist people also need a cause for celebration, a cause for joy, a cause for hope. So I think that's what music has given them. So it's multi-dimensional. There's the element of survival and there's also the element of resistance.

RG: Do you think music became a method for them to convey their message to the wider Australian community. Through music, through their talents, for example, on social media and in the media in general?

OT: Certainly, I think that it was a good medium. But at the same time for music to gain traction it needs to be both ways. So people making the music, sending out the message is one thing. But I think the Australian public really needs to respond to that, not just in artistic ways, not just in creative ways, but also in political ways to make sure that this system doesn't continue. I think this is one of the things that we need to think about – I hope this project actually creates a discussion around this issue; that is, that there needs to be the right infrastructure for these forms of resistance, these sorts of expressions, to have a place and to be leveraged for real change, sustainable change. So I think we need the right support base. We need the right people to listen. We need the right people to be able to interpret as well, and also for it to lead to other kinds of transformation.

RG: Coming back to symphony, what can you tell us about the project and how involved have you been?

OT: I was contacted by Luke Styles, who is the composer. And that was quite some time ago, well over a year ago. I can't remember exactly, but he contacted me because he'd read the book and he was trying to communicate with Behrouz. And so I put Luke in touch with Behrouz and also wrote support letters for him so that he could get his own support and funding for this project. And I was really impressed with the work that Luke had done in the past, the people involved, and the reviews that had been written about his work. So I thought this would be a perfect fit, and I was impressed to see how things developed. Once the symphony was created I started to work with Luke and with Margot and George who are involved in this event, as well.

And we've started to work with different organisations and promoted it through different channels. I think the way that they've consulted with us has been important. I think that was vital for getting this right, for communicating this in the right way and for sending the right message. And I think that we're just at the beginning now. I think that it's got a huge future and I think hopefully more projects like this will develop. But I also think transforming this into political change is also vital, so that it's not just left at the cultural, artistic level.

RG: The production is named *No Friend but the Mountains: a Symphonic Song Cycle*. Have you had a chance to listen to the music itself, and what did you think of it?

OT: Yes, I have. I've listened to different excerpts and I think Adrian does a wonderful job of transforming the text into song. And yeah, I'm really interested to see how the whole thing comes together because, you know, listening to parts of it is one thing, but listening to the symphony as a whole, I think, will be a whole different experience. And, of course, something like this is much better live. So I hope so, if borders allow and I can come to Melbourne to see it.

RG: The premiere will be on 21st of March in Melbourne at the Sydney Mayor Musical Bowl. Dr Omid Tofighian, thank you so much for your time and all the wonderful insight you've given us today.

Note

1 One of my earliest interactions with Satah was when he supplied me with an image for my article 'Sanctions, refugees and the marginalised: Iran uprisings are Australia's concern too.' (2018a) He organised men held in Manus Prison to gather in a show of solidarity with protestors demonstrating throughout Iran during late 2017/early 2018 and recorded the action by arranging for a photograph: the sign they held reads 'Freedom for Iran from Manus Island.' Protestors in over 140 Iranian cities were risking their lives as the government began a brutal crackdown, something that significantly impacted Satah and the other incarcerated men due to their own experiences of persecution and discrimination in Iran and the distressing updates they had been receiving from family and friends at the time.

I am particularly grateful to Satah for assisting in my research and thinking for this book, including the references in this note. For reporting on Satah's leadership and activism inside the prison camp see Laughland, 2014; Doherty, 2015; Doherty, 2015; ABC, 2015; Thomas, 2015; Courier Mail, 2015; Regional, 2015; Lomai, 2016; Gordon, 2016; Mcauliffe, 2016; Guardian Australia, 2016; Cohen, 2016; Pokiton, 2016; Chalmers, 2016; Refugee Action Campaign, 2016; Doherty, 2016; Cousens, 2016; Tlozek, 2016; Parke, 2016; Parke, 2016; Siegel, 2016; Wells, 2016; Irish Times, 2016; Cohen, 2016; Moi, 2016; Naime, 2016; Kampmark, 2016; Pokiton, 2016; Hasavi Jr., 2016; Gordon, 2016; Gordon and Ellinghausen, 2017; McKenzie-Murray, 2017; Cave, 2017; Parkes, 2017; Hamilton, 2017; Doherty, 2017; Roberts, 2017; Roberts, 2017; Gordon, 2017; Gordon, 2017; SBS, 2017; RNZ, 2017; RNZ, 2017; SMH, 2017; Newman and Head, 2017; Gregoire, 2017; RCA and Amnesty, 2017, pp. 10, 15-16; Gordon, 2017; Robinson-Drawbridge, 2017; Burnside, 2017, pp.5-6; Burnside, 2018; Boochani, 2018b; Zable, 2018; Wahune, 2018; Green, July 2018; National, 2018; Post-Courier, 2018; Davidson and Boochani, 2019; SBS, 2019; Whiting, 2019; Duffin, 2019; Somaliland Standard, 2019; AAP,

2019; Lewis, 2023; McNevin, 2019; Knaus and Davidson, 2019; McNevin, 2022, p. 212; Parker, 2023.

Bibliography

AAP (2019) 'Refugee on Manus Island Sets Himself on Fire', *news.com.au*. www.news.com.au/national/refugee-on-manus-island-sets-himself-on-fire/news-story/5968430c9971c0b3d7c85103f5547221

ABC (2015) 'Reza Barati: Trial of Pair Accused of Killing Asylum Seeker Adjourned, Main Witness Fears for Life', *ABC News*. www.abc.net.au/news/2015-09-25/pair-accused-of-killing-asylum-seeker-appear-in-court/6804682

ABC (2019) 'The Invisible Man – Behrouz Boochani', *Australian Story*. www.abc.net.au/news/2019-03-28/the-invisible-man/10950080

ABC (2020) 'The Great Escape – Behrouz Boochani', *Australian Story*. www.abc.net.au/news/2020-09-03/the-great-escape/12626448

Abdile, H. (2018) 'My mother tongue, and: untitled, and: home far from home', *Transition: The Magazine of Africa and the Diaspora* 126: pp. 25–30. www.muse.jhu.edu/article/702738

Adam, M. (2018) 'Betrayal. A Prison under siege', *Transition: The Magazine of Africa and the Diaspora* 126: pp. 19–24. www.muse.jhu.edu/article/702737

Adam, M. (2021) 'The Autobiography of Mohamed Adam (Chapter One)'. Translated by Noman Ahmed Ashraf. *Southerly – Writing Through Fences: Archipelago of Letters* 79(2)pp. 124–133. www.southerlylitmag.com.au/shop/writing-through-fences-archipelago-of-letters/

Arvin, M. (Spring 2020) 'Close the Eyes of your Conscience', translated by Tofighian, O. *Meanjin*. Melbourne: Melbourne University Press. www.meanjin.com.au/fiction/close-the-eyes-of-your-conscience/

Arvin, M. (2020a) 'This is My Eighth Christmas Locked Up in Immigration Detention. Next Year I Hope to Celebrate as a Free Man', translated by Tofighian, O. *The Guardian*. www.theguardian.com/commentisfree/2020/dec/24/this-is-my-eighth-christmas-locked-up-in-immigration-detention-next-year-i-hope-to-celebrate-as-a-free-man

Arvin, M. (2020b) 'Navid vs Australia's Border Regime: Wrestling against Indefinite Detention', translated by Tofighian, O. *Overland*. www.overland.org.au/2020/12/navid/

Arvin, M. (2020c) 'Australians Complain about Weeks in Quarantine. I've been In Immigration Detention for Almost Eight Years', translated by Tofighian, O. *The Guardian*. www.theguardian.com/australia-news/commentisfree/2020/sep/14/australians-complain-about-weeks-in-quarantine-ive-been-in-immigration-detention-for-almost-eight-years

Arvin, M. (2020d) 'From Manus to Melbourne: We Do Not Even Know What We Are Being Punished for', *The Guardian*. www.theguardian.com/commentisfree/2020/aug/08/from-manus-island-to-melbourne-we-do-not-even-know-what-we-are-being-punished-for

Arvin, M. (2021) 'Pokun the Little Black King', translated by Tofighian, O. *Southerly– Writing Through Fences: Archipelago of Letters* 79(2) pp. 164–171. www.southerlylitmag.com.au/shop/writing-through-fences-archipelago-of-letters/

Arvin, M. (2021) 'Ode to Reza Barati on the Seventh Anniversary of His Death', translated by Tofighian, O. *Critical Legal Thinking*. www.criticallegalthinking.com/2021/02/17/ode-to-reza-barati-on-the-seventh-anniversary-of-his-death/

Barseghian, A. (2020) 'che gooneh behrouz boochani ketab-e khod ra dar noskheh-ye nashr-e cheshmeh((momayezi))va((akhteh))kard',*hadeaghalkalanshahr*:metropolatleast.ir. www.metropolatleast.ir/%da%86%da%af%d9%88%d9%86%d9%87-%d8%a8%d9%87%d8%b1%d9%88%d8%b2-%d8%a8%d9%88%da%86%d8%a7%d9%86%db%8c-%da%a9%d8%aa%d8%a7%d8%a8-%d8%ae%d9%88%d8%af-%d8%b1%d8%a7-%d8%af%d8%b1-%d9%86%d8%b3%d8%ae%d9%87%d9%94/

Bielsa, E. (2023) *A translational sociology: interdisciplinary perspectives on politics and society*. London: Routledge.

Boochani, B. and Tofighian, O. (Summer 2018) 'The Last Days in Manus Prison', *Meanjin*. www.meanjin.com.au/essays/the-last-days-in-manus-prison/

Boochani, B. (2020) *hich doosti be joz kouhestan*. Tehran: Nashr-e Cheshmeh. www.cheshmeh.ir/Book/4565/16059/___%20_____%20__%20__%20_____

Boochani, B. (2017a) 'A Letter from Manus', translated by Tofighian, O. *The Saturday Paper*. www.thesaturdaypaper.com.au/news/politics/2017/12/09/letter-manus-island/15127380005617#hrd

Boochani, B. (2017b) 'I Write From Manus as a Duty to History', translated by Tofighian, O. *The Guardian*. www.theguardian.com/commentisfree/2017/dec/06/i-write-from-manus-island-as-a-duty-to-history

Boochani, B. (2017c) "'This is Hell out Here'. How Behrouz Boochani's Diaries Expose Australia's Refugee Shame", translated by Tofighian, O. *The Guardian*. www.theguardian.com/world/2017/dec/04/this-is-hell-behrouz-boochani-diaries-expose-australia-refugee-shame

Boochani, B. (2017d) "There was Our Silence and their Violence as Manus Camp was Evacuated,' They said", *The Guardian*. www.theguardian.com/commentisfree/2017/dec/01/there-was-our-silence-and-their-violence-as-manus-camp-was-evacuated

Boochani, B. (2017e) "Manus Police Pulled My Hair and Beat Me. 'You've Damaged Our Reputation,' They said", translated by Tofighian, O. *The Guardian*. www.theguardian.com/australia-news/commentisfree/2017/nov/24/manus-police-pulled-my-hair-and-beat-me-youve-damaged-our-reputation-they-said

Boochani, B. (2017f) 'All We Want is Freedom – Not Another Prison Camp', translated by Tofighian, O. *The Guardian*. www.theguardian.com/commentisfree/2017/nov/13/all-we-want-is-freedom-not-another-prison-camp

Boochani, B. (2017g) 'The Night we Tried to Save a Life Among Hundreds of Starving Men', translated by Tofighian, O. *Huffington Post*. www.huffpost.com/archive/au/entry/the-night-we-tried-to-save-a-life-among-hundreds-of-starving-men_au_5cd38366e4b0acea9501fa49

Boochani, B. (2017h) 'The Breath of Death on Manus Island: Starvation and Sickness', translated by Tofighian, O. *The Guardian*. www.theguardian.com/commentisfree/2017/nov/03/the-breath-of-death-on-manus-island-starvation-and-sickness

Boochani, B. (2017i) 'Manus is a Landscape of Surreal Horror', translated by Tofighian, O. *The Guardian*. www.theguardian.com/commentisfree/2017/nov/02/manus-is-a-landscape-of-surreal-horror

Boochani, B. (201j) 'The Refugees Are in a State of Terror on Manus', translated by Tofighian, O. *The Guardian*. www.theguardian.com/commentisfree/2017/oct/31/the-refugees-are-in-a-state-of-terror-on-manus-behrouz-boochani

Boochani, B. (2017k) 'Diary of Disaster: The Last Days Inside Manus Island Detention Centre', translated by Tofighian, O. *The Guardian*. www.theguardian.com/commentisfree/2017/oct/30/diary-of-disaster-the-last-days-inside-manus-island-detention-centre

Boochani, B. (2017l) 'Days Before the Forced Closure of Manus, We Have No Safe Place to Go', translated by Tofighian, O. *The Guardian*. www.theguardian.com/commentisfree/2017/oct/27/days-before-the-forced-closure-of-manus-we-have-no-safe-place-to-go

Boochani, B. (2017m) 'Rising Tension on Manus Island', translated by Tofighian, O. *The Saturday Paper*. www.thesaturdaypaper.com.au/news/politics/2017/07/29/rising-tension-manus-island/15012504004995#hrd

Boochani, B. (2018a) *No Friend but the Mountains: Writing from Manus Prison*, translated by Tofighian, O. Sydney: Picador-Pan Macmillan.

Boochani, B. and Tofighian, O. (summer 2018) 'The Last Days of Manus Prison', *Meanjin*. www.meanjin.com.au/essays/the-last-days-in-manus-prison/

Boochani, B. and Tofighian, O. (2021) 'Many Prisons, Many Borders, Many Islands: Spicy's Story', *Overland*. www.overland.org.au/2021/03/many-prisons-many-borders-many-islands-spicys-story/

Boochani, B. (2018b) 'Four Years after Reza Barati's Death, We Still Have No Justice', translated by Tofighian, O. *The Guardian*. www.theguardian.com/commentisfree/2018/feb/17/four-years-after-reza-baratis-death-we-still-have-no-justice

Boochani, B. (2018c) 'Manus Prison poetics/our voice: revisiting "A letter from Manus Island", a reply to Anne Surma', *Continuum: Journal of Media & Cultural Studies* 32(4): pp. 527–531. https://doi.org/10.1080/10304312.2018.1501796

Boochani, B. and Tofighian, O. (2020) 'A Human Being Feels They are on a Precipice: COVID-19's Threshold Moment', *Andrew and Renata Kaldor Centre for International Refugee Law*. www.unsw.edu.au/kaldor-centre/our-resources/legal-and-policy-resources/commentaries/human-feels

Boochani, B. and Tofighian, O. (2023) 'A Human Being Feels They are on a Precipice: COVID-19's threshold moment', in Boochani, B. (ed), *Freedom, only Freedom: the prison writings of Behrouz Boochani*, translated and edited by Tofighian, O. and Mansoubi, M. London: Bloomsbury Academic, pp. 219–222.

Boochani, B. (2023) *Freedom, only Freedom: the prison writings of Behrouz Boochani*, translated and edited by Tofighian, O. and Mansoubi, M. London: Bloomsbury Academic.

Burnside, J. (2017) '2017 Malcolm Fraser Oration – A Human Rights Legacy', *The University of Melbourne*. www.about.unimelb.edu.au/__data/assets/pdf_file/0025/28375/2017-Malcolm-Fraser-Oration.pdf

Burnside, J. (2018) 'Excerpts of 2018 Hobart Oration Delivered by Julian Burnside QC', *Howling Eagle Productions*. www.howlingeagle.com/julian-burnside-speech-2018

Cave, D. (2017) 'Refugees Trapped Far From Home, Further From Deliverance', *New York Times*. www.nytimes.com/interactive/2017/11/18/world/australia/manus-island-australia-detainees.html

Chalmers, M. (2016) 'Labour MP Calls for Witness of Reza Barati Murder to be Brought to Australia', *New Matilda*. www.newmatilda.com/2016/02/11/labor-mp-calls-for-witness-of-reza-barati-murder-to-be-brought-to-australia/

Cohen, R. (2016) 'Australia's Island Prisons are an Exercise in Cruelty', *The Sydney Morning Herald*. https://www.smh.com.au/opinion/australias-island-prisons-are-an-exercise-in-cruelty-20161212-gt8wae.html

Cohen, R. (2016) 'Broken Men in Paradise', *New York Times*. www.nytimes.com/2016/12/09/opinion/sunday/australia-refugee-prisons-manus-island.html

Courier Mail (2015) 'Finger Pointed at Australia Over Manus Island Murder Witness', *The Courier Mail*. www.couriermail.com.au/news/queensland/chinchilla/finger-pointed-at-australia-over-manus-island-murder-witness/news-story/e9e7650f42bb903e9e168e12b3cde86f

Cousens, D. (2016) "Reza Barati Witness on Manus Warned: 'It's Very Easy to Kill You'", *The Saturday Paper*. www.thesaturdaypaper.com.au/news/politics/2016/01/23/reza-barati-witness-manus-warned-its-very-easy-kill-you/14534676002802#hrd

Davidson, H. (2017) 'Manus Island Detainees Launch Legal Action Over Australian Centre's Closure', *The Guardian*. www.theguardian.com/australia-news/2017/oct/31/manus-island-detainees-launch-legal-action-over-australian-centres-closure

Davidson, H. and Wahlquist, C. (2017) 'Power Shut Off to Final Manus Compounds as 600 Men Refuse to Leave', *The Guardian*. www.theguardian.com/australia-news/2017/nov/01/power-shut-off-to-final-manus-compounds-as-600-men-refuse-to-leave

Davidson, H. and Boochani, B. (2019) 'Asylum Seekers Approved for Medivac Transfers Detained in Port Moresby', *The Guardian*. www.theguardian.com/australia-news/2019/oct/10/asylum-seekers-approved-for-medevac-transfers-detained-in-port-moresby

Doha Debates (2020a) 'Exiled on Manus Island: a message to the world', *Doha Debates*. www.dohadebates.com/human-rights/exiled-on-manus-island-a-message-to-the-world/

Doha Debates (2020b) 'Refugees on Manus Island Speak Out', *Doha Debates*. www.dohadebates.com/human-rights/refugees-on-manus-island-speak-out/

Doherty, B. (2015) 'Witness in Reza Barati Murder Trial Says he is Dogged by Death Threats', *The Guardian*. www.theguardian.com/australia-news/2015/oct/23/witness-in-reza-barati-trial-says-he-is-dogged-by-death-threats

Doherty, B. (2015) 'Manus Island: violent clashes break out between PNG police and detainees', *The Guardian*. www.theguardian.com/australia-news/2015/jan/16/manus-island-peter-dutton-says-refugee-workers-coached-detainees-to-self-harm

Doherty, B. (2016) 'Key Witness in Reza Barati Murder Trial Fears he will be Killed on Manus Island', *The Guardian*. www.theguardian.com/australia-news/2016/jan/16/key-witness-in-reza-barati-trial-fears-he-will-be-killed-on-manus-island

Doherty, B. (2017) 'Decay, Despair, Defiance: Inside the Manus Island Refugee Camp', *Gulf News*. www.gulfnews.com/world/oceania/decay-despair-defiance-inside-the-manus-island-refugee-camp-1.2130018

Doherty, B., Davison, H. and Karp, P. (2016) 'Papua New Guinea Court Rules Detention of Asylum Seekers in Manus Illegal', *The Guardian*. www.theguardian.com/australia-news/2016/apr/26/papua-new-guinea-court-rules-detention-asylum-seekers-manus-unconstitutional

Dreher, T., Michael G., Timothy L., and Tofighian, O. (2021) 'Afterword: Reconstructing Voices and Situated Listening', in Dreher, T., Griffiths, M., and Laurie, T. (eds),

Unsettled voices: beyond free speech in the late Liberal Era. New York: Routledge, pp. 149–159.

Duffin, P. (2019) 'Refugee Sets Fire to Himself on Manus', *Hawkesbury Gazette*. www.hawkesburygazette.com.au/story/6210106/refugee-sets-fire-to-himself-on-manus/

Galbraith, J., Abdile, H., Tofighian, O. and Boochani, B. (eds) (2021) *Southerly – Writing Through Fences: Archipelago of Letters* 79(2). www.southerlylitmag.com.au/shop/writing-through-fences-archipelago-of-letters/

Germian, R. (2023) 'Kurdish Identity and Journalism: Reporting to Record History', in Boochani, B. (ed), *Freedom, Only Freedom: the prison writings of Behrouz Boochani*, translated and edited by Tofighian, O. and Mansoubi, M. London: Bloomsbury Academic, pp. 62–65.

Gordon, M. (2016) 'Guards Accused of Building Tensions on Manus', *The Sydney Morning Herald*. www.smh.com.au/politics/federal/guards-accused-of-building-tensions-on-manus-20160201-gmj0z3.html

Gordon, M. (2016) "Manus Island Witness 'Terrified' After Reza Barati's Accused Killer Escapes'", *The Sydney Morning Herald*. www.smh.com.au/politics/federal/manus-island-witness-terrified-after-reza-baratis-accused-killer-escapes-20160405-gnyjja.html

Gordon, M. (2017) 'Sustained Gunfire Breaks Out at Manus Island Detention Centre', *The Sydney Morning Herald*. www.smh.com.au/politics/federal/sustained-gunfight-breaks-out-at-manus-island-detention-centre-20170414-gvlcnh.html

Gordon, M. (2017) 'Asylum Seekers Under Attack as Sustained Gunfight Breaks Out at Manus Island Detention Centre', *Stuff*. www.stuff.co.nz/world/australia/91594320/asylum-seekers-under-attack-as-sustained-gunfight-breaks-out-at-manus-island-detention-centre

Gordon, M. (2017) "'Bashed' Asylum Seekers on Manus Island 'Deserved What They Got': PNG minister', *The Sydney Morning Herald*. www.smh.com.au/politics/federal/bashed-asylum-seekers-on-manus-island-deserved-what-they-got-png-minister-20170102-gtkv2w.html

Gordon, M. and Ellinghausen, A. (2017) 'Waiting for America', *The Sydney Morning Herald*. www.smh.com.au/interactive/2017/waiting-for-america/

Green, M. (July 2018) 'No Exit: The Ongoing Abuses of Australia's Refugee Policy', *Harper's Magazine*. www.harpers.org/archive/2018/07/no-exit-australian-immigration-manus-island/

Gregoire, P. (2017) 'NYE Bashing of Two Asylum Seekers on Manus Island', *Sydney Criminal Lawyers*. www.sydneycriminallawyers.com.au/blog/nye-bashing-of-two-asylum-seekers-on-manus-island/

Guardian Australia (2016) 'Alleged Witness to Murder of Reza Barati is Forcibly Taken to Court – Video', *The Guardian*. www.theguardian.com/australia-news/video/2015/sep/25/manus-alleged-witness-reza-barati-death-forcibly-taken-to-court-video

Guardian (2019) 'Manus Island Refugee No QNK002: Abdul Aziz Muhamat wins international human rights prize', *The Guardian*. www.theguardian.com/australia-news/2019/feb/14/manus-island-refugee-no-qnk002-abdul-aziz-muhamat-wins-international-human-rights-prize

Hamilton, R. (2017) 'Manus and Nauru: this is how the world sees Australia's refugee policy', *Australian Financial Review*. www.afr.com/policy/foreign-affairs/manus-and-nauru-this-is-how-rest-of-the-world-sees-australias-refugee-policy-20170227-gulz6e

Hasavi Jr., T. (2016) 'Manus Asylum Centre Killing – Key Witness', *EMTV Online*. www.emtv.com.pg/manus-asylum-centre-killing/

Hassaballa, H. (2018) 'Time, torture... and tomorrow, and: artist's statement', *Transition: The Magazine of Africa and the Diaspora* 126: pp. 31–33. https://doi.org/10.2979/transition.126.1.05.

Hassaballa, H., Abdul, S., Boochani, B., Adam, M., Zazai, W. and Kanapathi, S. (2021) 'Siege', *Southerly – Writing Through Fences: Archipelago of Letters* 79(2): pp. 266–289. www.southerlylitmag.com.au/shop/writing-through-fences-archipelago-of-letters/

Human Rights Law Centre (2019) 'Former Manus Detainee Addresses the UN to Call for Freedom', *Human Rights Law Centre*. www.hrlc.org.au/news/2019/6/26/former-manus-detainee-addresses-the-un#:~:text=Abdul%20Aziz%20Muhamat%2C%20a%20refugee,on%20Nauru%20and%20Manus%20Island.

Irish Times (2016) "Australian Minister Warns of 'Illiterate, Innumerate' Refugees: Sharp Criticism as Immigration Minister Peter Dutton Makes Issue Central to Election", *The Irish Times*. www.irishtimes.com/news/world/asia-pacific/australian-minister-warns-of-illiterate-innumerate-refugees-1.2651897

Jeffreys, S. (2019) "Using Humour to Humanise Suffering: 'Where the Bloody Hell are You?'" *9 News*. www.9news.com.au/world/manus-island-detention-satirical-youtube-video-dan-ilic/ca0a4832-bff1-4eb9-9221-0356e7c0f6e2

Jensen, E. (2023) 'Words That Escaped from Prison', in Boochani, B. (ed), *Freedom, only Freedom: The Prison Writings of Behrouz Boochani*, translated and edited by Tofighian, O. and Mansoubi, M. London: Bloomsbury Academic, pp. 127–129.

Kampmark, B. (2016) 'Mild Punishment and Exoneration: The Killing of Reza Barati', *Counterpunch*. www.counterpunch.org/2016/04/21/mild-punishment-and-exoneration-the-killing-of-reza-barati/

Kanapathi, S. (2021) 'Australia's Abandoned Refugees: Nine Years of Exile in Offshore Purgatory', *OpenDemocracy*. https://www.opendemocracy.net/en/beyond-trafficking-and-slavery/australias-abandoned-refugees-nine-years-of-exile-in-offshore-purgatory/

Kanapathi, S. (2021) 'A Lesson for Australia on Love and Community: can the town of Biloela help free their Tamil friends from Australia's border regime?', *Southerly – Writing Through Fences: Archipelago of Letters* (Long Paddock – online) 79(2). www.southerlylitmag.com.au/wp-content/uploads/79_2/LP-79-2-SHAMINDA-KANAPATHIA-Lesson-for-Australia-on-Love-and-Community-1.pdf

Kanapathi, S. (2023) '23 Days of Resistance Alongside Behrouz Bocohani', in Boochani, B. (ed), *Freedom, Only Freedom: the Prison writings of Behrouz Boochani*, translated and edited by Tofighian, O. and Mansoubi, M. London: Bloomsbury Academic, pp. 124–126.

Knaus, C. and Davidson, H. (2019) 'Australia's Offshore Contracts: How Millions Were Spent for Dubious Outcomes', *The Guardian*. www.theguardian.com/australia-news/2019/feb/23/australias-offshore-contracts-how-millions-were-spent-for-dubious-outcomes

Laughland, O. (2014) 'Witnesses to Death of Reza Barati Apply for Protection in Australia', *The Guardian*. www.theguardian.com/world/2014/apr/30/eyewitnesses-to-death-of-reza-barati-apply-for-protection-in-australia

Lewis, L. (2023) 'Witness to Brutal Murder in Manus Detention Centre Fights on for Justice', *Radio New Zealand*. www.rnz.co.nz/international/pacific-news/496058/witness-to-brutal-murder-in-manus-detention-centre-fights-on-for-justice

Lomai, P. B. (2016) 'Application by Behnam Satah and 301 Others SCAPP No 03 of 2015 in the Supreme Court of Justice at Waigani, Papua New Guinea', Letter by Ben Lomai to Australian High Commissioner, uploaded, *Refugee Action Coalition*. www.refugeeaction.org.au/wp-content/uploads/2016/10/Letter-to-Australian-government.pdf

Lucashenko, M. (2021) 'Response to *Writing Through Fences*', *Southerly – Writing Through Fences: Archipelago of Letters* 79(2): pp. 21–23. www.southerlylitmag.com.au/shop/writing-through-fences-archipelago-of-letters/

Mcauliffe, A. (2016) 'Australia: Appeal to Free Detainee Receiving Threats', *Aljazeera*. www.aljazeera.com/news/2016/2/11/australia-appeal-to-free-detainee-receiving-threats

McKenzie-Murray, M. (2017) 'Safety Fears for Manus Island Murder Witness', *The Saturday Paper*. www.thesaturdaypaper.com.au/news/immigration/2017/03/04/safety-fears-manus-island-murder-witness/14885460004302#hrd

McNevin, A. (2019) 'From Offshore Detention of Refugees to Indigenous Incarceration', *Public Seminar*. www.publicseminar.org/essays/from-offshore-detention-of-refugees-to-indigenous-incarceration/

McNevin, A. (2022) 'Against Crisis: Violence and Continuity in Manus Island Prison', in Fassin, D. and Honneth, A. (eds), *Crisis under critique: how people assess, transform, and respond to critical situations*. New York: Columbia University Press, pp. 211–232.

Moi, C. (2016) 'Ruling Brings Joy to Asylum Seekers', *The National*. www.thenational.com.pg/ruling-brings-joy-to-asylum-seekers/#:~:text=By%20CHARLES%20MOI&text=He%20said%20after%2034%20months,this%20suffering%2C%E2%80%9D%20he%20said.

Naime, Q. (2016) 'Man Accused of Murdering Manus Island Detainee Escapes Jail', *Loop PNG*. www.looppng.com/content/man-accused-murdering-manus-island-detainee-escapes-jail

National (2018) 'Church Raises Concerns Over Refugees at Manus Centre', *The National*. www.thenational.com.pg/church-raises-concerns-over-refugees-at-manus-centre/

Newman, M. and Head, M. (2017) 'Australian High Court Sanctions Illegal Detention of Refugees in Papua New Guinea', *World Socialist Website*. www.wsws.org/en/articles/2017/08/24/refu-a24.html

No Friend but the Mountains – A Voyage Through Song (2021) Aurora Films/Good Vibes Only, Conti Bros. Films, Zelman Symphony, Wise Music Group, and Arts Centre Melbourne. www.wisemusicclassical.com/news/4250/ABC-TV-BROADCAST-No-Friend-But-the-Mountains---A-Voyage-Through-Song/

Parke, M. (2016) 'House Debates: Statement by Members – Asylum Seekers', *Open Australia Beta*. www.openaustralia.org.au/debates/?id=2016-05-03.15.2

Parke, M. (2016) 'Melissa Parke Tables Petition for Behnam Satah 11 February 2016', *YouTube*.

Parker, J. (2023) 'Remember Reza Barati and Demand Protection for Asylum Seekers', *Green Left Weekly*.

Parkes, Z. (2017) 'Australian Government Violates its Own Refugee Policy', *Green Left Weekly*.

Piotrowski, D. (2019) 'No Joke: Australian Comedian is Arrested in Manus Island over Visa Stuff-Up – But the Situation Turns to Farce When Cops LOSE Keys to the Cell', *Daily Mail Australia*. www.dailymail.co.uk/news/article-6655639/Australian-comedian-Dan-Ilic-arrested-Manus-Island.html

Pokiton, S. (2016) "'Residents' in Manus Seek Summary Judgment', *Loop PNG*. www.looppng.com/content/%E2%80%98residents%E2%80%99-manus-seek-summary-judgment

Pokiton, S. (2016) 'Asylum Seekers Frustrated and Now Holding Protest in Manus', *Loop PNG*. www.looppng.com/content/asylum-seekers-frustrated-and-now-holding-protest-manus

Post-Courier (2018) 'Refugees Seek Court Petition to Decide their Fate', *Post-Courier PNG*. www.postcourier.com.pg/refugees-seek-court-petition-decide-fate/

Refugee Action Campaign (2016) 'Demand to Protect Witness to Reza Barati Death', *Refugee Action Campaign*. www.refugeeaction.org/20160223/demand-to-protect-witness-to-reza-barati-death/

Refugee Council of Australia and Amnesty International (2017) 'Until When: The Forgotten Men of Manus Island', *Refugee Council of Australia*. https://www.refugeecouncil.org.au/manus-island-report/

Regional (2015) 'Witness Describes Killing', *Cook Islands News*. www.cookislandsnews.com/regional/witness-describes-killing/

Reilly, A. (2019) 'Explainer: The Medivac Repeal and What It Means for Asylum Seekers on Manus Island and Nauru', *The Conversation*. www.theconversation.com/explainer-the-medevac-repeal-and-what-it-means-for-asylum-seekers-on-manus-island-and-nauru-128118

RNZ (2017) '"No-one Safe at Detention Centre"', *Cook Islands News*. https://www.cookislandsnews.com/regional/no-one-safe-at-detention-centre/

RNZ (2017) 'Refugees in Crisis', *The Fiji Times*. www.fijitimes.com.fj/refugees-in-crisis/

Roberts, B. (2017) 'Manus Asylum Seeker Benham Satah Speaks to SBS World News', *SBS News* [audio]. www.soundcloud.com/sbsnews/manus-asylum-seeker-benham-satah-speaks-to-sbs-world-news-reporter-brianna-roberts

Roberts, B. (2017) 'Detainees Warn of Violence if Forced to Leave Manus Island Detention Centre', *SBS News*. www.sbs.com.au/news/article/detainees-warn-of-violence-if-forced-to-leave-manus-island-detention-centre/ji80ycq66

Robinson-Drawbridge, B. (2017) "Manus Detainees Want NZ Asylum as PNG 'Not Safe'", *Radio New Zealand*. www.rnz.co.nz/international/pacific-news/331610/manus-detainees-want-nz-asylum-as-png-not-safe

SBS (2017) "'Reasonable Force': PNG Police Defend Actions against Iranian Refugees', *SBS News*. www.sbs.com.au/news/article/reasonable-force-png-police-defend-actions-against-iranian-refugees/rgcjicijc

SBS (2019) 'Reports of Suspected Typhoid Outbreak on Manus Island', *SBS News*. www.sbs.com.au/news/article/reports-of-suspected-typhoid-outbreak-on-manus-island/sbve4m4ho

Siegel, M. (2016) "Australian Minister Warns against 'Illiterate, Innumerate' Refugees", *Khmer Times*. www.khmertimeskh.com/7357/australian-minister-warns-against-illiterate-innumerate-refugees/

SMH (2017) 'Locals Threaten Violence against Manus Island Asylum Seekers Ahead of Camp's Closure', *The Sydney Morning Herald*. www.smh.com.au/national/locals-threaten-violence-against-manus-island-asylum-seekers-ahead-of-camps-closure-20171029-gzam1l.html

Somaliland Standard (2019) 'Somali Migrant Sets Himself on Fire in Australian Detention Centre', *Somaliland Standard*. www.somalilandstandard.com/somali-migrant-sets-himself-on-fire-in-australian-detention-center/

Styles, L. (2020) *No Friend but the Mountains: a symphonic song cycle*, words by Boochani, B. www.wisemusicclassical.com/work/60895/No-Friend-But-The-Mountains-A-Symphonic-Song-Cycle--Luke-Styles/

Surma, A. (2018) 'In a different voice: 'A letter from Manus Island' as poetic Manifesto', *Continuum: Journal of Media & Cultural Studies* 32(4): pp. 518–526. https://doi.org/10.1080/10304312.2018.1468414

Surma, A. (2023) "Boochani's 'Political Poetics': Subverting and Reimagining the Fiction of Politics", in Boochani, B. (ed), *Freedom, only Freedom: the prison writings of Behrouz Boochani*, translated and edited by Tofighian, O. and Mansoubi, M. London: Bloomsbury Academic, pp. 223–227.

Thomas, A. (2015) 'A Glimpse of Australia's Manus Island Refugee Prison', *Aljazeera*. www.aljazeera.com/features/2015/12/1/a-glimpse-of-australias-manus-island-refugee-prison

Tlozek, E. (2016) 'A Dangerous Testimony: The Man Who Witnessed Reza Barati's Murder on Manus Island', *ABC News*. www.abc.net.au/news/2016-11-19/a-dangerous-testimony/8036212

Tofighian, O. (2018a) 'Sanctions, Refugees and the Marginalised: Iran Uprisings are Australia's Concern Too', *ABC News*. www.abc.net.au/news/2018-01-06/iran-uprising-australia-manus-island-political-refugees-islamic/9305756

Tofighian, O. (2018b) 'Black bodies for political profit: Sudanese and Somali standpoints on Australia's racialized border regime', *Transition: The Magazine of Africa and the Diaspora* 126: pp. 5–18. www.muse.jhu.edu/article/702736

Tofighian, O. (2018c) 'Behrouz Boochani and the Manus Prison narratives: merging translation with philosophical reading', *Continuum: Journal of Media & Cultural Studies* 32(4): pp. 532–540. https://doi.org/10.1080/10304312.2018.1494942

Tofighian, O. (2018d) 'Translator's Tale: A Window to the Mountains', in Boochani, B. (ed), *No Friend but the Mountains: Writing from Manus Prison*, translated by Tofighian, O. Sydney: Picador-Pan Macmillan, pp. xiii–xxxiv.

Tofighian, O. and Boochani, B. (2021) 'Spicy's Story', *PEN – Transmissions*. www.pentransmissions.com/2021/03/12/spicys-story/

UNHCR (2018) 'UNHCR Fact Sheet on Situation of Refugees and Asylum-Seekers on Manus Island, Papua New Guinea: Key Findings and Recommendations', *UNHCR: The UN Refugee Agency*. www.unhcr.org/au/media/unhcr-fact-sheet-situation-refugees-and-asylum-seekers-manus-island-papua-new-guinea-1

Wahune, T. 'Refugees Want Answers to Delayed Cases', *The National*. www.thenational.com.pg/refugees-want-answers-to-delayed-cases/

Walkowitz, R. (2015) *Born translated: the contemporary novel in an age of world literature*. New York Chichester, West Sussex: Columbia University Press.

Wells, M. (2016) "Ignoring the Facts, Australia's Immigration Minister Calls Refugees 'Illiterate and Innumerate'", *Vice News*.

Whiting, N. (2019) 'Marisa Payne to Visit PNG, New PM Pressured Over Asylum Seeker Issue', *ABC AM* [Radio]. www.abc.net.au/listen/programs/am/marise-payne-to-visit-png/11219318

Whitlock, G. (2020) 'No *Friend but the Mountains*: how should I read this?', *Biography: An Interdisciplinary Quarterly* 43(4): pp. 705–723. https://doi.org/10.1353/bio.2020.0102

Zable, A. (2018) " 'You're Strong': Refugees Remember the Friendship and Support of Michael Gordon", *The Age*. www.smh.com.au/national/youre-strong-refugees-remember-the-friendship-and-support-of-michael-gordon-20180208-h0vs9p.html

Zamiri, H. (2021a) 'The passenger of time', translated by Sarwari, S. *Southerly – Writing Through Fences: Archipelago of Letters* 79(2): pp. 141–143. www.southerlylitmag.com.au/shop/writing-through-fences-archipelago-of-letters/

Zamiri, H. (2021b) 'I Speak', translated by Sarwari, S. *Southerly – Writing Through Fences: Archipelago of Letters* 79(2): p. 179. www.southerlylitmag.com.au/shop/writing-through-fences-archipelago-of-letters/

Zamiri, H. (2021c) 'Life in the Shadow of the Pandemic', *Unheard Journalism Project* 1.1. www.journal.unheardproject.com/life-in-the-shadow-of-the-pandemic/

Zamiri, H. (2022) 'In the Darkness of the Night, I was Dreaming of the Light', *Unheard Journalism Project* 3. www.journal.unheardproject.com/homaira-zamiri-in-the-darkness/

Zhang, D. (2016) 'Always Already Translated', *Public Books*. www.publicbooks.org/always-already-translated/

4
TRANSLATION, PUBLIC PHILOSOPHY AND COLLECTIVE WORK

Translation and knowledge production: knowing border violence

Working closely with displaced, exiled and incarcerated peoples within Australia's detention industry, it has been difficult in most cases gaining acceptance from individuals and institutions with power and privilege. Long-term and sustainable support for producing different kinds of creative resistance has proved elusive. It is difficult and perplexing when constantly aiming to work within exclusionary systems; that is, according to institutional and elitist standards and norms. The refugees I have collaborated with understand the value and dynamism in our new approaches and new languages of resistance. They recognise the indispensable role of different kinds of collaboration and support; that is, the formation of networks and strategies that centre the experiences and visions of incarcerated refugees and are dedicated to collectively challenging and changing many interconnected forms of bordering.

In the collaborative work with people involved in the siege – before, during and after the situation – we worked to upend the language and conventions in experimental ways. The representational and philosophical aspects of the resistance involved creating a counter-discourse with its own constellation of terms. In fact, these aspects have been evolving with every act of defiance related to all incidents and periods. Throughout their incarceration, refugees within Australia's detention industry have contributed to the formation of a history from below; produced place-based and situation-specific intellectual and creative works; engaged in radical acts of naming to oppose state-authorised terminology; and insisted on the primacy of their narratives, representations and languages of resistance. These aspects are particular to every phase and carceral site in the colonial continuum and archipelago of indefinite detention.

In the context of the early years of my collaboration with Boochani, we were careful about using terms such as 'regional processing centre' – we had already begun developing new terminology and ways of thinking prior to the siege. Instead of accepting the language of the state, we insisted on referring to the carceral-site as 'Manus Prison' (a literal translation of the term Boochani uses in Persian). Boochani was already using this term when we met and as soon as we began collaborating we developed its meaning and philosophical significance. Soon I suggested we use Manus Prison as the basis for a complex philosophical, artistic and political theory: Manus Prison Theory (I capitalised 'prison' to introduce the new aspects and present the term as both compound noun and proper noun). This is one example amongst many which I examine in this section. This concept functions within an interdisciplinary and transdisciplinary system of critical thought; it derives from embodied and embedded experiences of systematic torture and both draws from and galvanises practices of creative resistance.

Collaborative philosophical, artistic and political work with refugees has expanded using approaches similar to the model related to Manus Prison Theory. In my work with people who were incarcerated in Nauru I have developed Nauru Prison Theory. In a co-authored article with Elahe Zivardar about Nauru Prison Theory as a form of public philosophy I explain how the theorising began and progressed:

> I have engaged with all of these not individually, but as a shared philosophical activity. I describe the significance of this briefly in my translator's note to Behrouz Boochani's 2018 book, *No Friend but the Mountains: Writing from Manus Prison*, and related articles, interviews, talks and seminars. While editing and translating the many rough text messages that made up the book, Behrouz and I had daily conversations. This shared philosophical activity, together with other examples of our creative resistance, helped form what we refer to as Manus Prison Theory – similar collaborative projects produced with Zivardar and explored in this paper have developed into Nauru Prison Theory.
>
> (Tofighian and Zivardar, 2024, p. 24)

In the same article we discuss the significance of combining different forms of collective work and advancing them into philosophical theories. The emergence of Nauru Prison Theory and its formation resembles that of Manus Prison Theory but has a stronger intersectional dimension because of the context of Nauru and the fact that Zivardar and other women are direct collaborators. It is also distinct from Manus Prison Theory due to the specialised skills and training of the people involved; in Zivardar's case her architecture and artistic talents and experience help enhance critical knowledge pertaining to what we now refer to as the weaponisation of space and the weaponisation of design. We combine our critique of these instruments of torture with critical methods I developed earlier with Boochani: the weaponisation of identity and the weaponisation of time. I introduce the background to these epistemic processes:

> Elahe realised the need for collaboration in order to create new concepts and theories for representing and unpacking the fluid and unpredictable nature of the situation in indefinite offshore detention. She understood that collective resistance was necessary; she worked together with others inside the facility, while also connecting with people outside. The interpretations and critical analyses that have emerged combine elements related to her identity, history and influences; the different individuals and communities incarcerated in Nauru; and the people and groups she has been collaborating with outside. These elements involve cultural heritage, training and skills, lived experiences, artistic and intellectual approaches, political visions, and more. Working with a range of people, she has developed new terms and perspectives appropriate for addressing the interlocking systems of oppression, domination and submission – our own collaboration soon developed into a shared philosophical activity, and this collective and creative resistance now forms the basis for Nauru Prison Theory. She realised that previous theories and concepts for interpreting and exposing this form of border violence, displacement and exile are insufficient, inaccurate or misleading. In this context, literature, art, philosophies of resistance, traditions of women's struggle, customs of care, and cultural heritage have been vital not just for survival and healing but also for consciousness raising and action.
> *(Tofighian and Zivardar 2024, pp. 30–31)*

In collaborative projects involving both people imprisoned in Manus Prison and Nauru Prison we were able to develop rich conversations between histories of struggle and other radical narrative frameworks for interpretation (Tofighian, Boochani, Mira and Zivardar, 2022). As a result, we were able to devise different critical terms and imagine more empowering ways for engaging with each other. In a co-authored piece of writing I was involved in the collaborators share views and experiences related to each other, regarding others who supported each other inside the prisons, and pertaining to interactions with people outside the prisons. Mira (a pseudonym) is another woman and collaborator who was imprisoned in Nauru and after she was released she shared with me her writings in English and Persian about psychology and wellbeing. She was trained in psychology in her homeland

and would engage in research and analysis while incarcerated in Nauru so that she could help herself and others to survive, feel empowered, resist and heal.

In our conversations she described a remarkable fact related to her reading and reflection inside the prison: she began studying a Persian translation of Viktor Frankl's *Man's Search for Meaning* – in addition to many other books, especially biographies and autobiographies. Mira continued her engagement with Frankl's book after her release and while struggling with her precarious visa status. She explained to me that she drew strength from his writings and experiences and used her reading and epistemic insights to empower others in the prison camp. In her contribution to our co-authored chapter and our conversations during the collaboration she describes the notion of Post Traumatic Growth (PTG) and the role of storytelling for healing and empowerment. Mira also shares her research and reflection on narratives by writers such as Frankl and made important connections with dialogues she had with other refugees in the prison camp. Over the years that they were imprisoned in Nauru they shared stories as a way of supporting and learning from each other. "Reading others' stories allowed me to see the world through their eyes. In their narrative vision, I could track a process of transformation, locate ideas, structures and techniques that could be applied to my own story. In this sense storytelling is a form of social support and PTG, and I see my own writing, research and resistance as part of this collective movement." (Tofighian, Boochani, Mira and Zivardar, 2022, p. 132) In this example we witness some of the ways creative resistance operates together with sharing stories; in combination, they enable us to imagine alternative forms of emplotment which helps with reinterpreting and rearranging our experiences, encounters and activities. Regarding the collective work I have been involved in I noticed that new narratives of resistance always involve new languages of resistance and knowledge production; they interweave to produce special forms of public philosophy. They are examples of shared philosophical activity where many diverse elements emerge and merge simultaneously to produce unique and transformative instances of creative resistance.

Working with Mira on her contribution exemplified the nature of the shared philosophical activity in numerous important ways that reflect collaboration, activism, translation and storytelling. We discussed and planned in Persian but the writing she submitted to me was in English. I edited her drafts of English text while in regular conversation in Persian. During the early stages Mira reversed the dynamic common in support and research involving refugees. She interviewed me and wanted to know more about my past and why I was involved in the kind of activism I had been doing for years. She wanted to encounter, understand and interpret my stories in order to engage more productively and better situate our collaborative work – hearing each other's narratives helped us move forward with our work and generate knowledge, and they also helped us reflect and contribute more meaningfully in our collaborations. This experience made me think what kind of academic and political projects might be possible if the roles were reversed in radical ways; if displaced and exiled peoples interviewed and studied researchers from related fields and supporters from different societies and published their dialogues, reflections and critical analyses (as articles and books). Later in our collaboration on the multi-author piece Mira shared writing in Persian which helped in the editing and development of her contribution in English. All this work culminated in her important role in the co-authored chapter. What took place can be interpreted as a form of intralingual translation with elements of interlingual translation. It is important to note that the planning was conducted in Persian, drafts were written mainly in English, the development process involved writing in English and Persian with discussions in Persian, and the overall product published in English.

In the same chapter we construct and employ the term 'Nauru Imprisoned Exiles Collective'; a name devised and used to refer to different groups that have been in communication since their time held in Nauru Prison. These groups are still organising and supporting each other in their various projects and plans. The introduction to the piece explains the connection between the collective and Manus Prison Theory:

> Manus Prison Theory emerged organically through years of collaboration, sharing and consultation between Behrouz – who was incarcerated in the Australian-run Manus Island immigration detention centre from 2013 to 2019 – and Omid, who supported and translated for him on the outside, communicating via WhatsApp. Manus Prison Theory explores the racial imaginary driving border regimes, the colonial logic underlying them and the debordering work necessary to dismantle them. The Nauru Imprisoned Exiles Collective addresses similar concerns with a specific focus on gendered violence from the lived experience of women locked up in the Australian run Nauru immigration detention centre. Both movements work to disrupt and dismantle the material and epistemic conditions, the symbolic aesthetic and social imaginary underpinning systemic attacks against displaced and exiled people. Both centre joy, hope, celebration, love and pride within their intellectual, creative and political perspectives in radically challenging and generative ways. These interventions are introduced as embodied knowledges, deeply ingrained in different antiracist, anticolonial and feminist struggles. This work is transgenerational and aims to be transnational.

Manus Prison Theory and Nauru Imprisoned Exiles Collective are deconstructive and iconoclastic interventions into debates about forced migration and border violence. Our work does not play off distinctions between creative praxis, intellectual and theoretical efforts, political activism and cultural heritage.

(Tofighian, Boochani, Mira and Zivardar, 2022, pp. 125–126)

Considering these examples, it becomes clear how new concepts and forms of philosophical thinking can aggressively oppose a whole system. Similarly, names such as Manus Prison and Nauru Prison contrast with the state-sanctioned term 'regional processing centre'. The term is a euphemism and an inaccurate title introduced by the state, normalised in discourse about Australia's border regime, and reinforced and disseminated by the media. In contrast to terms that function within the lexicon of power, and which help fortify coloniality, Manus Prison and Nauru Prison rename these manifestations of colonial violence by emphasising the fact that they are recent neocolonial experiments: locations of exile, systematic torture and exploitation. They are introduced to identify offshore detention facilities as particularly perverse carceral-sites – like prisons, but also different to prisons in so many tortuous and extralegal ways. Both offshore and onshore immigration detention centres function essentially as warehouses for those deemed undesirable by a neocolonial system and ideology. They are spaces where local and multinational companies and corporations can make profit from the incarceration of vulnerable people. Onshore facilities operate as a form of prison enclave, and offshore facilities are extraterritorial prisons for exiling refugees; human beings who politicians can also exploit for political profit.

> Australia first established an architecture of racial oppression to enslave and exploit the labour of Aboriginal and Torres Strait Islander peoples, and South Sea Islanders. The country now applies a relatively new method—a reconfiguration—on its borders based on the same colonial logic, and it has now begun to export this violent program to other Western nations.
>
> This brutal transportation of refugees over borders and into detention centres is a form of human trafficking. After a horrific boat journey from Indonesia to the shores of Australia, that country exiles them to indefinite, charge-less imprisonment on Manus Island and Nauru. Australia forces these people to survive in an unfamiliar and harsh natural environment with scant services, and in the midst of communities hostile to their presence. An already horrific situation is worsened when these detention centres bar these people access to their communities living in diaspora. No longer can they participate in ceremonies and cultural activities that help give their lives meaning and purpose. Nor do these centres allow more than extremely limited communication with loved ones at home.

All of this is happening for the most craven of purposes: the accumulation of political capital. Simply put, members of both major political parties imprison and exploit refugees in order to leverage the racism of their electorates.

(Tofighian 2018, pp. 11–13)

Manus Prison, Nauru Prison and the rest of the carceral-border archipelago are built on the foundations of colonial violence and have developed into unprecedented examples within the history of incarceration in Australia (El-Enany & Keenan, 2019; Dehm, 2020; Whitlock, 2018; Vogl, 2015, 2017, 2021; Galbraith, 2015; Pugliese, 2013, 2015; Giannacopoulos, 2013; Perera, 2002, 2007, 2009). The onshore and offshore cages are set up, in most cases, far away from urban areas within the nation or on islands at a great distance from the mainland. They are presented as necessary instruments within a campaign built on the cynical creation of national security fears and laboratories for developing and testing technologies of abandonment, exclusion, expulsion, control and submission.

On Christmas Eve 2016 I received a message from Boochani about the death of Faysal Ishak Ahmed. He was a Sudanese refugee who had been sick for six months and denied proper treatment from the private company contracted to provide medical care in the detention centre: International Health and Medical Services (IHMS). At the same time that I received the WhatsApp message I also read the news online about the tragedy. Boochani asked me to translate an article about the death which conveyed important background information about his death and his connections to family and friends. He just needed a couple of days to investigate and interview people in the prison and Ahmed's family back in Sudan. I translated the piece which was published on 30 December in the *Guardian* and included Ahmed's ID card with his photo (Boochani, 2016).

For the article Boochani interviewed Ahmed's friends in the detention centre in English with some assistance from a friend who interpreted from Arabic. He also managed to acquire comments from Ahmed's brother in Sudan. This was arranged through one of Ahmed's Arabic-speaking friends inside the prison who interpreted into English for Boochani, who then paraphrased and wrote on his phone in Persian, and finally sent to me as part of the article for translation into English. Once again, the role of interpreters and translators from among the detained refugees proved vital for supporting each other, in this case by contributing to reportage conducted on the ground and conveying important information about Ahmed's life and struggles. Salih, Ahmed's brother in Sudan, expressed the following over the phone which was published in the article:

When we were told that Faysal died we were shocked! Because Faysal was the only person we were counting on to transform our lives from the

> *refugee camp to a safe world. We don't actually know how he died and the only thing we know is he was sick. He told me so many times that he was sick but I have no idea how he injured his head.*

Ahmed was a close friend of Adam and Hassaballa whose work I have already discussed in this book. In fact, the articles we wrote (together with poems by Abdile) for the special issue of *Transition* is dedicated to Ahmed who died almost a year before the siege (the dedication appears at the beginning of my article which discusses the writing and resistance of the other three contributors; Tofighian, 2018).

Both Adam and Hassaballa replied to my message of condolence on the one-year anniversary of Ahmed's death, as we were preparing our articles for publication. I also suggested that we dedicate the series of publications to Ahmed. Parts of their responses featured in my paper.

Adam: "I was busy today preparing a small ceremony and memorial for our brother Faysal." "Our memories of him and his vision will remain with us and will always be on our minds. Faysal, you will never be forgotten. RIP brother."

Hassaballa: "Yeah bro, it's already a year now. Hope he's in a better place and has found some peace... What an amazing idea, bro. He absolutely deserves it... good idea, I'll get a photo."

(Tofighian, 2018, pp. 17–18)

Part of the border regime's strategy of deterrence involves slow and multilayered acts of punishment, and complex forms of signalling throughout the world that communicate the realities and consequences of indefinite detention (as part of the discourse of deterrence). At the same time, the strategy aims to deflect responsibility and criticism. Regardless of the evidence that indicates that the systematic torture encountered in Australia's immigration detention industry is by design and wilful, deaths and injuries are presented by authorities as unintended, mishaps, the result of negligence, or the responsibility of service providers or the authorities who are part of or under the control of the PNG/Nauru governments. Like in so many other instances of death and injury, one important aspect related to Ahmed's death is the fact that he was subject to a form of epistemic injustice (Fricker, 2007). The IHMS medical staff never seriously responded to Ahmed's alarming symptoms and many pleas for help over six months, and proper interpreters at crucial moments were unavailable or incompetent. At most times the only people who he could share his thoughts, feelings and health problems with were close confidants detained with him.

IHMS have lucrative contracts with the Australian government to provide adequate health and medical services in the detention centres; however, the lived experiences and accounts of refugees proves something contrary to their stated aims and purpose – formal agreements to help can be interpreted as acts of bad faith. Here, bad faith is weaponised as an instrument of torture. Is Ahmed's case an example of someone who suffered from testimonial injustice? As part of the strategy of deterrence and program of slow punishment we can conclude that the system functioned exactly as intended; there was never any real intention to respond adequately to Ahmed's requests for help. His testimony was discredited because there already existed a wilful intention to punish, an intention that was masked in a humanitarian discourse of care. In these circumstances even competent and concerned interpreters and translators would not have made a difference. Even the presence of any number of sympathetic medical staff in the detention centre could not change the operations of the machine, the kyriarchal system. Ahmed was flown to a Brisbane hospital after he collapsed for the last time, but it was too late – soon after he arrived he lost his life.

Australia's neocolonial experiment in the form of onshore and offshore indefinite detention (in addition to other forms of containment such as community detention and temporary visas) is another manifestation of the racial exclusivism that has always been part of the nation-state's immigration policies. This form of systemic violence and discrimination is consistent with the ideologies and practices that go back to the invasion of the land by the British Empire, the establishment of a penal colony, and the dispossession and displacement of First Nations peoples. As part of the most recent mechanisms for controlling human movement, manipulating national narratives, and engineering the country's racial and socio-cultural landscape, people seeking asylum find themselves "locked within a brutal labyrinth of futile settlement processing and malignant health services." (Tofighian, 2018, p. 7)

The roots of these and similar mechanisms of oppression, domination and submission (kyriarchal mechanisms) have connections with earlier colonial narratives and practices. These include myths about *terra nullius* which functioned to justify the dispossession, displacement and genocide of Indigenous peoples. New colonial narratives and practices helped justify forcing people from traditional lands and into cattle stations, missions and reserves for purposes of control and forced labour; erasure of identity, culture and sovereignty; and many other atrocities (Nethery, 2021). It is helpful to compare this colonial history with the idea of the carceral-border as a neocolonial experiment. In the context of mandatory indefinite detention, extralegal tactics are employed, international law is violated and human beings and land are exploited for the purposes of racial capitalism.

The carceral-border pertains to physical locations, and it is also symbolic and epistemic. It targets bodies, minds, emotions, and spirits. More accurately, carceral borders refer to evolving processes, institutions, narratives, concepts, and categories—the border is not just a thing, bordering is not an event. Processes of bordering cover a whole range of different features, notions, and factors from the demarcation of spaces and processes of territorialisation to the multiple dimensions of boundaries which extend to different kinds of meaning-making, meaning imposition, and methods of sustaining meaning. Processes of bordering also determine how movement is controlled using ideas, emotions, and wills. The events, ideas, and processes that determine all forms of bordering are contingent; the carceral-border shifts and morphs in line with other socio political and cultural phenomena in Australia and globally. Social elements and facets such as law, racialisation, economy, religion, trade, and other determining factors interweave, and this makes identifcation of the roots of marginalisation, stigmatisation and exclusion of asylum seekers difficult. When bordering practices are arranged and directed to embolden and maintain colonial manifestations then territorialisation becomes a horrific phenomenon.

(Tazreiter and Tofighian, with Boochani, 2022, p. 79)

Thinking about the carceral-border as a neocolonial experiment intertwined with racial capitalism renders concepts such as Manus Prison and Nauru Prison as manifestations of global and transhistorical theorising. Therefore, Manus Prison Theory, Nauru Prison Theory, the kyriarchal system, and the other place-based and situation-specific concepts, theoretical frameworks and philosophical tools can be interpreted and employed in ways that reach far beyond the structures, positionalities, territories and narratives from which they emerged. The kind of knowledge production we propose – the ways of knowing border violence we arrive at – are debordering practices in every sense: they aim to cross barriers pertaining to disciplines, histories, cultures, structures of oppression, and more.

In relation to all our collaborative projects we usually begin outlining and examining the built environment, natural environment, and internal power relations within the carceral site/s. All collaborators then follow up by deliberating over the workings of the broader detention industry and the way it marks life inside. We engage in conversation and deep analysis often through many text and voice messages – and real time conversation when circumstances allow. In cases where detained people have access to phones there have been times when connection is difficult or impossible because Wi-Fi reception in the prison is often too weak to support phone calls. Whether by WhatsApp messaging (text or voice) or through calls, we discuss the system people are up against and base our critiques on reflection and analysis of the relationships, experiences and actions of those inside (mostly refugees, staff and in some cases supporters/visitors).

When working with people who are still struggling in community detention, temporary visas, and other forms of systemic and targeted discrimination after release, the dynamics and approaches are similar. Communication becomes easier; however, people who are no longer held inside detention or who have been granted permanent residency in various countries face other difficulties particular to their socio-economic situations, visa status, racism and related issues. We also connect our analyses to the events, activities, relationships and discourses in Australia and other countries. Our exchanges involve deep consideration and interweaving of the physical environment of the detention centres (both built and natural), the techniques of systematic torture, and the complex social and political relationships with people inside and outside. Engagement with these issues includes making meaningful and productive links between cultural, aesthetic and philosophical features and factors and the border-industrial complex.

We also share our educational and research histories, our intellectual perspectives, and cultural backgrounds and traditions. We explore literary methods and topics and themes related to aesthetics, culture and belonging. During our discussions we suggest websites worth viewing, online readings, films, music, different examples of popular culture and research ideas. These dialogues make up part of the essential groundwork for later more complex collaborations.

In addition to acquiring important and unique knowledge about the experience of indefinite detention (onshore, offshore, community detention, also living with temporary visa status) regular conversations between collaborators also help inform our understanding about our positionalities within the projects. Socio-political context, environment, experiences and interactions condition both *what* and *how* one gains knowledge about the world. What people are confronted with in indefinite offshore and onshore detention is remarkably ruthless and extraordinarily relentless – the knowledge we are producing in our exchanges reflects these dimensions in detailed ways. The repressive conditions and limitations of the offshore and onshore carceral-sites generate more than testimony and narratives about encounters within the prisons; they initiate radically new concepts and theoretical frameworks, complex methods, and criteria for richer interpretation and inquiry. New ways of knowing border violence emerge even from the very first weeks of conversation.

The cultural worlds we occupy and our social positioning within structures and systems combine to impact our ways of knowing. Therefore, the theory of knowledge necessary for interpreting and translating must be in respectful and consistent dialogue with the dynamics shaping the lived experience of those in offshore and onshore indefinite detention (the situation is different but nevertheless absurd and terrifying for people in community detention or living in limbo on temporary visas, which are still forms of indefinite containment). The perspectives developed after consultation and collaboration with incarcerated refugees must be appropriate on many levels and correspond with their ways of thinking, imagining and doing. In this kind of activism there is always the risk of reinscribing the damaging and demeaning refugee stereotypes and tropes ingrained and circulating within public and political discourses and media representations. To avoid this, we theorise methods and strategies to directly challenge harmful and misleading ascriptions and reductions. We have come to realise that one of the best approaches is to prioritise the literary, philosophical and political influences and histories characterising refugee life worlds. That is, their ways of being and knowing, the traditions of resistance they are familiar with, and how they produce creative and intellectual outcomes.

On 22 April, 2018 I translated and edited a poem by Dana sent to me from Indonesia about an incident that had occurred in Afghanistan, killing members of the persecuted Hazara community which he belonged to (it was published in the special issue of *Southerly* in 2021; Dana, p. 209). Translation of this texts involved deep consideration of the experiences and identity of the writer together with the history of his community in Afghanistan. My decisions regarding format, style and word choice had to reflect this history in addition to details about the contemporary situation and the associated resistance expressed and practiced by Hazaras in Afghanistan and in diaspora.

Shoes that left home with the spirit of hope… never to return.

> These shoes…
>   These shoes are the remnants of a horrific crime.
>   A terrible injustice committed today in Kabul.
>   A horrific crime that has left us mourning, left us in grief… once again.
>   Today the lives of at least forty Hazara children, women and men were taken.
>   I am anxious what tomorrow will bring, I fear what the future holds.
>   I am terrified that I must once again write about the disaster in my homeland.
>   I must once again accept fate and suffer.
>   The government of Afghanistan targets my people and kills them for being Hazara.
>   My people are peace-loving people, my people are forced to flee persecution.
>   My people leave their homes in search of a peaceful existence.
>   But when we seek asylum in another land we are punished and detained for being refugees.
>   Locked up for an indeterminate amount of time, and returned to Afghanistan once again.

Deported to the slaughterhouse called Afghanistan, sent away to fade away.
Banished to disappear from the annals of human history.
How agonising…
how heart-rending…
… to be a Hazara.

(Dana, 2021, p. 209)

Translation and experimentation

The translation and editing process for *No Friend but the Mountains* represented radical forms of experimentation in order to present the multiple layers of literary, philosophical and political influences and histories pertaining to the author, translator/collaborator, and others involved in the shared philosophical activity. I began the translation of the book in December 2016 and by that time mobile phones were permitted. We had worked for many months together while mobile phones were contraband (before 26 April 2016) and Boochani risked losing his phone whenever he used it. During this time I had started translating numerous articles for various media organisations. After the 2016 PNG Supreme Court ruling we were finally able to communicate without those pressures. In addition to text and voice messages we started having conversations through phone calls since refugees were now able to leave the prison and enter areas with better internet connection for the first time after three years. A ruling by the PNG Supreme Court that Australia's detention centre in Manus Island was illegal and unconstitutional meant that refugees could no longer be locked in; they could now leave the detention centre for periods of time and phones were no longer contraband.

After many months of being limited to text and voice messages, Boochani called me for our first phone conversation when visiting the main town of Lorengau. This had an important impact on our working relationship, our theorising of the prison and the wider political situation. It also helped with the different political actions we wanted to organise. However, these changes now meant that the whole island became Manus Prison, and the new possibilities created other difficulties and dangers. As a result, Manus Prison Theory became more complex, the edited translation and other collaborative work incorporated many new insights, and we often experienced more profound instances of philosophical discovery. Manus Prison Theory now became about more than the caged enclosures and the rules and regulations within the prison camp. We expanded our thinking about Manus Prison Theory to represent more examples of debordering; our critical approach and practice developed in more global and transhistorical terms.

No Friend but the Mountains is a multilayered work, and my edited translation was produced in a way that helps illuminate complex points about the many diverse dimensions represented throughout the narratives. In addition to the paratexts (both the peritexts and epitexts), which explain many of the important details of the translation process and the writing/translation contexts, the translation itself indicates special features about the unique mode of production, and the methods used to construct the book.

In Chapter 3 Boochani describes his second journey to Australia, an attempt to seek asylum after his first attempt resulted in tragedy. On July 23, 2013 a boat travelling to Australia from Indonesia carrying people seeking asylum was rescued in Australian waters by a British tanker. The people were first taken on board the tanker where they waited to be transferred to an Australian navy ship. Boochani was amongst them. This was his second attempt to reach Australia after the first boat he travelled on sank in Indonesian waters. Disaster struck that initial journey and the cohort were rescued by Indonesian fishermen. In Chapter 2 of *No Friend but the Mountains* Boochani documents the death of one of his friends who was also from Ilam: he was named in the book as The Blue Eyed Boy. On the second attempt, Boochani's boat was rescued by the Australian navy; July 23 is also Boochani's birthday (on the same day in 2020 he received notification that his refugee status was accepted in New Zealand).

> Moments later a number of young sailors heave my bony, wounded body up over the sides of their ship; their arms smell like the sea. They lay me out on the dry deck. I lie flat on my face and my ears register the wailing and crying of our traumatised group.
>
> *The ocean has performed its sacrifice /*
> *That river ... this sea ... /*
> *The meeting of both at this juncture.*
>
> The Blue Eyed Boy is dead.
>
> (Boochani 2018, pp. 43–44)

- See notes on translation at the end of this chapter.

In an example of intertextuality, Arvin refers to the death of the same young man; he refers to him as Saeed. They had all been on the same boat when it sank (one of the characters, The Friend of the Blue Eyed Boy, in the first four chapters is based on Arvin). In the first story I translated for him, which was published in the literary journal *Meanjin*, Arvin writes from the perspective of a woman psychologist in the Manus Prison and includes a fictionalised version of himself – a story that mixes fiction and non-fiction – he states: "I sought protection! Between bad and worse, I chose worse. From a distance seeking asylum looked good. But now it's different. When our boat sank I was rescued. But Saeed drowned. His kicking and waving, his cries for help … I heard his pleas and I couldn't do anything. Right there and then I saved my own life and got away. Saeed is watching me now. He is everywhere. He's right there in the corner of that damn room. Even up there near the sun.'" (Arvin, Spring 2020) In these examples we see how narratives from different texts interweave to complete a story that exists in fragments throughout different examples of writing. Many parts of this same story have also been described to me as part of the oral history of the forced migration and connections between Boochani, Arvin, Satah, and others.

After escaping death on the first attempt to reach Australia by boat, Boochani was subsequently jailed in Indonesia. He managed to flee with other refugees held in the prison with him and found a way to engage another people-smuggler for a second journey to Australia. These important details are not mentioned in the book but were part of our consultation and sharing process while I was translating and editing.

All refugees who travelled by boat to request protection from Australia express that when the navy arrived to meet them they believed that their ordeal would be over. They imagined they would now be safe and free – they assumed that they would be granted protection by the Australian government. Their expectation was reasonable. Australia is a signatory to the Refugee Convention and refugees were exercising their right under international law.

July 19, 2013 marks the introduction of a new draconian law (in relation to Boochani this was just four days before his boat arrived in Australian waters, while they were still stranded at sea). The Labor Party prime minister at the time, Kevin Rudd, announced that from that day forward anyone arriving in Australia to seek asylum by boat would be sent offshore and barred from ever entering Australia (ABC News, 2016).

Refugees travelling by boat around this time were usually first imprisoned on Christmas Island (an Australian territory) for a short time before being exiled to Manus Island in Papua New Guinea (PNG), a former colony of Australia, or the Republic of Nauru, a former protectorate. Manus Island and Nauru became synonymous with the notorious offshore immigration detention centres: Manus Island set up for men traveling alone and Nauru for families, women and unaccompanied minors.

No Friend but the Mountains is possibly the first book written via WhatsApp text messaging – possibly all our work produced collectively over WhatsApp has this same unique aspect. Similar original features and factors pertain to the collaborative work with others. However, Boochani's different forms of writing and speech were the first examples of this kind that I translated and collaborated in. By sending several hundred text messages of different lengths (including a small number of early voice-texts to Mansoubi in which he read handwritten sections for her to transcribe) Boochani wrote his book during the first five years of his incarceration in Manus Prison. The technology used was a smuggled mobile he obtained by trading cigarettes within an underground economy – an experience that applies to other people I have collaborated with.

The reception to *No Friend but the Mountains*

No Friend but the Mountains was first published in 2018 by Picador-Pan Macmillan (Sydney) and received critical acclaim in Australia, won many prestigious awards, and attracted international recognition (see Sparrow, 2018; McNevin, 2019; Coetzee, 2019). We experienced a modest level of interest in the first few months of the book's release. We were monitoring the response at the time but, in general, our expectations for this initial period were not very high. We would often discuss the impact while we were working on the project. We thought it would probably take a generation for the edited translation to be fully appreciated, and Boochani originally had no intention of publishing the Persian source text. Since I was not involved I am unsure about the technical details related to the editing and publication of the Persian edition (Boochani, 2020). In our early conversation about the book's co-creation/collaboration we discussed how a Persian edition would take a long time and involve a lot of work if it were to reach the quality and complexity of the English edited translation. This is because of all the additions, changes and improvements that were implemented during the complex and experimental translation and editing process. I have already discussed some of these features in this book.

Regarding the English edited translation, we had hopes of eventually achieving a powerful and transformative response on many levels; but from the beginning we anticipated that this may take more than a decade. We were gauging our evaluation based on our research of the socio-political climate, the direction of the dialogues we were monitoring, the political discourse in the media and as presented by different politicians, our own personal encounters, and those of our many collaborators. For us, the project was a duty to history – an investment that we felt would be better received by future generations. Our judgement was also based on reaction to the years of translated journalism work that we had produced, which lacked the long-term institutional support and intellectual and cultural investment required to sustain it. And we factored in the response to the co-directed film *Chauka, Please Tell Us the Time* (2017; co-directed with Arash Kamali Sarvestani), for which I created the subtitles.

After *Chauka, Please Tell Us the Time* enjoyed an excellent reception at its world premiere at the Sydney Film Festival, and a strong response at its international premiere at the BFI London Film Festival, there were several well-attended screenings in different locations across Australia and internationally (including screenings at universities). Following this initial period there was only a relatively small amount of interest in the film and the circumstances around its creation. *Chauka* is available on Vimeo, released for viewing after it toured festivals. Over the first few months – maybe six or seven months – it received a surprisingly modest number of views considering the media attention and the remarkable conditions under which it was shot, directed and produced. Based on these facts, and a range of other factors, we were not anticipating anything remarkable regarding the immediate reception to the book. We certainly believed in it, and we invested so much into co-creating it; we knew how important it was, and how significant it could be as part of a wider strategy to challenge the border-industrial complex. However, we were being realistic due to our previous experiences. We thought we would have to wait some time before it garnered serious attention and audiences began to share our enthusiasm for its power and potential. This seemed true within the first few months of the books release; the response was not particularly impressive.

Everything changed once we won the 2019 Victorian Prize for Literature (Loughnan, 2019). The success of the translation launched our creative resistance into a whole new sphere. Similar to the events related to the siege of 2017, the plight of people held in indefinite detention (especially the offshore prisons), and Australia's border regime in general, entered an intense period of international attention. We witnessed something extremely special occurring at that moment.

The role of the Wheeler Centre was critical and game changing. Their decision to include the book even though Boochani was not an Australian citizen was transformative. Apart from appreciating the quality of the translated book, they understood what was at stake and the potential in including it in the national discourse, not just politically but also intellectually and artistically. Entering the competition was the first obstacle, and we had overcome that barrier. The Wheeler Centre was assigned the task of judging the prize for the Victorian government; they evaluated all the books that were nominated for the different prizes. We asked two of the judges for that prize to contribute to the edited collection *Freedom, Only Freedom*: Jordana Silverstein (2023) and Fatima Measham (2023). They have both also published other works on Boochani's writing and Australian border violence (see Silverstein, 2023 and Measham, 2019).

After winning the 2019 Victorian Prize for Literature and many other awards, we experienced a massive increase in requests from the media, festivals and various institutions; we received an influx of invitations to present or appear in different places, and for interviews. We also received many offers to collaborate on different kinds of projects (including emails with requests for me to translate other books). However, it is important to acknowledge that the international response to the protests and translation of journalism in 2017 – during and immediately after the 23-day siege – played a vital role in creating the possibilities for the subsequent success involving *No Friend but the Mountains*. This point has been overlooked amongst the enthusiasm and attention regarding the book and its many awards. Although some studies have situated the release of the book and its critical acclaim within broader narratives of resistance from Manus Prison, the role of the 23-day siege, the work of the main leaders involved in the period leading up to and during the standoff, together with the ways translation and collaboration functioned to produce writing in English, have been generally neglected in many examples of research and reviews pertaining to the book. In some cases, scholars and critics do not examine the book as both a translation and collaboration, or they discuss important features of the book that are exclusive to the English edited translation – and based on specific translation techniques, decisions and strategy – without investigating the collaboration between author, translator and others; frequent examples include the introduction of terms like kyriarchal system and the shifting prose-poetry format.

Regardless of the mostly isolated focus on *No Friend but the Mountains* at the expense of other work we have produced over the years, we are generally thrilled by the high number of extremely positive reviews and research conducted about the book and, by extension, Australia's border regime. For instance, I have had heartening and profound interactions with PhD researchers and other students, and early career researchers who provide new perspectives, support, encouraging suggestions, and proposed fascinating research trajectories. I read articles and reviews by established scholars and writers who conducted thoughtful and philosophically potent research about the book, drawing comparisons with esteemed literary figures of the past and marking the book as an important literary and scholarly contribution. For only some significant examples see Bielsa, 2023; Inghilleri, 2022; Stonebridge, 2021; Lloyd, 2019, 2021; Tazreiter (Boochani and Tofighian), 2021 and Tazreiter (and Tofighian, with Boochani), 2022; Walker, 2022; Namer, Düzen and Razum, 2022; Razavi, 2020, 2023; Lee, 2021; Hawas, 2019; Allayari, 2022; Galip, 2020; Zolkos, 2019; Vardoulakas, 2019; Coetzee, 2019; Sparrow, 2018; Cooke, 2019; Poletti, 2020, 2020; Whitlock, 2018, 2020, 2024; Qualey, 2020; Hill, 2019; Mckinnon, 2020; Bhatia and Bruce-Jones, 2021; Agozino (co-editor with Giannacopoulos of *Globalizations* 17[7] including my scholarly article and edited translation of Boochani's poem); Giannacopoulos, 2020a and 2020b; Loughnan, 2019 (with Giannacopoulos); Peter Mathews, 2019; Sarah Keenan, 2019; Alimardanian, 2020; Kebsi, 2024 and In press; Ozguc, March 2020; Olubas, 2019a and 2019b; McDonald, 2019; Paik, 2021;

Bal, 2022; work in Japanese by Megumi Kato and Sayoko Iizasa; Tomoko Ichitani (Japanese scholar and translator who was involved in the English to Japanese translation); and all contributors to *Freedom, Only Freedom* [2023]. Also, consider the Kurdish edition of *No Friend but the Mountains* (translated from English, approximately twenty translations have been made from the English edited translation; I wrote new introductions which were translated for the Arabic and Japanese editions) by scholar and translator Hashem Ahmadzadeh who published his translation in 2019 with Arzan (Sweden) which includes a new introduction by Ahmadzadeh (he works in Kurdish, Persian, English and other languages). The Kurdish translation was also published by Ghazalnus in 2019 in Sulaymaniyah (Slemani), Kurdish Region of Iraq (see my comments on Ahmadzadeh's Kurdish translation and his use of the English translation rather than Persian during a seminar with Anna Poletti and Onno Kosters: Tofighian, 2023). Ahmadzadeh has also published a scholarly article on *No Friend but the Mountains* and his translation of the English edition (article in Kurdish).

These outcomes were achieved because of a variety of aspects including the authors vision and unique critique, the book's decolonial and debordering commitments, its multi-generic approach (or anti-genre), the conditions the book was written under, and the experimental nature of the edited translation; the awards, reviews, the different paratexts, and our many events and activities. Together, these factors helped create special moments of interest and support, ruptures and resistance.

Notes on translation

The passage in this chapter quoted from *No Friend but the Mountains* (Boochani, 2018, pp. 43–44):

- The prose passage highlighted below from the Persian text messages corresponds with the poetry part of the quoted English passage below. (see Figure 4.1).

لحظاتی بعد ملوانانی جوان با دستانی که بوی دریا می دادند، بدن استخوانی و زخمی ام را از دیواره های کشتی بالا کشیدند، و مرا روی عرشه ی خشک کشتی رها کردند. با شکم افتاده بودم و تنها صداهای گریه و زاری جمعیتی هراسان به گوشم می رسید. دریا قربانی اش را گرفته بود،رود و دریا به هم رسیده بودند،سعید مرده بود.

FIGURE 4.1 Excerpt from Boochani's text messages; the highlighted line within the sentence was translated from Persian prose to English verse. The previous sentence and the subsequent line in the passage remain as prose after translation and editing.

- The creative use of punctuation is significant for these prose-to-verse interpretative translations.
- The prose-poetry part from the English text below corresponds with the section in the Persian text. Again, one part of the sentence is highlighted, which is the line that was translated as verse. The preceding and subsequent lines remain as prose. Also, past tense was translated into present tense.
- The Blue Eyed Boy appears in the source text as Saeed (as mentioned, Arvin also refers to him as Saeed in his short story). The mention of 'river' and 'sea' refers back to a conversation in Indonesia between The Blue Eyed Boy and Boochani in chapter 1 (Boochani, 2018, pp. 5–6). The Blue Eyed Boy confesses his fear of the ocean and describes a story from back in Kurdistan when he witnessed his brother drown to death in a river.

Moments later a number of young sailors heave my bony, wounded body up over the sides of their ship; their arms smell like the sea. They lay me out on the dry deck. I lie flat on my face and my ears register the wailing and crying of our traumatised group.

The ocean has performed its sacrifice /
That river … this sea … /
The meeting of both at this juncture.

The Blue Eyed Boy is dead.

Appendix

Excerpts from Samaak Audio Mag *and* Hafteh *Magazine*

Samaak Audio Mag published a program derived from the recording of a seminar held at McGill University, Montreal Canada: 21 September, 2019. This was our first public event in Persian.

Moderator and organiser: Farshid Sadatsharifi.

Participants: Omid Tofighian (via video from Cairo, Egypt), Behrouz Boochani (via video from Port Moresby, PNG) and Arash Kamali Sarvestani (in person).

Language: Persian.

Hafteh magazine published an article which included interviews with myself, Boochani and Kamali Sarvestani, with commentary by Sadatsharifi. It was published in Montreal, Canada on 19 September, 2019. This was our first interview published in written form in Persian (Fatemeh Hashemi from SBS Persian conducted a radio interview with me earlier that same year; see appendix 1 in Chapter 3).

All excerpts from the audio recording and magazine (including questions from Sadatsharifi) are my translations. I have indicated the source of the dialogues represented below; I thank Sadatsharifi for permission to translate and publish here.

McGill Seminar (from Samaak Audio Mag *recording)*

OT: I have contact with many who are in detention centres, or they are living in limbo within the community – they are not sure what will happen to them in the future. I wanted to say that it is correct that they are no longer on the island, no longer in Manus Prison or held in Port Moresby. But they have now entered another system of torture. A lot of things have occurred over the last 20 or 25 years under this policy, people committed suicide when they were no longer detained, when they were living freely in the community. This bureaucratic manipulation, this psychological and emotional manipulation, drove them to suicide. It is a major concern of mine to find out where this comes from, who designed it, who is administering this, and why do the people of Australia vote for these politicians. A majority of Australians agree with these policies, with this program. It is really interesting, this goes back to the phenomenon of colonialism in Australia. I mean, these instruments, these structures, these forms of violence, are exactly the reproduction of things that first occurred over two hundred years ago. Over time these transformed as new minorities were sought, new people were subjected to harms under this process and destroyed. Now we see that what is occurring on the Australian border is practically the latest version. However, the roots are within what happened over two-hundred years ago in relation to Indigenous peoples. We do not know what will happen in future, it may be that they implement this on citizens like me. We really need to take this seriously, if democracy is valuable to us then we need to resist. The rights of these people must be our central concern.

FS: Some have asked if possible to outline what you mean by this reference to two-hundred and fifty years ago, reference to the new laws that people voted for. Where can one learn more about this, what is the narrative?

OT: There are two points that I can refer to that allow me to explain briefly. When Australia was made a colony by the British Empire there were some differences to what occurred in other parts of the world like in the US, Canada or New Zealand. By creating a lie they made claim over to this land, this society, this culture, this civilization. This lie was that no humans existed here (*terra nullius*). In those times there were international laws by which the British Empire conducted its imperialism. For them, there were laws that determined how to engage in their colonies, with First Nations peoples… they had their own rules and regulations. But there was something different about Australia, it was based on the construction of a lie, a myth: no one existed here. By virtue of this they felt entitled to engage in many things. If you notice what is happening on the Australian border, clearly, what is happening is in violation of international law. They also constructed a myth that refugees arrived illegally, they are dangerous people. They created a story, a narrative, that frames refugees, that shapes the way they are seen.

Second, Australia itself, this former colony, when the British Empire arrived they established it as an offshore prison. In the same way that Manus and Nauru are Australian offshore prisons, Australia itself was transformed into a prison when the British came. Convicts, marginalised peoples, those whose rights had been violated for different reasons, were placed on a boat, a ship, and sailed to what became the penal colony of Australia. Similar was also inflicted on Indigenous peoples, they were taken from their societies and traditional lands, and put into prisons across the mainland. Sometimes they also converted islands into prisons. What we see happening now is based exactly on the same design established 250 years ago, something that has continued after that time.

Interview published as part of an article with **Hafteh** *magazine.*

An Absurd and Senseless Situation: an exclusive **Hafteh** *interview with Omid Tofighian, translator into English of Behrouz Boochani's acclaimed work.*

1. *FS:* Omid Tofighian, where did the initial inspiration for cultural work come from, how did this come into your life?

    OT: Storytelling, narrative, poetry and music played important roles in my childhood and youth. My interest in cultural production was a result of a number of factors: my mother and father were both very influential, and also growing up amongst multicultural communities in Australia provided me with many diverse experiences. I regularly engaged with many different cultural groups and events, but when I began studying at university and travelling I broadened my views regarding cultural production; I began looking at cultural production through a more academic and socio-political lens. My main source of inspiration has always been cultures of resistance and marginalised and stigmatised communities from all over the world.

2. *FS:* Omid, considering that you were brought up outside Iran, how did you learn Persian/Farsi language so well that you were able to produce a translation that attracted so much attention?

   OT: When my family left Iran I was three years old, this was around the time of the revolution. My family were first in the US for nearly five years and then we went to Australia when I was seven years old. As the eldest child I grew up interpreting for my parents a lot of the time and helping our family with daily tasks and with many of the demands of migration and establishing a life in a new place. My language skills began there but I never imagined I could use these experiences in the future to translate.

3. *FS:* How did your journey lead you towards the book *No Friend but the Mountains*?

   OT: As I have mentioned before, so much of the meaning and style of Behrouz's book relates to my own experience of displacement, exile and migration; and others I know who have had similar experiences. And because of my scholarly approach within a university context. Therefore, I was in a good position to work with Behrouz.

Moreover, I have always been concerned with other political topics such as incarceration and systemic exclusion and since I was an undergraduate student I have been involved in initiatives supporting refugees. This continued when I lived abroad in the Middle East and Europe. When I returned to Australia, I drew on the experiences I gained when travelling and started to develop projects related to cultural production and forced migration.

Actually, I only learned to read and write Persian/Farsi as an adult, much later than some was brought up in Iran. But my mother did teach me some basics for almost year when I was a child. I was not interested to learn reading and writing Farsi until I was an adult and I did very little written translation before I met Behrouz. After I met him, he asked me to help with translating journalism and I noticed immediately that I could do it well (much better than I had thought), especially because the topic and situation was deeply connected with my identity, research and activism.

Also, my father died just before I met Behrouz. My immediate family and I commemorated and honoured his life by using art and culture, particularly philosophy, poetry, music and storytelling. In fact, my work with Behrouz is a culmination of all these factors.

4. *FS:* What different stages were involved, and what obstacles did you face with this translation?

   OT: When I accepted the book translation project I was worried about the difficulty in shifting from journalism to literature. In addition, the translation process was also an editing process – the text required fundamental editing because the Persian version was like one long unedited text message without the redrafting and copy-editing necessary for a book. Based on our discussions – and after Behrouz considered my advice – many things had to be changed. I applied these changes to the text while I was busy doing the translating, I was engaged in both simultaneously.

Then I shared the first draft of my translation with Behrouz's first translator, Moones Mansoubi, and a friend who is a researcher, Sajad Kabgani. Their feedback and ideas were valuable and I became more confident. I shared my translation with both of them all throughout the process in order to receive different comments and ideas. One of the most difficult parts of the translation process was communicating with Behrouz who was isolated and with very bad internet connection. Another problem was the violent and unpredictable situation on Manus Island which made it hard to concentrate and work smoothly. I started translating after Behrouz wrote one third of the book and the other two-thirds were written at the same time I was translating. So it was a very unique project with a lot of disruption and obstacles, but also involving a lot of productive and positive consultation and sharing.

5. *FS:* Did you focus more attention on the importance of the content in Behrouz's work, or where formal and technical issues also important as aspects that interested you?

   OT: Behrouz's work is unique and powerful because of the way content, form and technique are integrated and reinforce each other. The disrupted, fragmented, disjointed and shattered nature of the content also penetrates the form and techniques. In this way, different genres, styles and symbols are used to connect to reflect the experiences and events depicted in the narratives. I was aware of these interconnected features while I was translating, and these gave me a lot of inspiration, they helped provide ideas during the project.

6. *FS:* With all its complexity, followed by all the success, did this work take you in directions you did not expect? Could one say that what has emerged as a result surprised you?

   OT: After reading the first few pages of Behrouz's work I knew it was going to be turned into a masterpiece and a classic. But I did not think it would happen so quickly. Therefore, I was not surprised by the success, but I thought it would take many years to happen. However, winning the Victorian Prize for Literature made a huge difference and many awards and support followed immediately.

7. *FS:* You raised the issue of awards, over the past year Behrouz's book won the Victorian Prize for Literature at the Victorian Premier's Awards which is the most important literary award in Australia; the Special Award at the NSW Premier's Literary Awards; and Australian Book Industry Awards Non-Fiction Book of the Year. And on 12 August this year the book also won the National Biography Award (Australia). However, Behrouz's was unable to attend any of the ceremonies to accept his award because the Australia government would not allow him leave Manus Island. What are your feelings regarding this?

   OT: The fact that Behrouz has been winning awards from the same political system that imprisons and tortures him, and then wins prize money he cannot access, is totally absurd. Our literary term 'horrific surrealism' is used to describe the content, structure, style and vision of the situations, and the book itself. There are many reasons why this is a relevant concept not just for Behrouz's literary imagination but also for his reality. From the situation of the author and his relationship with me as translator, to the experience of travelling to accept prizes on his behalf at these award ceremonies (many times from abroad), to using my WhatsApp connection to enable him to speak at least and have some presence there; all of it is ridiculous and ironic. And when he won two major Australian literary awards (Victorian and NSW) awards it was the first and only time I had ever heard a politician from the two major parties say his name or praise his book in a public space. Everything about this whole situation is paradoxical.

8. *FS:* Behrouz wrote: "What I have tried to reveal in my book is exactly the same system that is in place within hospitals, schools, universities, prisons, and other social systems, in the military, and school education. However, the original, the most complete version, is found in this island. Actually, Manus Prison is the purist example of a system that strips

human beings of their identity, human freedom and individuality." By producing this translation and also accepting awards on behalf of Behrouz in different places, attended by their various audiences. Do you see the response of the audience reactions as representative of Behrouz achieving his goal?

> OT: At literary awards, festivals and other cultural and political events the majority of the people are very supportive. They represent a part of Australian society that is opposed to the government's policies. Therefore, in these spaces the response to Behrouz's success has been great, and the literary community has been particularly supportive. But we have had very few opportunities to interact with people who are anti-refugee. In any case, I am not sure how those conversations would be productive anyway.[1] To change those people's views we need to take a more systemic approach. We have started this by organising activities in high schools because it is important that we address the next generation and prepare them to make substantial and sustainable changes. But *No Friend but the Mountains* is for everyone (people from all parts of the political spectrum). Also, it raises questions about structural issues in civil society and how immigration detention centres, and anti-refugee and anti-immigration policies in general, can continue to expand. The book also reveals how contemporary border politics is an integral part of Australian society and politics and connected with Australia's history of colonial violence. The treatment of non-citizens influences the treatment of citizens in profound and disturbing ways.

9. *FS:* I know that there are campaigns being run to free Behrouz. In your view can these efforts and plans (also contributing like you and Arash have here in Canada) accelerate his release or increase the impact of his book? Why and how?

> OT: Behrouz and I were realistic from the start – we knew that his journalism, film, speeches, art projects and book would not secure his release. But we were actively collaborating on these initiatives because we knew it was important for documenting history and that it has the potential to influence future generations. As long as Australian politicians benefit from demonising refugees and the detention industry profits from it the situation will not change; it will only get worse (Australia is now a model for many other countries!). More action needs to be taken to leverage Behrouz's work so that campaigns address

the ideology driving the border regime and also the political economy around it. I think engagement with Behrouz's work and the different campaigns have started this, but a lot of work still needs to be done. This could take many years.

10. *FS:* Are there plans to publish this text in Persian in future?

> *OT:* Behrouz is now focused on editing the original Persian and he also has a contract with Nashr-e Cheshmeh [Iranian publisher]. He is reviewing the English translation to make sure the changes made are all incorporated into the original.[2]

> *FS:* We thank you very much for your time and contributions to *Hafteh*.

McGill Seminar (from Samaak Audio Mag recording) – continued

FS: I was not able to ask this question when I interviewed you for the magazine due to limitations of space. You are an academician with a very diverse resume, you bring together work related to a lot of different areas, which in my view it is very impressive. Since I have been working within the university my question is about the conservativism associated with universities. How does it impact the work you have been doing? It is, nevertheless, a part of the colonialism, the university is an important feature of it, it cannot be separated. However, it also has the power to stand against it.

OT: I am really happy that you asked this question, it is an excellent question. I have thought about this issue a lot. Thank you. Behrouz and I have discussed this at length and we are planning to write about it and research it further.

My own view is, or actually the view that I subscribe to, is that the university is an institution and a structure, and it is also a way of thinking or an ideology. Like you described, it goes back to the issue of colonialism. Consider the way the university distances itself from the community, the borders that exist to separate it in society and from diverse spaces. Consider how knowledge is something always linked specifically to the university, it can only be produced there and then introduced or delivered to the rest of society. The various schools of thought, or the methodologies or the different disciplines, are all practically the organs or instruments of colonialism, related to controlling the colonies. In particular countries like Australia, Canada, New Zealand and the US that are settler colonial countries, which differs from places in North Africa, for instance Egypt where I live at the moment.

What I want to say in relation to your compelling question is that I think I could not have translated this book in the way that I did, and I could not have understood Behrouz's critical depth so quickly, if I were not already working within the university. The violence and form of conservativism I see in the university, the incidents that take place involving both right-wing people, people who identify as centre of politics, or the left, the incidents that occur in the university involving all of them – not just students but I also mean staff – in my view these incidents are different to what takes place in other institutions and organisations. It is not just something related to neoliberalism, it is certainly part of capitalist culture but it also has another dimension. For example, in companies people are concerned with production, they have their programs and ways forward and ways of making profit. But there is a different state of affairs in the university, a different kind of violence exists, it seems they just want to silence people, drive people into submission, marginalise them, and even when they remain on the fringes they try to banish them through different approaches – actually expel them or expel their thought. I think that the concept that Behrouz introduced in his book, *system-e hākem*, is connected exactly to the system I see in the university. For this reason, I adopted a feminist term for the English translation.: 'the kyriarchal system'. It is derived from a feminist philosopher and theologian who created a term to describe a particular kind of lord/master/sovereign, like a slave master or similar to a merciless ruler. I just wanted to say that the roots of Manus can be found in the university.

FS: I have a literary question about the book. Were you only the translator or something more than that? For example, during the translation process result in changes to the Persian/Farsi text for the purposes of conveying the message better?

OT: A very interesting question that can be answered in two ways. One of them is a bit complex. The simple response is that Behrouz wrote this during five years of enduring torture. The spirit and power and all the qualities of this book come from his blood and experience. This cannot be forgotten. I put a lot of pressure on myself and transformed my way of thinking to understand this book, something that comes from Behrouz's soul and lived experience. When I received the book it was not edited, it was practically one WhatsApp text message. Everything was stuck together. What I did along with Moones Mansoubi, another translator working with Behrouz, we divided the text into paragraphs and made various decisions.

FS: An editor is someone who makes an intervention during the process. I want to know what kind of edits helped build the text.

OT: I was editing the text with Moones and Sajad and we were in touch with Behrouz during the process. After that there was another stage of editing that I engaged in with the editor from the publisher (Picador). A lot of the things that were changed during the translation process were things that Behrouz and I debated over and then modified in the English translation, but there was no time to change the original text. Now Behrouz has gone back to edit the original text so that it matches the way he agreed in line with the outcomes from engaging in the English translation. It can roughly be described in this way.

There is something that people will find interesting. For a term such as *system-e hākem* I chose a philosophical and feminist word for its translation: the kyriarchal system. Now this was something Behrouz and I debated over and discussed before we came to this conclusion, I decided to translate *system-e hākem* in this way. One can say that specific things like this occurred which reflect my own perspective but they were things that Behrouz supported.

Notes

1 This particular sentence is different from the Persian interview since there must have been an error when editing for publication. This English translation is accurate.
2 The Persian edition was published after Boochani edited the original text messages himself together with an editor from the Iranian publisher. The Persian edition was also censored according to the restrictions in Iran.

Bibliography

ABC News (2013) 'Asylum Seekers Arriving in Australia by Boat to be Resettled in Papua New Guinea', *ABC NEWS*. www.abc.net.au/news/2013-07-19/manus-isl and-detention-centre-to-be-expanded-under-rudd27s-asy/4830778

Alimardanian, M. (2020) 'Ethnography of a nightmare: public anthropology, indefinite detention and innovative writing', *American Ethnologist* 47(1): pp. 86–89. https://doi.org/10.1111/amet.12870

Allayari, K. (2022) 'The Boochani effect: public feeling and the limits of refugee authorship', *Journal of Postcolonial Writing* 59(2): pp. 143–156. https://doi.org/10.1080/17449855.2022.2124881

Arvin, M. (Spring 2020) 'Close the Eyes of your Conscience', translated by Tofighian, O. *Meanjin*. Melbourne: Melbourne University Press. www.meanjin.com.au/fict ion/close-the-eyes-of-your-conscience/

Bal, M. (2022), 'Refugees and representation: an impossible necessity', *Humanities* 11(1): p. 29. https://doi.org/10.3390/h11010029

Bhatia, M. and Bruce-Jones, E. (2021) 'Time, torture and Manus Island: an interview with Behrouz Boochani and Omid Tofighian', *Race & Class* 62(3): pp. 77–87. https://doi.org/10.1177/0306396820965348

Bielsa, E. (2023) *A translational sociology: interdisciplinary perspectives on politics and society*. London: Routledge.

Boochani, B. (2016) 'Faysal Ishak Ahmed's Life was Full of Pain. Australia Had a Duty to Protect Him', translated by Tofighian. O. *The Guardian*. www.theguardian.com/commentisfree/2016/dec/30/faysal-ishak-ahmeds-life-was-full-of-pain-australia-had-a-duty-to-protect-him

Boochani, B. and Kamali Sarvestani, A. (dir.) (2017) *Chauka, Please Tell Us the Time*. Sarvin Productions. www.vimeo.com/ondemand/chauka

Boochani, B. (2018) *No Friend but the Mountains: Writing from Manus Prison*, translated by Tofighian, O. Sydney: Picador-Pan Macmillan.

Boochani, B. (2020) *hich doosti be joz kouhestan*. Tehran: Nashr-e Cheshmeh. www.cheshmeh.ir/Book/4565/16059/___%20_____%20__%20__%20_____

Boochani, B. (2023) *Freedom, only Freedom: the prison writings of Behrouz Boochani*, translated and edited by Tofighian, O. and Mansoubi, M. London: Bloomsbury Academic.

Boochani, B., Tazreiter, C. and Tofighian, O. (2021) 'The Multiple Faces of the People Smuggler', in Balint, R. and Kalman, J. (ed), *Smuggled: an illegal history of journeys to Australia*. Sydney: NewSouth Publishing, pp. 177–190.

Coetzee, J. M. (2019) 'Australia's Shame', *The New York Review of Books*. www.nybooks.com/articles/2019/09/26/australias-shame/

Cooke, R. (2019) 'Australia's Most Important Writer Isn't Allowed into the Country', *The New York Times*. www.nytimes.com/2019/02/08/opinion/australia-behrouz-boochani-victorian-prize.html

Dana, E. (2021) 'Shoes that Left Home with the Spirit of Hope... Never to Return', translated by Tofighian, O. *Southerly– Writing Through Fences – Archipelago of Letters*: 79(2): p. 209. www.southerlylitmag.com.au/shop/writing-through-fences-archipelago-of-letters/

Dehm, S. (2020) 'Outsourcing, responsibility and refugee claim-making in Australia's offshore detention regime', in McGuirk, S. and Pine, A. (eds), *Profit and protest in the asylum industry*. Oakland: PM Press, pp. 47–66.

El-Enany, N. (2015) 'On pragmatism and legal idolatry: fortress Europe and the desertion of the refugee', *International Journal of Minority and Group Rights*, 22(1): pp. 7–38. http://dx.doi.org/10.1163/15718115-02201001

El-Enany, N. and Keenan, S. (2019) 'From Pacific to traffic islands: challenging Australia's colonial use of the ocean through creative protest', *Acta Academica*, 51(1): pp. 28–52. http://dx.doi.org/10.18820/24150479/aa51i1.2

Fricker, M. (2007) *Epistemic injustice: power and the ethics of knowing*. Oxford: Oxford University Press.

Galbraith, J. (2015) 'Vulnerable, brutalised and returned to Nauru', *The Saturday Paper*. www.thesaturdaypaper.com.au/topic/law-crime/2015/07/04/vulnerable-brutalised-and-returned-nauru/14359320002071#hrd

Galip, O. (2020) 'From Mountains to Oceans: the Prison narratives of Behrouz Boochani', *Biography* 43 (4): pp. 724–735. https://doi.org/10.1353/bio.2020.0103

Giannacopoulos, M. (2013) 'Offshore hospitality: law, asylum and colonisation' *Law Text Culture* 17: pp. 163–183. www.ro.uow.edu.au/cgi/viewcontent.cgi?article=1311&context=ltc

Giannacopoulos, M. and Loughnan, C. (2019) '"Closure" at Manus Island and carceral expansion in the open air prison', *Globalizations* 17(7): pp. 1118–1135. https://doi.org/10.1080/14747731.2019.1679549

Giannacopoulos, M. (2020a) 'Without love there can be law but no justice', *Globalizations* 17(7): pp. 1085–1090. https://doi.org/10.1080/14747731.2019.1706918

Giannacopoulos, M. (2020b) 'Kyriarchy, nomopoly, and patriarchal white sovereignty', *Biography* 43(4): pp. 736–747. https://doi.org/10.1353/bio.2020.0104.

Hawas, M. (2019). 'On Refugee Literature and the Art of Giving a Fuck', *Politics/Letters*. www.quarterly.politicsslashletters.org/on-refugee-literature-and-the-art-of-giving-a-fuck/

Hafteh 552 (Spring 2019), Montreal, Canada.

Hill, L. (2019). 'Behrouz Boochani charts the survival of asylum seekers– and himself– in the stunning memoir No friend but the mountains', *The Globe and Mail*. www.theglobeandmail.com/arts/books/article-behrouz-boochani-charts-his-survival-and-that-of-other-asylum-seekers/

Inghilleri, M. (2022) 'Migration, Materiality, and Structures of Feeling', in Petrilli, S. and Ji, M. (eds), *Intersemiotic perspectives on emotions: translating across signs, bodies and values*. London: Routledge, pp. 97–115.

Kebsi, J. (2024) 'A Decolonial Translation: Omid Tofighian's Collaborative Approach in Behrouz Boochani's No Friend but the Mountains', *Nawaat*. www.nawaat.org/2024/06/18/decolonizing-translation-omid-tofighians-collaborative-approach-in-behrouz-boochanis-no-friend-but-the-mountains/

Kebsi, J. (In press) 'The challenges of translating world prison literature: Omid Tofighian's contribution to *No Friend but the Mountains*', *Antipodes: A Global Journal of Australian/New Zealand literature*. https://researchers.mq.edu.au/en/publications/the-challenges-of-translating-world-prison-literature-omid-tofigh

Keenan, S. (2019) 'No Friend But the Mountains: Writing from Manus Prison' and Renisa Mawani's Across Oceans of Law: The Komagata Maru and Jurisdiction in the Time of Empire', *Antipode Online*. https://antipodeonline.org/2019/08/29/no-friend-but-the-mountains-writing-from-manus-prison-and-renisa-mawanis-across-oceans-of-law-the-komagata-maru-and-jurisdiction-in-the-time-of-empire/

Lee, B. (2021) *Who gets to be smart: privilege, power and knowledge*. Sydney: Allen & Unwin.

Lloyd, G. (2019) 'Rethinking Australia's Border', *Inside Story*. www.insidestory.org.au/rethinking-australias-borders/

Lloyd, G. (2021) '*No Friend but the Mountains*: an "Australian Reading"', *Southerly – Writing Through Fences: Archipelago of Letters* (Long Paddock – online) 79(2). www.southerlylitmag.com.au/wp-content/uploads/79_2/LP-79-2-GENEVIEVE-LLOYD-No-Friend-but-the-Mountains.pdf

Loughnan, C. (2019) 'No Friend but the Mountains by Behrouz Boochani', *International State Crime Initiative*. https://doi.org/10.13169/statecrime.8.1.0126

Mathews, P. (2019) 'Boochani Unbound: A Promethean meditation on refugee detention camps', *Westerly* 64(1): pp. 59–71.

McDonald, W. (2019) 'A Call to Action: Behrouz Boochani's Manus Island prison narratives', in Avieson, B., Giles, F. and Joseph, S. (eds), *Still here: memoirs of trauma, illness and loss*, Routledge Interdisciplinary Perspectives on Literature 98. New York: Routledge, pp. 238–254.

McKinnon, C. (2020) 'Enduring indigeneity and solidarity in response to Australia's Carceral colonialism', *Biography: An Interdisciplinary Quarterly* 43(4): pp. 691–704. https://doi.org/10.1353/bio.2020.0101

McNevin, A. (2019) 'What we owe to the refugees on Manus', *Inside Story*. www.insidestory.org.au/what-we-owe-to-the-refugees-on-manus/

McNevin, A. (2022) 'Against Crisis: Violence and Continuity in Manus Island Prison', in Fassin, D. and Honneth, A. (eds), *Crisis under critique: how people assess, transform and respond to critical situations*. New York: Columbia University Press, pp. 211–232.

Measham, F. (2019) "Love in a Time of Apocalypse," *Meanjin*. www.meanjin.com.au/essays/love-in-a-time-of-apocalypse/

Measham, F. (2023) 'On Mothers, Nature and the Body', in Boochani, B. (ed), *Freedom, only Freedom: the prison writings of Behrouz Boochani*, translated and edited by Tofighian, O. and Mansoubi, M. London: Bloomsbury Academic: pp. 160–164.

Namer, Y., Düzen, N. E. and Razum, O. (2022), 'What the Mountains Told Us: A Conversation on Behrouz Boochani's Book "No Friend but the Mountains"', in Razum, O., Dawson, A., Eckenwiler, L. and Wild, V. (eds), *Refugee camps in Europe and Australia*. Cham: Palgrave Macmillan, pp. 79–89. https://doi.org/10.1007/978-3-031-12877-6_6

Nethery, A. (2021) 'Incarceration, classification and control: administrative detention in settler colonial Australia', *Political Geography* 89: pp. 1–10. https://doi.org/10.1016/j.polgeo.2021.102457

Olubas, B. (2019a) 'We forgot our names', *Public Books*. www.publicbooks.org/we-forgot our-names/

Olubas, B. (2019b) '"Where we are is too hard': refugee writing and the Australian border as literary interface", *Journal of the Association for the Study of Australian Literature* 19(2): pp. 1–15. www.openjournals.library.sydney.edu.au/index.php/JASAL/article/view/13455

Ozguc, U. (March 2020) 'Borders, detention, and the disruptive power of the noisy-subject', *International Political Sociology* 14(1): pp. 77–93, https://doi.org/10.1093/ips/olz026

Paik, A. N. (2021) '"Create a Different Language": Behrouz Boochani and Omid Tofighian', *Public Books*. www.publicbooks.org/create-a-different-language-behrouz-boochani-omid-tofighian/

Perera, S. (2002) 'What is a camp…?', *Borderland e-Journal* 1(1): pp. 1–13. www.mcrg.ac.in/RLS_Migration_2020/Reading_List_2020/Module_E/Perera_what%20is%20a%20camp.pdf

Perera, S. (2007) 'A Pacific Zone? (In)Security, Sovereignty, and Stories of the Pacific borderscape', in Rajaram, P. K. and Grundy-Warr, C. (eds), *Borderscapes: hidden geographies and politics and territory's edge*. Minneapolis: University of Minnesota Press, pp. 201–227.

Perera, S. (2009) *Australia and the insular imagination: beaches, borders, boats, and bodies*. New York: Palgrave Macmillan.

Poletti, A. (2020) 'A forum on Behrouz Boochani's *No Friend but the Mountains*', *Biography: An Interdisciplinary Quarterly* 43(4): pp. 68--690. https://doi.org/10.1353/bio.2020.0100

Poletti, A. (2020) 'This place really needs a lot of intellectual work: Behrouz Boochani's innovation in life writing as a transnational intellectual practice', *Biography: An Interdisciplinary Quarterly* 43(4): pp. 755–752. https://doi.org/10.1353/bio.2020.0077

Pugliese, J. (2013) 'Technologies of extraterritorialisation, statist visuality and irregular migrants and refugees', *Griffith Law Review* 22(3): pp. 571–597. https://doi.org/10.1080/10383441.2013.10877013

Pugliese, J. (2015) 'Geopolitics of Aboriginal sovereignty: colonial law as "a species of excess of its own authority", Aboriginal passport ceremonies and asylum seekers', *Law Text Culture* 19: pp. 84–115. www.ro.uow.edu.au/cgi/viewcontent.cgi?article=1333&context=ltc

Qualey, M. L. (2020) 'Displaced Voices: Translating Writing by Refugee and Exiled Authors', *The London Book Fair – The Hub*. www.hub.londonbookfair.co.uk/displaced-voices-translating-writing-by-refugee-and-exiled-authors/

Razavi, H. (2020) 'Failures of Imagination: A Journey from Tehran's Prisons to Australia's Immigration Detention Centres', *Australian Book Review* 426. www.australianbookreview.com.au/abr-online/archive/2020/november-2020-no-426/897-november-2020-no-426/6998-failures-of-imagination-a-journey-from-tehran-s-prisons-to-australia-s-immigration-detention-centres-by-hessom-razavi

Razavi, H. (2023) 'Walking Dollar Signs: A National History Full of Puzzles', *Australian Book Review* 450. www.australianbookreview.com.au/abr-online/archive/2023/january-february-2023-no-450/986-january-february-2023-no-450/9985-hessom-razavi-reviews-freedom-only-freedom-the-prison-writings-of-behrouz-boochani-translated-and-edited-by-omid-tofighian-and-moones-mansoubi

Silverstein, J. (2023) 'Testifying to History', in Boochani, B. (ed), *Freedom, only Freedom: the prison writings of Behrouz Boochani*, translated and edited by Tofighian, O. and Mansoubi, M. London: Bloomsbury Academic, pp. 39–43.

Silverstein, J. (2023) *Cruel care: a history of children at our borders*. Melbourne: Monash University Publishing.

Sparrow, J. (2018) 'A Place of Punishment: No Friend But the Mountains by Behrouz Boochani', *Sydney Review of Books*. www.sydneyreviewofbooks.com/review/a-place-of-punishment-no-friend-but-the-mountains-by-behrouz-boochani/

Stonebridge, L. (2021) *Writing and righting: literature in the age of human rights*. Oxford: Oxford University Press.

Tazreiter, C. and Tofighian, O. with Boochani, B. (2022) 'Spectres of Subjugation/Inter-Subjugation/Resubjugation of People Seeking Asylum: The Kyriarchal System in Australia's Necropoleis', in Billings, P. (ed) *Regulating refugee protection through social welfare: law, policy and praxis*. London: Routledge, pp. 68–90.

Tofighian, O. (2018) 'Black bodies for political profit: Sudanese and Somali standpoints on Australia's racialized border regime', *Transition: The Magazine of Africa and the Diaspora* 126: pp. 5–18. www.muse.jhu.edu/article/702736

Tofighian, O., Boochani, B., Mira and Zivardar, E. (2022) 'Narratives of Resistance from Indefinite Detention: Manus Prison Theory and Nauru Imprisoned Exiles Collective', in Bennett, J. (ed), *The big anxiety: taking care of mental health in times of crisis*. London: Bloomsbury, pp. 125–138.

Tofighian, O. (2023) 'Translation in digital times: Omid Tofighian on translating the Manus Prison narratives', *Humanities* 12(1): p. 8. https://doi.org/10.3390/h12010008

Tofighian, O. and Zivardar, E. (Spring 2024) 'Nauru Prison theory as public Philosophy', *The Philosopher* 112(1): pp. 23–31.

Vardoulakis, D. (2019) 'Behrouz Boochani and the biopolitics of the camp: The new Primo Levi?' *Public Seminar*. www.publicseminar.org/2019/02/behrouz-bechani-and-the-biopolitics-of-the-camp/

Vogl, A. (2021) 'What is a Bogus Document? Refugees, Race and Identity Documents in Australian Migration Law', in Biber, K., Vaughan, P. and Luker, P. (eds), *Law's Documents*. London: Routledge, pp. 94–111.

Vogl, A. (2015) 'Over the borderline: a critical inquiry into the geography of territorial excision and the securitisation of the Australian border', *UNSW Law Journal* 38(1): pp. 114–145. www.classic.austlii.edu.au/au/journals/UTSLRS/2015/39.html

Vogl, A. (2017) 'Sovereign Relations? Australia's 'Off-Shoring' of Asylum Seekers on Nauru in Historical Perspective', in Epstein, C. (ed), *Against international norms: postcolonial perspectives*. Abingdon: Routledge, pp. 158–174.

Walker, M. B. (2022) 'Writing: the question as revolt in Kristeva and Boochani', *Humanities* 11(4): p. 78. https://doi.org/10.3390/h11040078

Whitlock, G. (2018) 'The diary of a disaster: Behrouz Boochani's 'asylum in space'', *The European Journal of Life Writing* 7: pp. CP176–CP182. https://doi.org/10.5463/ejlw.7.269

Whitlock, G. (2020) '*No Friend but the Mountains*: how should I read this?', *Biography: An Interdisciplinary Quarterly* 43(4): pp. 705–723. https://doi.org/10.1353/bio.2020.0102

Whitlock, G. (2024) *Refugee lives in the archives: a Pacific imaginary*. London: Bloomsbury Academic.

Zolkos, M. (2019) 'Registers of Undesirability, Poetics of Detention. Jean Améry on the Jewish Exile and Behrouz Boochani on the Manus Prison', in Ataria, Y. and Pitcovski, E. (eds), *Jean Améry: Whoever was tortured, stays tortured?* Houndmills: Palgrave Macmillan, pp. 55–84.

5
BORDER-INDUSTRIAL COMPLEX

Storytelling, cultural memory and experimentation

After completing the final draft of *No Friend but the Mountains* and as I was preparing my translator's note and reflection essay, the editor I was working with suggested that I express more personal experiences in the 'Translator's Tale' when explaining the process. All the work on the three texts (translator's note [Tofighian, 2018b], reflection [2018c] and edited translation [Boochani, 2018]) was done while crossing borders between Sydney, Cairo and Manus Island. I grew up in Sydney and my family established a new life there where we connected with new communities and tried to revive the cultures we had left behind; however, as an adult I travelled a lot and lived and worked in numerous countries. While I was working on the book I spent time in Cairo where I finished the edited translation of *No Friend but the Mountains* and my accompanying essays. In Cairo I learned about many new and important cultural, historical and intellectual themes and topics, especially those related to translation studies which I incorporated into my research (there I met many scholars of translation who invited me to give seminars or publish my work with them; for example Boochani and Tofighian, 2019 was published by Samia Mehrez in her edited book; and Tofighian, 2020b was published by Mona Baker [who I was introduced to by another scholar and translator, Randa Aboubakr] and colleagues in a co-edited encyclopaedic volume [also see Aboubakr, 2020 in the same volume]).

As I mentioned earlier, after completing about two-thirds of the translation in draft form (and before traveling to Cairo) I visited Manus Island where I met Boochani and other collaborators for the first time in person. While there I checked the unfinished draft manuscript with the author, collaborated on numerous changes and additions, and developed parts of my translator's note and reflection essay. Therefore, in response to the editor's request to incorporate personal narratives into my translator's note the first and strongest ideas and feelings that came to mind were about crossing borders. She explained that my text needed more stories to engage the reader and invite them into the experience of collaborating over borders: geographical, linguistic, cultural, political, generic and others. It was here that I incorporated two important stories: one about the way my immediate family honoured my father's death; the other about the death of a refugee in Manus Prison.

My late father's life and death are part of the network of influences on my collaborative translation, writing and activism. The impact of his memory on my cultural, intellectual, creative and political frameworks reinforces the role of story in the different forms of resistance I have engaged in over the years. My father suffered persecution in Iran; in fact, the persecution goes back generations before him. And after leaving Iran he ended up living the rest of his life in exile which involved other kinds of discrimination and exclusion. His namesake Manoutchehr is a mythical shah from the Persian epic the *Shāhnāmeh*. After his sudden passing I prepared a eulogy inspired by his connection to and love of literature, cultural heritage and storytelling at both his funeral and at his memorial (I gave similar talks at his 40-day memorial or *chehelom*, the one-year memorial ceremony and other events). In both presentations I drew on myth, legend and poetry and employed them in creative ways to describe his life. We also acknowledged and paid tribute to my uncle Iradj Towfighian who had died in Germany two years earlier, who was extremely close to my father, and whose name also has a connection to the *Shāhnāmeh*. When sharing narratives of my father's life I refigured the tale about the last days of the mythical shah to create a literary act of remembrance that also represented celebration, love, resilience and pride (using both the Persian original and Dick Davis' acclaimed English translation). My interpretation of Ferdowsi's *Shāhnāmeh* in this way, which was presented at numerous events organised in his honour (at the first memorial passages in English and Persian were read together with my sister-in-law Stephanie Huitema), coincided with presentations of poetry by Iranian cultural icons that my father loved including Omar Khayyam (read by my mother Akhtar and brother Navid at different events) and Ṭahirih Qurrat al-Ayn (read by my youngest brother Naysan at the first memorial). My father admired both and was deeply familiar with their work, often quoting them by heart. Significantly, the lives of these revered and influential individuals were impacted by marginalisation, stigmatisation and suppression. My mother also sang a well-known Persian song from the 1960s.

My immediate family and I made sure that commemorations of my father's life were transformed into literary and cultural festivals. The numerous events we organised over the first couple of years after his death featured performances and talks from our friends who had all established lives in diaspora (my mother also organised a memorial event for the second anniversary of his passing during one of her visits to their birthplace, Isfahan in Iran). At the first memorial event we played a message of condolence and tribute recorded by one of his childhood friends from Isfahan, Hooshmand Aghili, a well-known Iranian singer who has lived in the US (Los Angeles) since we left Iran together. These experiences were formative, and my translation methods embody a similar approach to storytelling, philosophy, memory and performance. My different forms of scholarship, cultural and community advocacy, and activism are interconnected in the approach I used to commemorate Manoutchehr.

I visited Manus Island for the first time in August 2017. My plane from Port Moresby landed in Manus Island early on 7 August 2017. I was able to interact with refugees on the island outside the prison since it was after the PNG Supreme Court ruling that determined that the detention centre was illegal and unconstitutional. After that decision the gates of the prison were left unlocked and refugees could come and go, but with no adequate support network to assist them. Therefore, their lives were always dependent on the prison; and now the whole island had become a prison. This fluidity, mutability and interconnectedness of barriers and borders informs the concept of Manus Prison and the philosophy behind Manus Prison Theory.

A refugee who was working at the hostel where I was staying had come to pick me up together with another person who had left the prison temporarily. While we were driving to my accommodation we noticed a group of people gathered on a reserve near the side of the road, including many children since it was close to a school. The road was blocked by police and after they stopped our vehicle for what was a tense moment we were allowed to pass – but our questions about the situation were left unanswered. The interaction with the police increased my anxiety about my trip to Manus Island and I was worried about whether I might create issues for the refugees I was visiting on the island.

Approaching and landing in Manus Island by plane was itself an uncanny experience since I was reminded of the passages I had translated just months earlier describing Boochani's arrival in Manus Island from Christmas Island by plane having been exiled by Australia. After collaborating with refugees in indefinite detention for decades I had acquired an intimate understanding of the personal narratives of people banished to offshore (and onshore) detention centres. With every new encounter the absurdity of the situation is reinforced and adds new dimensions to my reflections and analysis. In particular, the contrasts at every level between my positionality and the people I have been collaborating with provide the basis for some of the most paradoxical encounters. One striking difference, for instance, is the fact that Boochani and over 1,300 other men seeking asylum were forcibly taken and exiled to Manus Island by Australia to be incarcerated indefinitely, while I travelled there alone for a one week stay before returning to Australia. The strange feelings I had upon arriving in Manus Island proved to be ominous.

A lift was waiting for me when I landed in Manus Island and we reached the hostel soon after passing the roadblock and the crowd. At the lodgings we were informed immediately about the news of what had happened back at the location we just passed. Hamed Shamshiripour was found dead. Shamshiripour was a refugee from Iran who was relocated to a new detention centre in Lorengau from the original prison (the former naval base which held most other refugees at the time). The 23-day siege had not happened yet; Shamshiripour was amongst the refugees who had already been moved. His body had been found not long before we passed by that morning, but it was unclear exactly how long since he had died and how it happened.

Near a school in Manus Island and hidden behind trees, Shamshiripour lost his life. It was evident that he had been beaten (Doherty, 2017). He also had a noose around his neck. The refugees I talked to about it did not believe the basic narrative that PNG and Australian authorities announced. Everything about the events raised suspicions about the official narrative. When one analyses a range of factors leading up to the death including the accounts provided by people who had close ties with Shamshiripour, and subject to the same systematic torture that he endured, the 'official' narrative loses credibility. Shamshiripour had been mentally unwell for a long time and requesting help – authorities knew how emotionally and mentally fragile he was and that his overall situation was volatile (see Kamali Sarvestani's film *Tall Fences, Taller Trees* [2020] for a rendition of Shamshiripour's reflections before his death which depicts some sense of his personality, relationships and feelings; and also indicates that his mental health was in decline. I also created the subtitles for this film which uses Shamshiripour's own words verbatim).

Weighing up the evidence alongside the many testimonies from Manus Prison had convinced us that a more comprehensive investigation was needed. Shamshiripour and his family deserved that. We all deserve to know the truth about exactly what occurs in these carceral sites. However, the official narrative in the mainstream media remained the same. Mainstream journalists and others contacting Boochani and other refugees about the situation heard many of the suspicions and critiques by the people who had been privy to Shamshiripour's life and struggles. Numerous refugees were adamant that there were still many complex factors left unexplored. However, the official government narratives were the only ones published and discussed in the mainstream media.

Many Australian and international journalists would mostly reach out to people such as Boochani, Satah and a few others whenever there was a 'newsworthy' incident. Like on so many other occasions Boochani and several others experienced back-to-back interviews and discussions. While I was there I witnessed Satah working hard with different authorities he was acquainted with on the island to arrange a proper investigation and begin other important proceedings.

Just hours after arriving one of the refugees who met me at the airport took me to the central Lorengau bus stop in town to meet Boochani. It was our first in-person meeting after nearly two years of WhatsApp communication and collaboration. By that time I had already translated dozens of articles, statements, speeches and tweets, and I had translated about 70 to 80 percent of what would later become *No Friend but the Mountains*. Boochani could not meet me when I arrived but was waiting for me at the bus stop in Lorengau that afternoon. Due to the extremely traumatising and tense situation he had not eaten breakfast or lunch and had only been smoking cigarettes that day. The role of mobile phones in the creative resistance of refugees in Manus Prison was vital and Boochani was recognised as the journalist who wrote and organised his activism and writing through WhatsApp communication technology. The first time I saw him in person he was preoccupied with an interview by phone. I walked over to meet him while also greeting others at the bus stop.

There were many important reasons for visiting Boochani (and others) in Manus Island at that time, and one of the most pressing was working with him to improve my edited translation of the book. As I mentioned, I had completed about three-quarters up to that point. However, the translated English text was still a rough draft and the structure resembled the original text messages in Persian; for example, there were still no paragraph breaks, little consistency regarding important structural issues (for example, every chapter in the published English edition begins with a passage of poetry which I incorporated later in the translation and editing process), no headings, nor any kind of divisions between sections within chapters (also, one extremely long chapter still had to be split into two – what became Chapters 8 and 9). I had translated in a very experimental way and incorporated some editing while refashioning the text into English, but I did not apply the same experimental features and edits to the original text for reasons pertaining to the lack of time and because there were originally no plans to publish in the source language. As mentioned, Boochani's views on this changed after the release and success of the English edited translation. Although, as I explained earlier, I was not involved in the editing process and publication of the Persian text, which underwent a very different kind of editing process with the publisher (Nashr-e Cheshmeh – see Boochani, 2020). It is important to reiterate that it did not incorporate most of the changes or the experimental decisions and additions which I have discussed throughout this book. It may be considered a somewhat rewritten version since it was modified for publication in Iran; it ended up becoming its own (intralingual translation) product which I will discuss later (see Barseghian's review in Persian, 2020).

The original plan of my first trip to Manus Island was to spend every day checking many crucial elements related to my translation choices and overall approach to translating the book. From early in the process I realised that it would be necessary at a certain point for us to discuss in person the various details and modifications and the experimental methods and techniques I was implementing. Messages through WhatsApp and phone conversations (after refugees could leave the facilities and find stronger reception) were extremely helpful but we required a workshop setting where we could engage on a deeper level and have the physical texts in both languages in front of us to analyse, in the same way I had been doing on a regular basis with the Sydney-based translation consultants for the project, Mansoubi and Kabgani. Both Mansoubi and Kabgani had confirmed the suitability of my experimental approach, and when we communicated this with Boochani while we worked together he endorsed the approach and changes. But it was still necessary to conduct a close study of the translation together in person.

From the first hour into my visit to Manus Island everything transformed into something extremely different from what I had planned. I had entered something much more extreme and disturbing, it was a harsh introduction into life under systematic torture; the daily situation of offshore indefinite detention. The border-industrial complex makes torture an integral part of the everyday experience of refugees. As Michelle Nayahamui Rooney has discussed, the detention centre has also irreversibly disrupted the kinship networks, customs, moral framework and knowledge of the local people which has always dictated the rhythms of everyday life (Rooney, 2017, 2018, 2021). During the period while refugees had been forced into exile in Manus Prison it was the border-industrial complex that dominated and functioned as the new colonial ruler. The legacy of that time remains even after the prisons in Lombrum and Lorengau have been closed.

As translator and collaborator working with refugees who have experienced indefinite detention, it is difficult finding the best approaches and focus points for the different projects. Finding the balance between the main topic or theme for a project and incorporating multidimensional meanings has been difficult; developing ways to design and deliver a powerful and effective message requires selection of some at the expense of others. It is tempting to want to imbue a project with a wide range of critical and artistic perspectives, especially when it is a collaboration between two or more people. There is an expectation that direct political critiques using predominantly empirical approaches or an exposé about corruption and abuse should take precedence, or that data and reports related to urgent health concerns should be prioritised in representations. The expectation in these cases is usually that a form of realism is the best method of depicting the tragedies that occur in indefinite detention. Drawing connections with Rancière in her interpretation of Boochani's poetic and narrative approach to writing about Manus Prison, McNevin argues: 'What is real in history, including what is real in histories of the present, is only partially illuminated and frequently concealed by facts presented as evidence. Facts can be overwhelming, compiled in order to document the real by virtue of scale and repetition. But accumulated facts also banalize their constituent parts: irrevocable loss, for instance, or a man's depth of feeling for a creature with whom he shares a form of displacement. In fiction and in stories, paradoxically, the real becomes visible more precisely for what it is.' (McNevin, 2023, p. 84) Faced with the expectations and norms that demand a form a realism based on facts, data, 'official' statements and reports, it is hard to step back and explore new forms of creative resistance in translation, to develop different and multidisciplinary techniques that incorporate unconventional literary and artistic practices and approaches.

Regardless of the success so far, my view is that many of the different layers of collaborative projects such as *No Friend but the Mountains* and the intricacies of the experimental translation and editing process require a lot more time and attention to grasp fully. For one, apart from two articles (Kebsi, 2024 and In press), a study comparing the English edited translation and the Persian edition published later in Iran has not been conducted in English, one that considers the reception to the 2020 Persian edition. Some issues related to the philosophical influences behind key points require further analysis from experts in different fields: 1) the translation and editing decisions; 2) the experimental approach; 3) the socio-cultural and political conditions in which the book was written, translated and edited; 4) the different layers of meaning and messages; 5) the historical and literary background; 6) and the mode of production.

Also, the existential difficulties associated with working in this space are worth closer examination. Finding closure on many issues and themes will only ever be possible when every single person is free and the onshore and offshore prison camps have been permanently closed. In addition, the Australian government and the individuals who made decisions and designed the policies need to be held accountable for the deaths and damage to people's lives. Confronted with this reality, closure may be impossible. However, this is not necessarily a cause for withdrawal or resignation. In fact, translators know well this feeling regarding the limited (or no) possibilities for closure. The act of translation and the commitment to activism against border violence share this quality. It is by living and struggling through this uncertainty and unpredictability that new languages of resistance emerge.

Synecdoche: part/whole relationships of border violence

Boochani's description of the absurd experience of demanding an answer from the Boss in *No Friend but the Mountains* resembles so many kyriarchal situations we encounter in our lives as citizens living within the nation-state:

> Whatever the question, whoever you ask within the prison, the answer is the same: 'The Boss has given orders.' Whenever a stubborn prisoner makes inquiries and finds The Boss of that individual who has said 'The Boss has given orders' and then confronts that person, that person also responds with 'The Boss has given orders'. It is just a pointless effort. All the rules, all the regulations, and all the questions about those rules and regulations are all referred back to one person: The Boss. It is astonishing how The Boss also responds with 'The Boss has given orders'. A long chain ascending through the hierarchy.
> *(Boochani, 2018, pp. 211–212)*

- See notes on transition at the end of this chapter.

Operation Sovereign Borders is the continuation of the Pacific Solution and is ongoing. We are still witnessing the oppression and containment of people in Port Moresby (PNG) and in Nauru (new groups of people were sent there at the end of 2023 and in 2024), in Australian-run detention facilities in Indonesia, and in detention centres across Australia (including Christmas Island). The conditions do not allow me to make a fair evaluation about the impact of the collaborative work we have produced so far. What evaluative and hermeneutical framework is necessary to study the impact of this work on the Australian public, on its politics and culture, on its social and colonial imaginary? Horrific surrealism as a hermeneutical schema is extremely useful and productive, I feel it is necessary – but it is insufficient.

During the second phase of the Pacific Solution and then Operation Sovereign Borders seven people have been killed as a result of indefinite detention in Manus Prison, four in Nauru and one in Christmas Island. Fourteen deaths in total. However, this does not factor in the many who have died after being deported and which we know little or nothing about (or the many who have died in onshore detention or after release). People have been killed by the offshore system since 2002, the first iteration of the Pacific Solution:

Mohammed Sarwar (Nauru, 2002)
Fatima Irfani (Christmas Island, 2003)
Saeed Qasem Abdalla (Christmas Island, 2013)
Reza Barati (Manus, 2014)

Sayed Ibrahim Hussein (Nauru, 2014)
Hamed Khazaei (Manus, 2014)
Fazal Chegani (Christmas Island, 2015)
Omid Masoumali (Nauru, 2016)
Rakib Khan (Nauru, 2016)
Kamil Hussain (Manus, 2016)
Faysal Ishak Ahmed (Manus, 2016)
Hamed Shamshiripour (Manus, 2017)
Rajeev Rajendran (Manus, 2017)
Mohammad Jahangir (Nauru, 2017)
Salim Kyawning (Manus, 2018)
Fariborz Karami (Nauru, 2018)
Sayed Mirwais Rohani (died in Brisbane after transfer from Manus, 2019)
Abdirahman Ahmed Mohammed (died in Perth after transfer from Manus via imprisonment in Nauru and then Brisbane, 2021)

The collaborative and creative resistance I discuss in this book is a direct response to the illegal detention of refugees by the Australian government, part of a border regime that has inseparable connections with the global border-industrial complex. This form of resistance is not limited to border politics but is also part of multifaceted discourses about coloniality and other intersecting structures of discrimination and violence from the modern history of Australia (Nethery, 2021; Tofighian, 2020; Tazreiter and Tofighian with Boochani, 2022). However, the struggle against the border-industrial complex must be interpreted using a global approach; while our collective work is a scathing critique of Australia's border regime it also applies to the situation in other Western liberal democracies and beyond (see Miller, 2019, 2021; Paik, 2016; Bhatia, 2020a, 2020b; Bosworth, 2008, 2014; Bosworth, Fili, & Pickering, 2014; Canning, 2017a; Canning, 2017b; El-Enany, 2015; Esposito et al., Winter 2019; Esposito, Ornelas, Briozzo, and Arcidiacono, 2019; Kebsi, 2019; Khosravi, 2010; Khosravi, 2019; Sirriyeh, 2018).

Surrealism pervades so much about the relationships I have built over the years and the work we have produced together. The fact that we communicate, collaborate, resist, and produce art and knowledge regardless of the differences between our circumstances and the opportunities available to us causes deep reflection about the absurdities of border regimes, and the ever-shifting, intersecting and perplexing nature and role of bordering in the modern globalised world. My own critical interpretation of border politics has taken shape and moved in new directions as I engage in different collaborative projects and deliberate the meaning and purpose of theoretical, artistic and practical frameworks. Examples such as Manus Prison Theory and Nauru Prison Theory, for instance, are evolving philosophical and political projects that are enhanced and change with every new collaborator, interaction, experience and project. These theoretical, creative and practical models reflect the experiences of displacement, exile and incarceration endured by the immediate collaborators, many individuals and groups who become part of the collaborations, the many people we know who experienced similar situations at different points in their lives, our different histories of displacement and exile, and the contributions of larger groups of people from other marginalised and persecuted communities.

In the case of the collaborators who have experienced immigration detention, the experience of incarceration informs our processes and directions in multidimensional ways. At every step we factor in the specificities of our diverse experiences; in particular, persecution based on gender, ethnicity, social or citizenship status, religious belief, or political views and affiliations. Power imbalances are always a serious consideration and point of discussion. The fact that certain collaborators are incarcerated in offshore immigration detention or have recently been released marks clear differences with my experience of forced migration and deserves careful consideration in our working relationships. The citizen/non-citizen power differential is a crucial factor and must be engaged with as a serious issue when balancing and connecting our contributions.

Our analyses of the detention industry always aim to identify connections with diverse and intersecting forms of violence and domination. Theories developed from Manus Prison and Nauru Prison focus on systems of oppression and their interconnection within the context of what we consider to be neocolonial experiments. The theories represent the location of enunciation, the socio-political-economic context, colonial histories, and the intricate details of the built and natural environments on those islands – they are place-based and situation specific. Naming the theories by including the location relates to how we incorporate the way those islands and their people and cultures have been in a sense expropriated for the purposes of indefinite detention. In addition to identifying and engaging closely with the specific sites, the theories also represent unique concepts and methodologies that can be applied globally.

The carceral sites function within the colonial imaginary, in addition to ideologies of racial capitalism and the political entities, institutions and groups that initiate and sustain them. The nuanced intellectual frameworks developed for understanding the detention sites expose their brutal dimensions and their cruel historical and political foundations.

> The indispensable power of narrative in political ambition and garnering support for a socio-cultural vision based on violence and suppression is a frightening reality; mythmaking conditions all forms of biopolitics and all interactions with ecosystems, nowhere is it more fundamental than in the necropolis. One of the driving forces behind MPT is to expose, satirise,

and dismantle colonial narratives by imposing narratives of resistance and decolonisation, literature that reclaims and replaces: the myth of "illegal" refugees; the myth that allows for the false dichotomy of genuine and fake/political and economic refugee; the myth that evokes the sense of entitlement in settlers with citizen-privilege to demand performances of refugeehood and play off of deservingness; the myth of uniform, fair, and informed asylum claim determination systems; the myth that justification must precede humanity—one must first justify their humanity according to some "refugee imaginary" to then be treated as human; and, the myth of the errant traveller which constitutes border politics and bordering practices—it is intertwined with the colonial violence imposed on First Nations people and is, in fact, one extension of its technologies and ideologies. Crimmigration becomes both the narrative source for producing "illegals" in the intertwining of criminal and immigration law (Weber and McCulloch, 2018) and itself is the product of earlier mythmaking.

It is apt that MPT was born from a literary endeavour, a writing and translation process that crossed borders and genres and facilitated an emerging language that then supported storytelling about new horizons, characterised by abolition of immigration detention and debordering. It is apt to imagine *No Friend but the Mountains* as new language for a new way of knowing, it is an anti-genre about a new kind of subject created by late capitalism and experimented on by new bordering technologies. *No Friend but the Mountains* is also a myth about the future, a narrative with ravaging potential to become a far-reaching reality. MPT is as much a story as it is a theory.
(Tazreiter and Tofighian, with Boochani, 2022, pp. 76–77)

Intersectional and decolonial approaches help to reframe and redirect critiques of the border-industrial complex, and the role of kyriarchy in this discourse helps reveal the roots of border violence in coloniality (Quijano and Ennis, 2000; Schüssler Fiorenza, 2020). Border violence is one form of colonial thinking with a central aspect of its core ideology targeting and torturing refugees. The colonial imaginary in an Australian context has roots in the colonisation of Indigenous lands by the British Empire, and it continues to expand and reinforce the displacement, dispossession and repression of Aboriginal and Torres Strait Islander peoples (Moreton-Robinson, 2015; Giannacopoulos, 2006 and 2013; Keenan, 2014; Perera and Pugliese, 2018a and 2018b; Pugliese, 2015). 'The first wave of invading white British immigrants landed on our shores in 1788. They claimed the land under the legal fiction of *terra nullius*— land belonging to no one—and systematically dispossessed, murdered, raped, and incarcerated the original owners on cattle stations, missions, and reserves. In all these contexts, the lives of Indigenous people were controlled by white people sanctioned by the same system of law that enabled dispossession. Indigenous people were denied their customary proprietary rights under international law and their rights as subjects of the crown." (Moreton-Robertson, 2015, pp. 4–5) Legal fictions, and extralegal tactics, continue to be employed by the Australian government today, especially in the way it deals with people seeking asylum. '[M]ythmaking conditions all forms of biopolitics and all interactions with ecosystems, nowhere is it more fundamental than in the necropolis'. (Tazreiter and Tofighian, with Boochani, 2022, pp. 76) International law is consistently violated by a nation-state that has signed the 1951 Refugee Convention and the Protocol Relating to the Status of Refugees (which entered into force in 1967). A racial bias deeply ingrained in Australian society is interconnected with factors pertaining to capitalism: to be accepted and 'belong' means to fit within a socio-political-economic construct: the accumulation of capital, social worth, authority and ownership. (Tofighian, 2018, pp. 7–8)

Both empire building and crimmigration depend on narratives in fundamental and vital ways. New languages of resistance – decolonial and transnational approaches that interweave collaboration, activism, translation and storytelling – attempt to dismantle and replace fictions that conflate criminal and immigration law (Weber and McCulloch, 2018; Billings, 2019); fictions that are built on earlier colonial myths. Australia's carceral-border archipelago, its detention industry, is the consequence of many factors including recent chapters of dangerous and destructive colonial storytelling: 'the myth of "illegal" refugees; the myth that allows for the false dichotomy between genuine and fake/political and economic refugee; the myth that evokes the sense of entitlement in settlers with citizen-privilege to demand performances of refugeehood and play off of deservingness; the myth of uniform, fair, and informed asylum claim determination systems; the myth that justification must precede humanity—one must first justify their humanity according to some "refugee imaginary" to then be treated as human; and, the myth of the errant traveller which constitutes border politics and bordering practices—it is intertwined with the colonial violence imposed on First Nations people and is, in fact, one extension of its technologies and ideologies.' (Tazreiter and Tofighian, with Boochani, 2022, pp. 76)

There exists an interdependent relationship between Australian society and its detention industry which requires multifaceted interpretations and forms of engagement to unpack. A nuanced understanding of relevant tropes helps illuminate the dynamic and complex historical and contemporary relationships that exist between the state and the border, particularly as they relate to offshore detention. A transposable synecdochic (part/whole) relationship connects the nation-state with its detention industry. I employ this trope in my arguments to explicate the interchangeable active–passive exchanges between the nation and the border; that is, expose the links between Australian society and its institutions and the border-industrial complex.

Australia's detention centres are carceral sites created by the nation-state and conditioned by its history and the socio-political structures within it. The locations have symmetrical relationships with its progenitor, meaning that Australian society and detention centres determine each other. Using the example of an offshore carceral site, the island prison at times occupies a passive role. In this instance, the policies, rhetoric, phases of governance, and acts of violence against refugees are tested, further ingrained, and expanded in the offshore prisons. However, contemporary Australian society is not immune from the actions of leaders and stakeholders against refugees; citizens are also impacted by the containment of people seeking asylum, and the creation and maintenance of the sites themselves (Kukathas, 2021). The events, activities, decisions and justifications related to contemporary immigration detention represent interdependent links with Australia's colonial past and, therefore, it was inevitable that border violence soon became an integral part of Australia's collective imagination.

As explained above, at one point in the synecdochic relationship the offshore prisons functions as passive recipients in that Australia's historical, socio-cultural and political elements impact and shape what takes place in offshore carceral sites. However, at other random points in time the roles are reversed. In the inverse synecdochic relationship the nation-state occupies the passive role. That is, what takes place or is tested in the neocolonial experiment – in this example, the offshore detention centre – determines the socio-cultural and political climate, discourse and policies in Australia in uncanny and inescapable ways.

While translating for and collaborating with people held in indefinite detention or recently released, many political incidents reinforced the part/whole relationships between the border and the state, between the non-citizen and citizen. Numerous connections can be made between border politics and examples such as police raids on the ABC, discriminatory treatment of Australian citizens trying to return to Australia from India during the pandemic, or the use of detention centres to quarantine Australian citizens returning from China. Also, the border plays a crucial role in the way the Labor Party has adopted a permanent defensive posture against the conservative Liberal-National Coalition (regardless of whether Labor are in power or opposition) when addressing issues pertaining to border politics. The Labor Party has adopted and advanced many LNP policies – even those they were previously opposed to.

The Christchurch massacre is another case in point, with the terrorist being an Australian citizen living in New Zealand and expressing an extremely dangerous racist and anti-immigration attitude (see Tofighian, 2023, pp. 224–228. The interview with me cited here was conducted in English by Heba Abdel Sattar and then translated by the interviewer and published in the Arabic newspaper *Al Ahram* in 2019). In many ways Australia's social/colonial imaginary can be interpreted as the foundations for border violence, and this impacts how the carceral-border and the state are connected through a complex and interchanging synecdochic dynamic.

Identifying kyriarchy, exposing the kyriarchal system

As intellectual, artistic and political projects the objectives of our collaborative initiatives involve a combination of truth-telling, radical reinterpretations of underlying narratives, and a commitment to transformation. It is through these aims that we attempt to make unique contributions to the discourse about border violence. There is a particular vision involved in this work that is dedicated to driving change in the same way as many abolitionist movements which emerge from grassroots and transnational organising. This critique of Australia's border politics builds on transhistorical and cross-cultural domestic and global movements against xenophobic nationalism, neoliberal policies, securitisation, and the militarisation entangled with international humanitarian interventions. This critique also focuses on the way three particular industries have merged: the prison, military and border industries.

In a collaborative project with the Indigenous and intercultural dance theatre company Marrugeku, Boochani and I were commissioned as cultural dramaturgs together with Patrick Dodson (see Tofighian, et al., 2022). Titled *Jurrungu Ngan-ga* (Straight Talk) the development of the performance also included discussions with and contributions by Dylan Voller, who was incarcerated as a juvenile in a Northern Territory detention centre. The horrendous treatment of him and other youth by guards while imprisoned was caught on camera and featured in a documentary called *Australia's Shame* which exposed the treatment of Indigenous boys in detention. For the chapter I wrote about *Jurrungu Ngan-ga* (Tofighian, 2021) for Marrugeku's edited book (a testament to twenty-five years of creating performances committed to culture, community and justice edited by Helen Gilbert, Dalisa Pigram and Rachael Swain) I incorporate quotes from Voller to help highlight the connections between the tactics and weapons used within Australia's different forms of incarceration:

> Well, I think a lot of people don't realize that that video of me in the restraints was actually in the adult prison when I was only 16 years old. A lot of people think that I was older. I was actually 16 in an adult correctional facility (in Alice Springs). That actually happened because I was going off when they were trying to transfer me from Alice Springs

to Darwin, Don Dale. I didn't want to go back to Darwin. And I had only just come back to Alice Springs. I've got no family or friends in Darwin. I couldn't have visits there. I couldn't have anything.

I just said I wanted to stay. So I ended up getting put back to the adult prison for three nights and then flown up the next day in a police helicopter, strapped into belts on a police aeroplane and taken up to Darwin. I had no choice. That's a big factor when people run amok in incarceration. They've taken a lot of these Indigenous kids whose English is their second language. A majority of the time they're grabbing these kids, locking them up and then taking them 1,500 kilometres away from their family, from their Country, and then expecting them to abide by the rules. They're told to be quiet but most of these kids don't know what's happening. To take them away from Country, take them away from family, stuff like that – how – are they supposed to heal? How are they supposed to rehabilitate when they can't even have the one thing that's important in their lives? And that's culture, that's family.

(Voller, quoted in Tofighian 2021, p. 310)

As my work with Marrugeku and Voller illustrates, our diverse projects and activities involve a range of collaborators and are rigorous and scathing critiques of border violence which address coloniality in both Australian and international contexts. We build on various features and factors to develop theoretical, literary, artistic and political projects by employing comparative and genealogical approaches. I have explored the possibilities of using the notion of kyriarchy in this work and attempted to acquire a more multidimensional and relational understanding of its definition and use in order to help explain how incarcerated refugees, Indigenous peoples, settlers and other groups are all impacted in different ways by intersecting structures of oppression, domination and submission.

It is important to note that kyriarchy is not a synonym for general notions of structural oppression, systemic violence or institutional discrimination (these are necessary conditions for the definition, but are insufficient in accounting for all of the nuances that constitute the kyriarchal system/s). The term represents something much more complex, and when applied to Australia's border regime it helps describe a phenomenon that is much more brutal and ruthless than something that terms like 'oppression', 'violence' or 'discrimination' can represent. The kyriarchal system was developed through translation as a specific concept and a platform for richer discourses and more dynamic philosophical and political frameworks. The kyriarchal system is a translation of the term *system-e hākem*. The Persian word *hākem* has Arabic roots and is used in many languages throughout the world, making it a transnational term. In previous work and earlier in this book

I have described the reasoning behind my translation decision regrading the kyriarchal system and the significance of using Schüssler Fiorenza's notion of kyriarchy in this context (Tofighian, 2018b, pp. xxvii-xxviii; Tofighian, 2018c, pp. 369–370; Boochani, 2018, n. 6 p. 124; Tofighian 2020; Tofighian, 2023). However, the complex translation and philosophical processes involved in introducing this new term and theoretical framework require deeper critical analysis by scholars writing about *No Friend but the Mountains*. On many occasions, numerous scholars have left out necessary analysis of the translation *planning* and translation *process* and focused on an inaccurate or insufficient interpretation of the translation *product*; in many cases, the kyriarchal system is simply viewed as a general synonym for oppression or violence. In some cases a basic reading of intersectionality is acknowledged without the many other aspects associated with the translation planning, process and product. Usually, a serious engagement with Schüssler Fiorenza's scholarship is missing in addition to the way her work was adapted, developed and incorporated in our work (many examples have little or no citations to her scholarship). There are many missed opportunities here for acknowledging the importance and broad applicability of her radical feminist hermeneutics. There is enormous potential in studying the development and use of the term and situating it within the collaborative and creative resistance from indefinite detention. This would require researchers to draw connections with discourses central to translation studies, intersectional discrimination, literary and narrative studies, critical and cultural border studies, public philosophy, and other related perspectives and approaches.

One important example of writing that does engage with the kyriarchal system in serious ways is offered in a non-academic book by writer and researcher Bri Lee in *Who Gets to Be Smart: Privilege, Power and Knowledge* (2021). In her book she conducts a close and well-researched study of both Schüssler Fiorenza's scholarship and my own writing, philosophical work and public engagement. She indicates how I drew on different examples of research and activism and used them to develop the translation and philosophy related to the kyriarchal system.

Lee recounts the time we were in Indonesia for the 2019 Ubud Writers & Readers Festival and were discussing university study while traveling in a vehicle together. She asked me about academia, in particular about her ambitions to do a PhD. She describes my response and her reaction in *Who Gets to be Smart*:

'I would say that academia–'he moved his hands as though he were shaping something or holding a package–'is second only to Manus prison in terms of being the most violent and cruel institution I have ever encountered.'

His hands dropped back into his lap. I just stared at him, dumbfounded, while the vehicle bumped along the corrugated road.

When I'd gathered the pieces of my exploded brain, he patiently explained to me the concept of 'kyriarchy'–a way of thinking about and understanding the accumulation and exercise of power, particularly institutions, which we can call 'kyriarchal systems'.

Thinking back to this conversation later made me wince, because I was asking him about ideas and concepts articulated throughout *No Friend but the Mountains*. I am ashamed to admit I'd bought the book but skipped Omid's introductory translator's note...'

(pp. 46–47)

Throughout the chapter titled 'Kyriarchy', Lee continues to detail her subsequent research process regarding the concept, my scholarship and examples of public philosophy, particularly in connection to the kyriarchal aspects of universities. She refers to different examples including passages from *No Friend but the Mountains*, my translator's note, and my interview with Louisa Luong in *Vertigo* (the longer unpublished version is included here as the appendix to this chapter). I was very encouraged to read about her response to our conversation about academia. As I read and then reflected on her writing several feelings and thoughts were evoked: by reading Lee's account and analysis I began to develop an even stronger sense regarding the special and transformative power and importance of translation work.

Many times, in many different encounters, I got the impression that some people saw translators as something like machines who just happen to be the ones who conduct the 'mechanical transfer' from one language to another (or as people who are available simply and solely to assist with interpreting issues). Acknowledgement and credit for translation and collaboration has been an issue in many instances – and something incredibly difficult and awkward to address (personally, professionally, and especially culturally) considering the extreme circumstances. But when reading Lee's book I felt appreciated not just as a translator but as a writer and philosopher. It reminded me of an edifying passage by Edith Grossman:

> I believe that serious professional translator's, often in private, think of themselves – forgive me, I mean ourselves – as writer's, no matter what else may cross our minds when we ponder the work we do, and I also believe we are correct to do so. Is this sheer presumption, a heady kind of immodesty on our part? What exactly do we literary translators do to justify the notion that the term "writer" actually applies to us? Aren't we simply the humble, anonymous handmaids-and-men of literature, the grateful, ever-obsequious servants of the publishing industry? In the most resounding yet decorous

terms I can muster, the answer is no, for the most fundamental description of what translators do is that we write – or perhaps rewrite – in language B a work of literature originally composed in language A, hoping that readers of the second language – I mean, of course, readers of the translation – will perceive the text, emotionally and artistically, in a manner that parallels and corresponds to the esthetic experience of its first readers. This is the translator's grand ambition. Good translations approach that purpose. Bad translations never leave the starting line.

(Grossman, 2010, pp. 6–7)

However, reading Lee's admission about initially skipping the translator's note in *No Friend but the Mountains* and then returning to it after our meeting did make me wonder how many readers and researchers have overlooked it (and also the reflection essay at the end, or even my many articles and interviews on the topic). How many think the discussions about translation, editing and collaboration are inconsequential and unnecessary for understanding the book? I thought maybe some did not appreciate that what they were reading was an edited translation that involved so much more than a basic and mechanical transfer from one language to another, as I have argued in this book. In particular, my explanations regarding shared philosophical activity, the kyriarchal system, and horrific surrealism are vital for a multidimensional and culturally-informed reading that addresses coloniality, history, intersectional discrimination, literatures of resistance, storytelling practices and more.

I strongly believe in, and have argued for, the power and political importance of 'joy, hope, celebration, love and pride' in the context of displacement and exile (see appendix to Chapter 2): 'In order to resist people also need a cause for celebration' (see appendix 2 to Chapter 3). But I also argue that celebrating the success of a translation *product* without acknowledging, understanding, and investing in the translation *planning* and translation *process* (especially when they involve extensive, careful and experimental collaboration – what I have called a shared philosophical activity) can be interpreted as just another expression of liberal humanitarianism (see my comments in the introduction under 'The border-industrial complex: the refugee industry and pro-refugee/anti-refugee disposition'; also Kaus, 2019). That is, turning creative resistance into a politically non-threatening and philosophically impotent product for public consumption within the refugee industry. Acknowledging, understanding and investing in translation plans and processes are just some ways to help build empowering infrastructure for enabling future collaborations – necessary conditions for creative resistance against the border-industrial complex. More dynamic and transformative instances of creative resistance require broader and more diverse collectives. Success here means sustaining, maintaining and expanding the shared philosophical activity.

After reading Lee's writing about kyriarchy and academia and our subsequent conversations I was heartened by many aspects of her interpretation. In particular, how she connected collaboration, activism, translation and storytelling; how she understood the significance of fragmented, disrupted, disjointed and shattered phenomena; and how these linkages and associations help provide better intellectual experiences of *No Friend but the Mountains* and lead to more comprehensive literary and political perspectives.

The comment I shared with her about academia being the most violent and cruel institution after Manus Prison (and Australia's detention estate, in general) is, I think, a comparison worthy of a serious reflection and collective response. I often say that one of the reasons I was able to understand stories by refugees in indefinite detention – especially Boochani's writing – and was able to engage with their writing and other forms of creative resistance so quickly, and translate and collaborate with success, was because of my years working in domestic and international academic contexts (see reviews of Lee's book in which reviewers expresses the impact of my statement: Edwards, 2021; Miekus, 2021).

But the comparisons do not end with these two examples. The stories told by diverse people about what they have experienced and witnessed within so many contemporary institutions and societies (in Australia and abroad) constitute other kinds of kyriarchy. A comprehensive justification of other examples deserves specialised study beyond the scope of this book. In *Working for the Brand: how corporations are destroying free speech* (2024) Josh Bornstein draws on his legal expertise, experience and research to offer a detailed critique of the power wielded by companies and corporations in the twenty-first century to manipulate employees, suppress free speech, erode participatory democracy, and encourage tacit acceptance of repression; that is, they abuse power (in some cases they are more powerful than nations) through repressive and anti-democratic strategies and tactics designed to protect a brand. After sacrificing so much in their struggles against enmity and cruelty, so many people are left with little option but to reduce their narratives to: *'the matter has settled on a confidential basis.'* This is another example of how silencing strategies operate; how they conceal or rationalise using humanitarian or bureaucratic and corporate language. Here is where the role of creative resistance can make impactful, memorable and lasting ruptures. Creative resistance such as the examples of translation, art and public philosophy described in this book make cracks in the system – they render alternative ways to talk about and challenge kyriarchy.

In relation to the systematic torture of refugees in indefinite detention, a deeper understanding of the kyriarchal system requires examining how it weaponises identity, time, space and design. The architecture of systematic torture and the multidimensional process of dehumanisation, slow punishment and subjugation begins by first targeting identity, agency and personhood; a strategy employed within a matrix of various techniques associated with time, space and design. Identity, time, space and design are exploited by structures and mechanisms that interweave different tactics in gross and systemic ways. The reduction of refugees to numbers is one of the initial and most obvious markers of this attack, signalling an act of capture and subjugation against refugees at the border. Innumerable features of the detention centres and its bureaucratic system work to render detainees as insignificant bodies without agency. Creative resistance is committed to combatting the weaponisation of identity, in addition to the way it interweaves with the weaponisation of time, the weaponisation of space, and the weaponisation of design.

Consider this phenomenon within the synecdochic equation featuring the two islands. In relation to the island of Australia, offshore refugee prisons are neocolonial experiments that function to reduce the capacity for compassion among settler communities. The symmetrical dynamic also works to amplify and normalise the forms of aggression and enmity in the detention industry and then replicate them within the settler society. This hate and enmity are not only directed towards humans; it extends to animals and the environment where detention centres have been imposed. The offshore island prisons (and onshore detention centres) destroy intellectual insight and repress the moral imagination in Australia; by extension it is important to investigate the fluid and unpredictable interchangeability of the two-island dynamic.

There are distinct differences between the offshore island detention centres on Manus Island and Nauru and the detention centres on Australian territory. However, it is more productive to interpret these various forms of carceral-border containment as part of a network, all elements of the same industry, ideology and history. The different situations in which refugees are held (and forcibly moved between) embody the intersecting systems of violence or the kyriarchal system: onshore detention, community detention and temporary visas (See Briskman, 2013 and 2020; Zion, 2018, 2019a and 2019b; Fleay, 2017; Hartley and Fleay, 2017; Coddington, 2017; Briskman and Doe, 2016; Briskman and Zion, 2014). It is through this interpretation of the facilities as indispensably interconnected that we can then extend the analysis to border violence and bordering around the world, historically and transnationally.

A nuanced approach which centres issues pertaining to racial capitalism and coloniality illuminates the direct connections between Australian institutions, companies and multinational corporations (Dehm, 2020; Verma, 2019; Vogl, 2015 and 2017; xBorder, 2016; Verma and Mitropoulos, 2015; Sanggaran & Zion, 2015 and 2016; Kiem, 2014; Briskman & Zion, 2014; Australian Centre for Corporate Responsibility). The connections between the offshore prisons and the nation-state go beyond the economic and practical – they also involve ideology and culture. As I have indicated, one important entanglement within the border-industrial complex involves universities, a relationship which is disturbing and rapidly increasing. Dismantling the detention industry requires a specific strategy, a multifaceted approach that includes disrupting the dominant ideas, theories, scholarly approaches and language used to represent border regimes. Therefore, a critique of educational institutions plays a vital role.

Also, as part of the border-industrial complex, the 'refugee industry' includes an extensive cultural industry which capitalises on refugee stories and promotes the narratives and tropes I criticised earlier. In the collaborative work I have been engaged in we have tried to resist models and projects that replicate and reinforce damaging and reductive representations and approaches. In our work we refuse the easy categorisations such as refugee testimony, or simplifying refugee accounts by presenting and analysing them mainly as the experiences of victims or reflections on trauma.

In relation to *No Friend but the Mountains*, for instance, I attempted to find alternative ways of framing the book and have suggested understanding it as an example of clandestine philosophical literature, prison narratives, philosophical fiction, Australian dissident writing, political art, transnational literature, decolonial writing, or descriptions from other literary traditions (Tofighian, 2018c, p. 372). In addition, my research and experience in social epistemology, aesthetics and narrative studies have opened up clearer and richer ways to examine collaborative works such as *No Friend but the Mountains* and their potential for knowing border violence.

Notes on translation

The passage in this chapter is quoted from *No Friend but the Mountains* (Boochani, 2018, pp. 211–212):

- The highlighted passage below (Figure 5.1) is the Persian source text which corresponds to the paragraph from the subsequent English edited translation (the same passage quoted in this chapter).

هستند ناگهان در را باز کرد و محکم روی میز بیضی کوبید،باید آنجا فریاد کشید" حرامزاده ها گیر افتادید،رئیس کجاست"،اما باز هم رئیس بزرگ را پیدا نمی شد،در زندان از هر کسی سوال پرسیده می شد جوابش این بود"رئیس گفته است"،وقتی یک زندانی سمج پیگیری می کرد و رئیس آن کسی که گفته بود"رئیس گفته است" را پیدا می کرد و یقه اش را می گرفت او هم می گفت "رئیس گفته است"،و این یک تلاش بیهوده بود.همه ی قوانین و مقررات و سوالات پیرامون این قوانین و مقررات به رئیس می رسید،اعجاب آور بود که رئیس هم میگفت رئیس گفته است،خطی طولانی که به سمت بالا می رفت،سلسله مراتبی اداری که با قدرت ربط پیدا می کرد.هر رئیسی زیر دست یک رئیس دیگر

FIGURE 5.1   Excerpt from Boochani's text messages which were compiled into PDFs by Moones Mansoubi and sent to me. The translation of the highlighted passage corresponds to the passage above in English.

- Decisions regarding paragraph breaks proved significant in these sections.
- I also had to consider the best way to translate the hypothetical conversations that Boochani was imagining.
- As with the rest of the book, past tense is converted to present tense.
- It was vital when translating these kinds of passages to convey a particular form of satire and dark humour.

> Whatever the question, whoever you ask within the prison, the answer is the same: 'The Boss has given orders.' Whenever a stubborn prisoner makes inquiries and finds The Boss of that individual who has said 'The Boss has given orders' and then confronts that person, that person also responds with 'The Boss has given orders'. It is just a pointless effort. All the rules, all the regulations, and all the questions about those rules and regulations are all referred back to one person: The Boss. It is astonishing how The Boss also responds with 'The Boss has given orders'. A long chain ascending through the hierarchy.

Appendix

The following is the original long version of an interview conducted by Luisa Luong which was edited down and published in the October 2019 edition of the magazine *Vertigo*, produced by UTS (University of Technology Sydney). Luong contacted me for the interview after attending my event with Boochani (moderated by Richard Cooke) at the 2019 Sydney Writers Festival. This version includes important responses that were not published. I have included Luong's introduction from the magazine version and thank her for permission to publish here.

In conversation with Omid Tofighian (an interview with Louisa Luong)

The ease between Omid Tofighian and Behrouz Boochani was palpable at the panel for 'No Friend but the Mountains' at the 2019 Sydney Writers' Festival, despite Behrouz having to be livestreamed because he was – and still remains – in offshore detention on Papua New Guinea. The majority of the talk was in English, save for a few casual exchanges between the two men where Behrouz redirected phrases or questions in his native tongue to Omid for translation. Omid would then diligently scribble on the notepad on his lap, gaze up in deep thought, and deliver Behrouz's words with care and precision. This dedication to detail offers a small window into the tremendous trust between not just a translator and an author, but between respected friends.

In addition to being a lecturer, researcher, and community advocate specialising in philosophy, religion, rhetoric, myth, migration and displacement (just to name a few), Omid is a translator of Behrouz's book *No Friend but the Mountains* – an intimate account of Behrouz's five years of exile on Manus Island. Behrouz is an Kurdish-Iranian journalist, writer, filmmaker, philosopher and political activist who wrote his book via Whatsapp messages on contraband phones. His book, which weaves poetry, literature and philosophy serves as a powerful counter-narrative to the refugee archetype that dominates the imagination of the Australian populace.

Louisa Luong chats to Omid about his remarkable partnership with Behrouz, the significance of multidimensional resistance and storytelling, the influence of his own experiences of displacement in Iranian and Australian society, the repercussions of the white curriculum on the politics of nationhood and citizenship, and how hope can become a powerful political tool.

1. You've been translating Behrouz's work since 2016, what about him initially drew you to his work and how did your partnership evolve during the time spent working on the book?

I first read one of Behrouz's writing in February 2016 – I think it was the first article he wrote for the *Guardian* and just months after he began using his real name rather than a pen name. The article was remarkable on a number of levels. It was a critique of the prison and border politics by a writer incarcerated by the same system, and I realised immediately that I was reading something by an original and experienced intellectual. Actually, I have been involved in working with and supporting displaced and exiled peoples for two decades and have encountered many examples of testimony, critical analysis, creative response and resistance from people who have lived experience. My own family history involves displacement and exile so, in fact, I have been affected by similar issues and narratives my whole life. I noticed there was a special multi-dimensional and multi-layered feature in Behrouz's article which spoke to many themes and topics I had been working on in my own research and activism. So I sent him a Facebook message immediately and we began a conversation. When I told him I was an academic we started to discuss research ideas and engaged intellectual work and that's when he asked me to help with translation. There was a very good response to the first article I translated and we continued collaborating on articles, speeches, strategies and building networks. Throughout this time he mentioned that he was writing a novel and when he received a contract for the book he asked me to translate. I began the translation of the book in December 2016. The collaboration was very complex, innovative and unpredictable. In my translator's note I call it a "shared philosophical activity" because it involved a number of important people who all occupied – and still occupy – essential roles. In the same article I also describe what I call "literary experimentation"; this refers to the way we had to a mix genres, styles and techniques in original ways to represent the extraordinary nature of his literary work and ensure the different meanings and messages are communicated. Many things changed throughout the translation process but the project was always collective, collaborative and experimental. Empowerment and liberation were drivers and essential features – both in terms the poetics and political vision.

2. **What was it like translating a book described as "horrific surrealism"? Did you struggle with translating and dissecting someone else's intimate trauma, especially someone you know so personally?**

There are many reasons we decided to use the term "horrific surrealism". My experience translating the book was totally surreal. Also, the response to the book has enhanced this surreal factor. In fact, so much about our relationship and the work we have been doing together is surreal. We collaborate closely and understand each other very well; we are close friends who speak almost daily, we support each other regularly and in multiple ways, and there are many things about our identities that connect us. It is a remarkable partnership, but it is also totally surreal because of many stark contrasts between us and our circumstances. The power differential is striking in terms of citizenship status, mobility and so many related factors. And, of course, this surreal aspect is combined with the horrific reality of imprisonment in Manus, Australia's border regime and the psychological and emotional dimensions of the lived experience. But when we refer to the notion of horrific surrealism we mean something more than just the lived experience and identities. Horrific surrealism is a scheme – a form of epistemic and aesthetic framework – that helps understand 1) the identity of the author and his experiences of oppression and domination; 2) it is important for examining Australia's political situation in the context of global border politics; 3) it is central in explaining the mode of production in the making of the book and Behrouz's other projects; and 4) it opens up appropriate and heuristic spaces for interpreting the style, content, structure and tropes used in the book. One of the great strengths of the book is the fact that all four of these factors reflect horrific surrealism. In this way they mutually reinforce each other. Therefore, a deep reading of the text requires consideration of the interconnectedness of these dimensions in the framework of horrific surrealism. This matrix includes features such as fragmentation, disjointedness disruption; absurdity; the role of the subconscious; psychological horror; dreams visions; satire and irony; assemblages of objects and symbols from the built environment and natural environment; personification and anthropomorphism; a critical form of figuration; and exploring the possibilities of anti-genre. These interpretations are the result of collaborative intellectual and creative

work and involved deep consultation on all levels. This relationship and method helped with translating all the personal and traumatic aspects.
3. **The book is a literary resistance by its very existence because Behrouz wrote it in Farsi — the language of his oppressors. You've mentioned in a previous interview that you were initially unfamiliar with Behrouz's words because of the effects of intergenerational trauma on Kurdish people as a group that has endured systematic persecution. Can you talk us through this observation?**

Historical injustice, intergenerational trauma and systematic erasure are part of the reality of being Kurdish in the Middle East. In Iran there are many different groups that face various forms of systemic oppression and suppression; this is perpetrated by the state, ingrained within institutions and normalised in social interactions. Cultures of domination and exclusion and the ideas and traditions they embody infect each other and also travel beyond borders; they need to be resisted in multiple ways if positive, long-lasting transformation is to take place. These facts have determined my modes of engagement with Behrouz and my attitude to translation. I identify with the dominant ethnic group in Iran (Fars/Persian) and my language (Farsi/Persian) is the national language there; I am deeply aware of the consequences of Iran's modern nation-building program. This has involved a process of Persianisation and has been implemented at the expense of many identities, languages, histories and traditions. While translating I educated myself regarding Kurdish literature, folklore and resistance. Acknowledging and centering the political, cultural and symbolic features of Kurdish traditions were key and determined so many of my choices regarding terminology, style, voice and tropes. Also, my own experiences of displacement and exile, marginalisation and stigmatisation in Iranian society, and in Australian society, have influenced my interpretations and ethical stance. My background also taught me the importance of accountability and self-criticism in this kind of work. Therefore, I drew on my own lived experience and family networks for insight into historical injustice, intergenerational trauma and systematic erasure. This helped me see how these factors play out in transnational contexts and the subtle differences between various situations, encounters and periods. It is significant to mention that Behrouz combines a wide range of diverse cultural, political and literary traditions – some are Kurdish, others are better known in Iran or easily identifiable globally, some are more marginal, some are unique to his own socio-cultural background and upbringing, while others are new and specific to his displacement, exile and incarceration.

4. **You were tasked with conveying an intricate concept that you and Behrouz call the "Kyriarchal System"; a self-governing system of torture, control**

and oppression. What were the challenges of translating not only an elaborate language, but also an elaborate and abstract concept?

I realised early in the translation process that Behrouz was experimenting with theory and art. He was creating new languages and symbols, and interconnecting multiple frames of reference. His book is clearly part of various literary and political traditions, but it has also initiated a new tradition. There are many complex concepts and it is crucial to interpret them as rooted and imbedded in lived experience, lived endurance and active resistance. They are presented as abstract but are indispensible to knowing and engaging with Manus Prison in an embodied way, and they are inseparable from the narratives that emplot them. The book certainly offers theoretical reflections and theoretical frameworks, but the multi-dimensional style and attitude of the book grafts epistemological, instinctual and sensory elements. This is why I call it an anti-genre – philosophy is performance, theorising is advocacy, ruminating is action, thinking is embodied, theory is drama. So for both me and Behrouz the term *system-e hākem* had to be analysed and translated with this context in mind. It is a new term for a special way of thinking about oppression, domination and submission which emerges out of his prison experience in Manus but also links to colonisation of the Kurdish homeland, Western colonial violence, neoliberalism, border technologies, racism, misogyny, homophobia and transphobia and many other forms of violence. After struggling for a couple of months to find the right word I returned to some reading I had done on feminist theological hermeneutics. I revisited Elisabeth Schüssler Fiorenza's work and felt it was an excellent match with many things Behrouz was trying to communicate and critique. After discussing the connections with Behrouz we settled on the translation of the phrase. We appropriated Schüssler Fiorenza's term "kyriarchy" and created the "kyriarchal system". Interestingly, Schussler Fiorenza's notion developed in a context that involved interactions between Black feminists, Chicana feminists, feminists from South America and other transnational scholarly traditions and conversations.

5. A tremendous amount of trust was needed to tell this story. How did you maintain the integrity of Behrouz's words? Was it daunting to have so much control over someone else's narrative, especially for a story that will serve as a socio-cultural marker in our nation's collective narrative?

I refer to the translation process and other work I do with Behrouz as a shared philosophical activity. We began as a small cluster who were working toward the same political, cultural and intellectual goals; our collaborative work was not controlled or influenced by any institutions nor affiliated with any group or organisation. We consulted and cooperated with Behrouz at every stage and always felt our own interactions and mutual support were sufficient for creating a new language and new ways of knowing, sensing and acting. Behrouz has always been the main decision maker even though we discuss our strategies, methods and tactics at length – after suggestions, support and debates we find ways to move forward together and then involve others we are working with in integral ways. Trust was established in different ways with different people but every interaction and new collaboration shared common features: self-determination, reciprocity, understanding, commitment, reliability and respect. This was always the case – I think this is why the shared philosophical activity has continued to grow and become more influential. I knew from reading the first few pages of the book that it was going to be one of the most significant socio-cultural markers in the nation's collective narrative and I never doubted this at any point in our collaboration. But I was not sure how long it would take to be recognised in this way and whether we would attract the kind of support we needed to continue with our strategies and tactics. Based on the response to Behrouz's work prior to the book I honestly did not think it would happen as quickly as it has. But still I think there are a lot more organising and creative ways of taking action still to take place; firstly, human beings are still being incarcerated off-shore and on-shore and many lives have been irreparably damaged. The book project was a daunting task but throughout, and still now, I never lost sight of the fact that freedom and empowerment were the priorities and this work was about more than one person's story – Australia's border regime is intertwined with a vicious colonial vision that is pervasive in Australia and has been adapting, denying, concealing, transforming and strengthening since invasion. Trying to represent this in creative and powerful ways was the most daunting part. But as we worked together I also found it to be the most motivating and invigorating part. It would not have been so successful if it did not involve Behrouz himself in integral ways and if it did not evolve out of a shared philosophical activity.

6. **Refugees in Australia are the subject of polarising narratives; dehumanised as the Other, or burdened with a heavy onus to present a prescriptive (and therefore credible) story as the suffering victim. How does trauma and memory affect storytelling? Can it be a source of resistance and agency rather than contention?**

One idea I am working on at the moment pertains to the heavy onus placed on refugees to present a prescriptive story about a suffering victim or weak person which is then evaluated according to rigid, bureaucratic standards by people with citizen privilege. It is necessary to begin a critical and anti-colonial conversation about the pervasive culture of justification (or the control of a kind of justification thesis) that demands a particular response according to the norms, standards and narratives determined by nation-states and their institutions; that is, associated with power and violence. Behrouz deconstructs the binaries associated with refugees and his resistance is iconoclastic in this respect. Dangerous oppositions such as victim/saviour, beneficiary/benefactor, recipient/supporter are dismantled and exposed. This kind of response is decolonial and a core element of the book and other works – it is fundamental to Behrouz's multi-dimensional resistance and storytelling. In this way storytelling can transform the collective imaginary that depends on violent colonial and inequitable discourses about legitimacy. Behrouz's narratives reclaim the notion of validation and he reinterprets it on his own terms.

7. **How can refugees reclaim their narrative from politicians who use their bodies as voter currency?**

    Refugees have been reclaiming their narratives from politicians and antagonistic parts of Australian society as soon as their persecution began. I think it is important to acknowledge that even though politicians use refugee bodies for political profit voters are also involved in reinforcing and perpetuating damaging narratives. There are many different actors involved in demonising and exploiting refugees – politicians are an influential element but do not act alone. In terms of reinforcing and replicating the 'suffering victim' trope, people from across the political spectrum have been complicit. The imaginary that conditions certain perceptions of refugee bodies ignores, reduces or marginalises narratives of empowerment and self-determination presented by refugees. Therefore, so many discourses project the notion of the suffering victim and this often becomes the sole or dominant trope. Again, refugees have always been reclaiming their narratives, but being heard has been difficult. An epistemic shift needs to take place and this involves a vision of justice dedicated to changing the epistemic and cultural conditions as well as the material and social conditions. Behrouz's creative and intellectual resistance has always been part of a wider political project which is dedicated to abolishing the detention industry and centering freedom of movement, but it is also about knowledge production and knowledge sharing.

8. **Are we able to create a space for these stories of resistance in a country built on stories of oppression and colonialism dating back to our First Peoples?**

    In a number of publications and during talks we have both argued that there is a colonial logic governing the detention industry. By this we mean that the exile and incarceration of refugees is based on a colonial mentality and uses technologies inspired by or adapted from the dispossession, displacement and ongoing persecution of Aboriginal and Torres Strait Islander peoples. Particular colonial structures have been modified and improved for the purposes of contemporary border violence; there are many interconnections we have written and talked about and these are exemplified in themes such as systematic torture, the kyriarchal system, the pro-refugee/anti-refugee disposition, horrific surrealism, carceral-border violence and more.

9. **You've raised issues on the problematic nature of Australia's white curriculum, can you tell us more about this, and how you see its effect on our collective memory?**

I have been inspired by scholarship and activism focused on challenging and dismantling the white curriculum mainly in South Africa and the UK, and I have also been looking to other forms of resistance in the Middle East, North Africa and Continental Europe regarding education. I have tried to incorporate many of the gains made in other places into my own teaching and research and the different social and institutional environments I have been living and working within. It is important to explain that the curriculum involves more than subjects, themes and topics of study and reading lists. The white curriculum is also about pivotal issues like teaching methods and activities; constructions of history, legacies and traditions; creation of canons; amplifying certain questions, concerns and arguments and attenuating others; who determines what is legitimate and valid and why; representation in terms of who advances in higher education and ultimately moves on to becoming an educator and decision-maker; classroom setup and prioritising particular voices and views; whose complaints are supported and whose dismissed or ignored. The white curriculum is also about who is unwelcome in the university and who feels out of place in that space; it is about which communities border the physical space, who is situated at a greater distance, and what kind of relationships do they have with the university; it is also about the identities who work there in roles other than teaching and research. Considering these factors helps us understand the university as both an institution and an ideology. Therefore, the way refugees, borders, nationhood and citizenship are imagined and employed in society and politics are dependent on the white curriculum. Many serious questions need to be addressed in this context: Can the curriculum support and empower people who have experienced displacement, exile and colonialism to advance through the higher education system and then into academia? To what extent can displaced, exiled and colonised peoples be involved in the creation and distribution of knowledge? How is academia racialised and gendered and how do these factors intersect with other forms of marginalisation and stigmatisation? Challenging the white curriculum involves these issues and questions and many more. Therefore, I argue that the white curriculum is deeply connected with major aspects of Australia's border regime. Structural changes to teaching, learning and organisational networks in education are necessary. There are many issues that need serious consideration but systemic changes should consider: 1) knowledge systems (the dominant epistemologies); 2) hegemonic cultures (related to academic imaginaries); 3) borderless collegiality (what are the responsibilities of the academic publishing industry towards marginalised and system-impacted researchers?).

10. **Considering your work with youth cultures and communities, do you see young people playing a big role in this narrative shift?**

Behrouz and I have discussed the historical significance of his writing and resistance and realise that it is something that will only really be fully appreciated by the next generation. After struggling for six years and producing an amazing corpus of work it is disappointing that Behrouz has only recently been recognised as an intellectual, as a creative, as a knowledge producer and a central voice in debates about border politics. And still, this recognition is still limited to specific circles. We both feel the way in which the current generation has engaged with his work and tried to organise in order to free refugees and transform the political situation has, unfortunately, been unsuccessful – the reasons are complex and multifarious. We are now aiming to make Behrouz's work part of high school curriculum and also central to university teaching and research, all on a global scale. Our hope is for the next generation to ensure these atrocities are never forgotten and do not happen again. There are many examples of resistance involving young people – particularly by Indigenous young people and other racialised groups – which motivate and educate us.

11. **Are you hopeful for the future of Australia's treatment of refugees and asylum seekers?**

I cannot lose hope – it is essential to my personal and working relationship with Behrouz. In this context maintaining and increasing hope is a political act. Not just for me but for those I engage with. Actually, my name means hope in Farsi. But hope is fickle if not situated within a strategy and employed within a diversity of tactics. I think with the right methods and vision – and the right narrative – hope can become a powerful political tool.

Bibliography

Aboubakr, R. (2020) 'Popular Culture and Citizen Media', in Pérez-González, L., Blaagaard, B. and Baker, M. (eds), *Routledge Encyclopedia of Citizen Media*. New York: Routledge, pp. 305–310.

Australian Centre for Corporate Responsibility. www.accr.org.au/qantas-expert-statement/

Barseghian, A. (2020) 'che gooneh behrouz boochani ketab-e khod ra dar noskheh-ye nashr-e cheshmeh ((momayezi)) va ((akhteh)) kard', *hadeaghal kalanshahr*: metropolatleast. ir. www.metropolatleast.ir/%da%86%da%af%d9%88%d9%86%d9%87-%d8%a8%d9%87%d8%b1%d9%88%d8%b2-%d8%a8%d9%88%da%86%d8%a7%d9%86%db%8c-%da%a9%d8%aa%d8%a7%d8%a8-%d8%ae%d9%88%d8%af-%d8%b1%d8%a7-%d8%af%d8%b1-%d9%86%d8%b3%d8%ae%d9%87%d9%94/

Bhatia, M. (2020a). 'Crimmigration, imprisonment and racist violence: narratives of people seeking asylum in Great Britain.' *Journal of Sociology* 56(1): pp. 36–52. https://doi.org/10.1177/1440783319882

Bhatia, M. (2020b). The permission to be cruel: street level bureaucrats and harms against people seeking asylum. *Critical Criminology* 28: pp. 277–292. https://doi.org/10.1007/s10612-020-09515-3

Billings, P. (ed) (2019) *Crimmigration in Australia: law, politics, and society*. Gateway East, Singapore: Springer.

Boochani, B. (2020) *hich doosti be joz kouhestan*. Tehran: Nashr-e Cheshmeh. www.cheshmeh.ir/Book/4565/16059/___%20_____%20__%20__%20_____

Boochani, B. (2018) *No Friend but the Mountains: Writing from Manus Prison*, translated by Tofighian, O. Sydney: Picador-Pan Macmillan.

Boochani. B. and Tofighian, O. (2019) 'No Friend but the Mountains: Translation as Literary Experimentation and Shared Philosophical Activity', in Mehrez, S. (ed), *In the shoes of the other*. Cairo: Kotob Khan, pp. 131–146.

Bornstein, J. (2024) *Working for the Brand: how corporations are destroying free speech*. Melbourne: Scribe.

Bosworth, M. (2008) 'Border control and the limits of the sovereign state', *Social & Legal Studies* 17(2): pp. 199–215. https://doi.org/10.1177/0964663908089

Bosworth, M. (2014) *Inside immigration detention*. Oxford: Oxford University Press.

Bosworth, M., Fili, A. and Pickering, S. (2014) 'Women's Immigration Detention in Greece: Gender, Control, and Capacity', in Guia, M. J., Koulish, R. and Mitsilegas, V. (eds), *Immigration detention, risk, and human rights*. New York: Springer, pp. 157–170.

Briskman, L. (2013) 'Technology, control, and surveillance in Australia's immigration detention centres', *Refuge: Canada's Journal on Refugees* 29(1): pp. 9–19. https://doi.org/10.25071/1920-7336.37502

Briskman, L. (2020) 'The people's inquiry into detention: social work activism for asylum seeker rights', *Journal of Sociology* 56(1): pp. 100–114. https://doi.org/10.1177/1440783319882

Briskman, L. and Doe, J. (2016) 'Social work in dark places', *Social Alternatives* 35(4): pp. 73–79. www.ezproxy.uws.edu.au/login?url=http://search.informit.com.au/documentSummary;dn=872338259155085;res=IELLCC

Briskman, L. and Zion, D. (2014) 'Dual loyalties and impossible dilemmas: health care in immigration detention', *Public Health Ethics* 7(3): pp. 277–286. http://dx.doi.org/10.1093/phe/phu024

Canning, V. (2017a) 'Border (mis)management, ignorance and denial', in Barton, A. and Davis, H. (eds), *Agnotology, power and harm: the study of ignorance and the criminological imagination*. Basingstoke: Palgrave Macmillan, pp. 139–162.

Canning, V. (2017b) *Gendered harm and structural violence in the British asylum system*. Oxon: Routledge.

Coddington, K. (2017) 'Intimate Economies of Erasure and Ambiguity: Darwin as Australia's 2011–2012 "Capital of Detention"', in Hiemstra, N. and Conlon, D. (eds), *Intimate economies of immigration detention: critical perspectives*. London: Routledge, pp. 140–154.

Davidson, H. (2023) 'Australian Corruption and the Pacific: Dollars, Displacement and Deaths', in Boochani, B. (ed), *Freedom, only Freedom: the Prison writings of Behrouz Boochani*, translated and edited by Tofighian, O. and Mansoubi, M. London: Bloomsbury Academic, pp. 188–191.

Dehm, S. (2020) 'Outsourcing, Responsibility and Refugee Claim-Making in Australia's Offshore Detention Regime', in McGuirk, S. and Pine, A. (eds), *Profit and protest in the asylum Industry*. Oakland: PM Press, pp. 47–66.

Doherty, B. (2017) 'Manus Island Asylum Seeker's Friends Begged Australia for Help Before his Death', *The Guardian*. www.theguardian.com/australia-news/2017/aug/07/manus-island-asylum-seekers-friends-begged-australia-for-help-before-his-death

Edwards, A. (2021) 'Education and Elitism Under the Microscope in New Bri Lee Book', *The Sydney Morning Herald*. www.smh.com.au/culture/books/education-and-elitism-under-the-microscope-in-new-bri-lee-book-20210617-p581ul.html

El-Enany, N. (2015) 'On pragmatism and legal idolatry: fortress Europe and the desertion of the refugee', *International Journal of Minority and Group Rights* 22(1): pp. 7–38. http://dx.doi.org/10.1163/15718115-02201001

Esposito, F., Ornelas, J., Briozzo, E. and Arcidiacono, C. (2019) 'Ecology of sites of confinement: everyday life in a detention center for illegalized non-citizens', *American Journal of Community Psychology* 63: pp. 190–207. https://doi.org/10.1002/ajcp.12313

Esposito, F., Ornelas, J., Scirocchi, S. and Arcidiacono, C. (Winter 2019). 'Voices from the inside: lived experiences of women confined in a detention center', *Signs: Journal of Women in Culture and Society* 44(2): pp. 403–431. https://doi.org/10.1086/699344

Fleay, C. (2017) 'Bearing Witness and the Intimate Economies of Immigration Detention Centres in Australia', in Conlon, D. and Hiemstra, N. (eds), *Intimate economies of immigration detention: critical perspectives*. Croydon: Routledge, pp. 70–86.

Giannacopoulos, M. (2006) 'Terror Australis: white sovereignty and the violence of law', *Borderlands e-Journal* 5(1). www.link.gale.com/apps/doc/A169458000/AONE?u=anon~2e571aa3&sid=googleScholar&xid=b8d67987

Giannacopoulos, M. (2013) 'Offshore hospitality: law, asylum and colonisation', *Law Text Culture* 17: pp, 163–183. www.ro.uow.edu.au/cgi/viewcontent.cgi?article=1311&context=ltc

Grossman, E. (2010) *Why translation matters*. New Haven: Yale University Press.

Hartley, L. and Fleay, C. (2017) '"We are like animals": negotiating dehumanising experiences of asylum-seeker policies in the Australian community', *Refugee Survey Quarterly* 36(4): pp. 45–63. https://doi.org/10.1093/rsq/hdx010

Kamali Sarvestani, A. (director) (2020) *Tall Fences, Taller Trees* [film]. Sarvin Productions. www.watch.eventive.org/tallfences/play/5f59090b0b6a30007c7506c9

Kaus, A. (2019) 'Liberal humanitarianism: obscuring US culpability in James Disco and Susan Clark's *Echoes of the lost boys of Sudan* and Dave Eggers's *what is the what'*, *Contemporary Literature* 60(2): pp. 198–226. www.muse.jhu.edu/article/757960

Kebsi, J. (2019) 'Bridging the Mediterranean without papers: Tunisian francophone illiterature's representation of irregular immigration in the age of globalisation', *Journal of North African Studies* 25(6): pp. 980–994. https://doi.org/10.1080/13629387.2019.1654381

Kebsi, J. (2024) 'A Decolonial Translation: Omid Tofighian's Collaborative Approach in Behrouz Boochani's No Friend But the Mountains', *Nawaat*. www.nawaat.org/2024/06/18/decolonizing-translation-omid-tofighians-collaborative-approach-in-behrouz-boochanis-no-friend-but-the-mountains/

Kebsi, J. (In press) 'The challenges of translating world prison literature: Omid Tofighian's contribution to *no Friend but the Mountains*', *Antipodes: A Global Journal of Australian/New Zealand Literature.* https://researchers.mq.edu.au/en/publications/the-challenges-of-translating-world-prison-literature-omid-tofigh

Keenan, S. (2014) *Subversive property: law and the production of spaces of belonging.* Abingdon: Routledge.

Khosravi, S. (2010) *Illegal' traveller: an auto-ethnography of borders.* Basingstoke: Palgrave Macmillan.

Khosravi, S. (2019). 'What do we see if we look at the border from the other side?' *Social Anthropology* 27: pp. 409–424. https://doi.org/10.1111/1469-8676.12685

Kiem, M. (2014) 'Should artists boycott the Sydney Biennale over Transfield Links?' *The Conversation.* www.theconversation.com/should-artists-boycott-the-sydney-biennale-over-transfield-links-23067

Kukathas, C. (2021) *Immigration and Freedom.* Princeton and Oxford: Princeton University Press.

Lee, B. (2021) *Who gets to be smart: privilege, power and knowledge.* Sydney: Allen & Unwin.

McNevin, A. (2023) 'Epistemic Violence and the Man Who Loves Ducks', in Boochani, B. (ed), *Freedom, only Freedom: the prison writings of Behrouz Boochani*, translated and edited by Tofighian, O. and Mansoubi, M. London: Bloomsbury Academic, pp. 82–86.

Miekus, T. (2021) 'A Common World', *Sydney Review of Books.* https://sydneyreviewofbooks.com/review/lee-who-gets-to-be-smart/

Miler, T. (2021) *Build bridges, not walls.* San Franscisco: City Lights Books.

Miller, T. (2019) *Empire of borders: how the US is expanding its border around the world.* London: Verso.

Moreton-Robinson, A. (2015) *The white possessive: property, power, and indigenous sovereignty.* Minneapolis: University of Minnesota Press.

Nethery, A. (2021) 'Incarceration, classification and control: administrative detention in settler colonial Australia', *Political Geography* 89: pp. 1–10. https://doi.org/10.1016/j.polgeo.2021.102457

Paik, A. N. (2016) *Rightlessness: testimony and redress in U.S. prison camps since World War II.* Chapel Hill: The University of North Carolina Press.

Perera, S. and Pugliese, J. (2018a) 'Repetitions of Violence: On David Dungay's and Fazel Chegeni Nejad's Inquest', *Overland.* www.overland.org.au/2018/08/repetitions-of-violence-the-inquests-for-david-dungay-and-fazel-chegeni-nejad/

Perera, S. and Pugliese, J. (2018b) 'Sexual violence and the border: colonial genealogies of US and Australian immigration detention regimes', *Social and Legal Studies* 30(1): pp. 66–79. https://doi.org/10.1177/0964663918767954

Pugliese, J. (2015) '"Geopolitics of aboriginal sovereignty: colonial law as 'a species of excess of its own authority", Aboriginal passport ceremonies and asylum seekers', *Law Text Culture* 19: pp. 84–115. www.ro.uow.edu.au/cgi/viewcontent.cgi?article=1333&context=ltc

Quijano, A. and Ennis. M. (2000) 'Coloniality of power, Eurocentrism and Latin America', *Nepantla* 1(3): pp. 533–580. www.muse.jhu.edu/article/23906

Rooney, M. N. (2017) 'The Violence Engendered on Manus Island Cannot be Ignored', *Devpolicy Blog*, Development Policy Centre, Crawford School of Public Policy, College of Asia and the Pacific, Australian National University. www.devpolicy.org/the-violence-engendered-on-manus-island-cannot-be-ignored-20170331/

Rooney, M. N. (2018) 'Friday Essay: The Chauka Bird and Morality on Our Manus Island Home', *The Conversation*. www.theconversation.com/friday-essay-the-chauka-bird-and-morality-on-our-manus-island-home-90107

Rooney, M. N. (2021) '*As Basket* and *Papu*: making Manus social fabric', *Oceania* 91(1): pp. 86–105. https://doi.org/10.1002/ocea.5289

Sanggaran, J. and Zion, D. (2015) 'What Australia Hides in the Dark: Torture and the Need for Transparency', *ABC Religion and Ethics*. www.abc.net.au/religion/what-australia-hides-in-the-dark-torture-and-the-need-for-transp/10097732

Sanggaran, J. and Zion, D. (2016) 'Is Australia engaged in torturing asylum seekers? A cautionary tale for Europe', *Journal of Medical Ethics* 42: pp. 420–423. https://doi.org/10.1136/medethics-2015-103326

Schüssler Fiorenza, E. (2020) 'Biblical Interpretation and Kyriarchal Globalization', in Scholz, S. (ed), *The Oxford Handbook of Feminist Approaches to the Hebrew Bible*. Oxford: Oxford University Press, pp. 2–20. https://doi.org/10.1093/oxfordhb/9780190462673.013.1

Sirriyeh, A. (2018) *The politics of compassion: immigration and asylum policy*. Bristol: Bristol University Press.

Tazreiter, C. and Tofighian, O. with Boochani, B. (2022) 'Spectres of Subjugation/Inter-Subjugation/Resubjugation of People Seeking Asylum: the kyriarchal system in Australia's necropoleis', in Billings, P. (ed), *Regulating refugee protection through social welfare: law, policy and praxis*. London: Routledge, pp. 68–90.

Tofighian, O. (2018a) 'Black bodies for political profit: Sudanese and Somali Standpoints on Australia's racialised border regime', *Transition* 126: pp. 5–18. www.muse.jhu.edu/article/702736

Tofighian, O. (2018b) 'Translator's Tale: A Window to the Mountains', in Boochani, B. (ed), *No Friend but the Mountains: Writing from Manus Prison*, translated by O. Tofighian. Sydney: Picador-Pan Macmillan, pp. xiii–xxxvi.

Tofighian, O. (2018c) 'Translator's Reflections', in Boochani, B. (ed), *No Friend but the Mountains: Writing from Manus Prison*, translated by O. Tofighian. Sydney: Picador-Pan Macmillan, pp. 359–374.

Tofighian, O. (2020a) 'Introducing Manus Prison theory: knowing border violence', *Globalizations* 17(7): pp. 1138–1156. https://doi.org/10.1080/14747731.2020.1713547

Tofighian, O. (2020b) 'Citizen Media and Philosophy', in Pérez-González, L., Blaagaard, B. and Baker, M. (eds), *Routledge Encyclopedia of citizen media*. New York: Routledge, pp. 286–292.

Tofighian, O. (2021a) 'Australian border violence, race and translating no Friend but the Mountains: Al Ahram interviews Omid Tofighian in Cairo', *Southerly – Writing Through Fences: Archipelago of Letters*, 79(2): pp. 221–228. www.southerlylitmag.com.au/shop/writing-through-fences-archipelago-of-letters/

Tofighian, O. (2021b) 'Horrific Surrealism: New Storytelling for Australia's Carceral Border Archipelago', in Gilbert, H., Pigram, D. and Swain, R. (eds), *Marrugeku: telling that story— 25 years of trans-indigenous and intercultural performance*. Wales: Performance Research Books, pp. 306–319.

Tofighian, O., Swain, R., Pigram, D., Ra, B., Connell, C., Brown. E. J., Shaheen, F., Assaad, I. E., Currie-Richardson, L., Wheen, M., Bero, C. and Lopez, Z. (2022) 'Performance as intersectional resistance: power, polyphony and processes of abolition', *Humanities* 11(1): p. 28. https://doi.org/10.3390/h11010028

Tofighian, O. (2023) 'Manus Island and Manus Prison Theory', in Braidotti, R., Klumbyte, G. and Jones, E. (eds), *More posthuman glossary*. London: Bloomsbury Academic, pp. 77–80.

Verma, S. (2019) '"We Feed You'. The Real Cost of Undocumented Labour in Australia", *Overland*. woverland.org.au/2019/03/we-feed-you-the-real-cost-of-undocumented-labour-in-australia/

Verma, S. and Mitropoulos, A. (2015) 'Roundtable: Nauru, border force and the transformation of the detention complex', *xBorder*. www.xborderoperationalmatters.wordpress.com/2015/10/14/nauru-borderforce-detention/

Vogl, A. (2015) 'Over the borderline: a critical inquiry into the geography of territorial excision and the securitisation of the Australian border', *UNSW Law Journal* 38(1): pp. 114–145. www.classic.austlii.edu.au/au/journals/UTSLRS/2015/39.html

Vogl, A. (2017) "Sovereign relations? Australia's 'off-shoring' of asylum seekers on Nauru in historical perspective", in Epstein, C. (ed), *Against international norms: Postcolonial perspectives*. Abingdon: Routledge, pp. 158–174.

Weber, L. and McCulloch, J. (2018) 'Penal power and border control: which thesis? Sovereignty, governmentality, or the pre-emptive state?' *Punishment & Society*, 21(4): pp. 496–514.

xBorder Operational Matters (2016) 'Roundtable on #LETTHEMSTAY and #KIDSOUT', *xBorder*. https://xborderoperationalmatters.wordpress.com/2016/02/28/roundtable-on-letthemstay-and-kidsout/

Zion, D. (2018) 'Yes, The US Border Policy is Harsh– But Australia's Treatment of Refugee Children Has Also Been Deplorable', *The Conversation*. www.theconversation.com/yes-the-us-border-policy-is-harsh-but-australias-treatment-of-refugee-children-has-also-been-deplorable-98706

Zion, D. (2019a) 'On beginning with justice: bioethics, advocacy and the rights of asylum seekers', *Bioethics* 33: pp. 890–895. DOI: 10.1111/bioe.12660

Zion, D. (2019b) 'Dual Loyalty, Medical Ethics, and Health Care in Offshore Asylum-Seeker Detention', in Allotey, P. and Reidpath, D. (eds), *The health of refugees: Public health perspectives from crisis to settlement*. Oxford: Oxford University Press, pp. 260–272.

CONCLUSION

More translator's reflections

While writing this book I was involved in conversations with Satah about his leadership role in Manus Prison. As part of his role he was also the primary representative of the Iranian and Kurdish communities there. Over the years he has shared with me important information about his interpreting and translation work within the broader activism he was engaged in. So much of his oral histories and archive of documents, images, videos, and audio recordings (including from meetings and personal dialogues, some of which involve government and company representatives within the border-industrial complex) provide significant narrative threads that function as necessary additions to the work that many refugees, activists, friends, supporters, researchers and other collaborators, have been involved in. In particular, my own translation *plans*, *processes* and *products* have acquired new dimensions as a result of collaborations with people such as Satah (Manus and other carceral sites in PNG), Zivardar (Nauru; for a study of archives by people imprisoned in Nauru see Whitlock, 2024), and others. As I reflect on the many collaborations it is oral histories and archives such as these that add new dimensions to the creative resistance; they offer us multidimensional interpretations and contribute significantly to different examples of public philosophy.

Our theoretical and political works are experiencing radical forms of development and nuance as a result of oral histories and refugee archives. The shared philosophical activity is both expanding and rendering many more unique contributions. The potential for philosophical discovery and dynamic forms of public philosophy are unlimited.

In the weeks leading up to finishing the first draft of this manuscript I received a series of text messages from Satah explaining his recent

DOI: 10.4324/9781003455493-7

experience of visiting the International Criminal Court in The Hague. As a representative of a large group of survivors from Manus Prison and Nauru Prison he was there to follow up on his submission which he prepared with his lawyer and other members of the legal team involved. He contacted me because he wanted to collaborate on writing a statement about his encounter with the ICC authorities. After reviewing his series of text messages and voice messages in Persian/Farsi, and engaging in lengthy conversations about the situation in Persian, I translated/wrote the following statement for him to post on Facebook (another mix of translation, translated transcription, rewriting, co-writing – another example of born-translated literature):

Official Statement: Manus and Nauru survivors make formal submission to ICC.
Representative: Benham Satah

For the people who suffered years of torture in Australia's offshore immigration prisons in Manus Island-PNG and Nauru the struggle for justice is long and hard. Most of us are now trying to rebuild our lives in different countries, but we carry the scars from years of imprisonment, torment and humiliation. We will never forget what the Australian government put us through and we continue to support each other in any way we can. Also, we will always remember the people who lost their lives and honour their memory by continuing to expose and dismantle Australia's cruel and corrupt border-industrial complex. On Monday 6 of May, 2024 I visited the International Criminal Court in The Hague. I have been collaborating with many people who were illegally incarcerated in offshore prisons, and I worked with experienced lawyers to make a submission well in advance. I had the privilege of representing a large group of us at the ICC, our aim is to have our voices heard in the court and achieve justice for everyone who was targeted by Australia's border regime. We believe this is an important step in our plight. We aim to present to the court important evidence about what we endured over many years and convey crucial information pertaining to the ways people were killed or driven to suicide. Unfortunately, staff at the ICC were not open to engaging us on Monday and denied my request to address various representatives. I was also refused entry into the area within the ICC which is open to the public. The reasons they gave are unacceptable considering that we approached them six months ago with our submission by using their standard process. It is unfair, but these experiences are not uncommon for us. We will continue to pursue the matter – we will eventually address the court and arrive one step closer to making real systemic change. Our situation is complex and difficult but we always knew that it would take time before we can hold Australian authorities accountable. I am discussing next steps with our group and our legal team so we can make the appropriate plans going forward. No human being should be treated the way we were and we are doing our best to make sure it does not continue. We are confident that we will be heard and make progress next time.

Special thanks to the collaborators in this process: the group of survivors from Manus and Nauru; our legal team, including our lawyer Jay; and the individuals who supported me during this visit Yolie, Neil and Omid Tofighian.

(Facebook, posted 9 May, 2024)

The post on social media attracted multilingual responses from his partners and supporters in the form of online comments. He also received private messages of support in multiple languages in the form of texts and voice texts from people who were/are subject to Australian border violence. This collaboration represents one of the most recent examples of creative resistance I have explored throughout this book; a combination of *collaboration, activism, translation* and *storytelling*; a project that reflects *fragmentation, disruption, disjointedness* and *shattered* experiences and phenomena in productive and empowering ways.

My recent collaboration with Satah corresponds with elements from other stories he shared with me from his time incarcerated in Manus Prison involving interpreting and translation. The narratives pertaining to his experiences exemplify the power and potential of translation practice and theory. For instance, a negligence case related to an infant whose family was incarcerated in Nauru was settled in 2023 (see Rachwani, 2023); Satah met the mother involved by chance during the time she was transferred to PNG with her child and assisted her as an interpreter and translator when she was left powerless and vulnerable because authorities had not arranged for anyone to help with communication and administration in Persian. Satah used his skills, experience and connections in crucial ways to support them from the time he met the family until the settlement of their case (also assisting their resettlement process).

Many of Satah's stories depict how chains of multilingual interpreting and translation followed important meetings between head representatives of different communities in the detention centre when they met to organise. In instances when all the diverse groups were involved the discussions between representatives and the relevant documents were in English, after which the representatives interpreted/translated to members of their communities in their own languages (for members who spoke/read different levels of English or no English). In other instances, Satah had to interpret/translate crucial news reports and other important announcements for members of his community, in some cases after information had already been misunderstood by people who had limited understanding of English. These interpretations/translations were then shared through the multilingual chains in the prison for further translation/interpretation. The information discussed during meetings in languages other than English was often communicated through this multilingual chain by people who could speak many languages; for instance, Persian and Arabic, Kurdish and Persian, or Persian and Urdu. In some cases, the correct interpretations or corrections of misinterpreted information had enormous consequences throughout the prison and on people's wellbeing and futures. In one agonising and distressing story pertaining to mistranslation confusion, heartbreak and despair was caused when Satah had to explain to a large group of refugees the exact meaning of the word 'urged' in the context of an article written by his late friend and journalist Michael Gordon (2015) – a correction that then had to run through the multilingual chain of translation/ interpretation in Manus Prison.

The ideologies and practices of exclusion and division employed and perpetuated by nation-states on citizens are reflected in the violence of their border regimes. Exclusion and division based on language and lack of support for interpretating and translation become weapons against refugees on the border and instruments of systematic torture. But interpreting and translation become tools for fighting back, surviving, achieving freedom, and healing when refugees and their collaborators use them to engage in collective and creative resistance. Interpreting and translation helps all of us combine our struggles to resist the kyriarchal system. The racialisation, surveillance and militarisation that oppresses and limits the freedoms and safety of citizens transfer to the realities on the border. By extension, the ideologies enhanced and directed at the people subject to border control condition the epistemic resources and possibilities for imagining, thinking, creating and acting within Australian society and culture (see the two-island thought experiment in the appendix to Chapter 2). Essentially, border regimes help determine the function and development of the state. In this sense, the border-industrial complex is integral to political culture, social dynamics, and the potential for citizens to flourish on different levels. The ideologies and imaginaries in question here are global and inseparable from ideologies driving racism and capitalism. Meaningful discussion about the border-industrial complex involves addressing these ideologies and imaginaries in connection with the role of communication technology, media, political participation, and access to material and epistemic resources. A critical approach must engage with questions about complicity and censorship, the creation and distribution of media images and narratives, the role of journalism, and the often-ignored issues of interpreting and translation (or lack of support for them).

The original Persian text messages that became *No Friend but the Mountains* provide an uncompromising critique and a scathing exposé of Australian border violence. As I have described throughout this book, the original text messages were translated and edited into English with a commitment to challenging, exposing and transforming the situation. The Iranian publisher was very keen to publish the book in Persian since there had been so much interest in it after it won numerous prestigious awards and Boochni's plight received international attention. In unconventional fashion the English translation here does not constitute the afterlife of a Persian book; the development was inverted when the Persian edition (an edited version of the original Persian text messages) somehow became the afterlife of the target text (English). The conversations that emerged from the publication of the Persian edition are an example of the afterlife of a translation (rather than the afterlife of the source text), and an important topic for further specialised research.

In an interview with BBC Persian Boochani was asked about publishing his book in Persian in Iran and he clarified the situation (BBC Persian, 2020). There also exists a Persian language audiobook read by the famous Iranian actor Navid Mohammadzadeh (who like Boochani is also a Kurd from Ilam province).

By defining the book's development into distinct phases over time one may interpret four different examples of *No Friend but the Mountains*.

1) There are the original text messages in Persian (written by Boochani and converted into PDF chapters by Mansoubi) completed at the end of 2017 after almost five years.
2) The edited English translation by myself which involved collaboration and experimentation and was published in 2018.
3) The Persian volume published in Iran in 2020 based on Boochani's edited text messages.
4) And the ephemeral Persian volume which is based on the original text messages but became something else during our collaboration (over WhatsApp and during my visit to Manus Island) and my edited translation process. The changes and additions were discussed in Persian over a long period of time but only appear in the English edited translation (in the form of born-translated literature) and were never applied in writing to the rough text messages written in Persian.

These four versions are markedly different, so much so that they could be understood as four different interpretations.

In a fascinating dialogue Khalili and Stavans discuss the ambiguous and shifting dynamics involving censorship and incorporating other texts, stories and experiences in the context of translation plans, processes and products.

IS: The bureaucratic ordeal, not only of the Farrokhzad volume but the set you translated, makes me think of the administrative procedures Cervantes had to go through to get the two volumes of the manuscript of *Don Quixote of La Mancha* through the Holy Inquisition censors. Some of the sections in the novel are quite daring. Did the censors

	truly read them? If so, they must have been amused by Volume One, Chapter VI, in which the barber, the priest, and Alonso Quijano's niece go through Quijano's personal library while Don Quixote is ill. It's a hilarious scene that results in many volumes ending up in a bonfire. What was accepted and what rejected by the actual censors, not by Cervantes' characters, is less humorous but just as capricious. By the way, I am of the view—and I have stated it in *Knowledge and Censorship* (2008)—that censorship is useful in literature. Likewise, I believe in its cleansing power in terms of translation.
SK:	What do you mean by cleansing?
IS:	Purifying. We cannot live without censorship. Dictatorships regulate the flow of information. But so does an open-market economy, though under a different pretense. A self-translation, which is the most ubiquitous, defines everything we do, even this exchange.
SK:	Translators consciously sift, rewrite, reword, compromise, and to some extent filter while rendering a book into another language. We all do the same in our daily lives, but we do it far less consciously and less deliberately.
	Translation, by its very nature, shares these functions with censorship. Where the two differ is in their intentions. The translator strives to convey, whereas the censor aims to purge.
IS:	Going back to *Don Quixote*, the reader is told numerous times that the original narrative about the deranged knight was written by an Arab historian, Cide Hamete Benengueli, and that what we are reading is a poor, impromptu translation delivered by "*un morisco aljamiado*," which, loosely translated, is a Spanish-born Arab speaker with a lousy knowledge of his ancestral tongue.
SK:	"*Traduttore, traditore!*"

(Khalili and Stavans, Spring 2019)

Our imagination of the border and citizenship is conditioned by systems and practices of censorship, in addition to exclusion, division and abandonment. Through translation and collaboration, my approach has been to contribute new concepts and theoretical approaches and develop creative ways to speak back and expose intersectional discrimination as it pertains to the carceral-border and bordering practices – and the entities and dynamics they are connected to within the state. My aim is to create possibilities for distinct ways of knowing by collaborating with people who offer unique and critical positions, experiences and insights.

A critical analysis of the border-industrial complex in any context must also factor in the role of universities, the knowledge produced in tertiary institutions about borders and bordering, and question to what extent they are contributing to futures without border violence. In addition, the border-industrial complex is an environmental concern and the political economy sustaining detention centres is inseparable from degradation of ecosystems.

The positionality of refugees held in indefinite detention is unique and inherently critical because they constantly have to navigate and survive a perverse system of physical, psychological, emotional and bureaucratic control. This space of interlocking oppressive structures has rendered them as simultaneously 1) banished through the creation of racially targeted laws that disempower them and restrict opportunities for crossing borders; 2) people held at the border and denied access to the law; 3) and direct victims of laws that allow for the use of bad faith as an instrument of torture – laws that shift frequently to expel, exclude and exile. In the Australian context, the state commits acts of border violence by breaking laws, denying rights, creating laws, changing laws and, at the same time, justifying violence using the law. And since refugees are non-citizens and have been exiled to an extraterritorial location (or extralegal enclaves on the mainland) their access to law is skewed, they have limited or no access to a judicial system that will hear them and process their claims appropriately. It has been proven that even international law is difficult to enforce in these circumstances.

What has occurred is brutal and absurd in so many respects. People seek asylum under the international convention and are selected randomly and exiled by force to remote island prisons because of their mode of transport (by boat rather than by plane). With no reliable judiciary or processing, they are kept there indefinitely for years. During their imprisonment refugees are constantly pressured to accept settlement in the nation where they have been banished to and imprisoned. Very few people have accepted to live in PNG or Nauru, and the situation of the people who have agreed to settle involves commitments to the new families established there. When New Zealand offered to resettle a number of people from offshore detention Australia refused for an excruciatingly long period of time. And in instances when someone is killed by the system Australia denies responsibility.

Australia's border regime has global ramifications, it is a model for a new global form of violence since there are so many elements which are being exported (and imported; also co-devised and co-developed by many transnational stakeholders). As I have tried to illustrate in this book, the magnitude of the violence is highlighted and addressed in profound ways through individual stories that help expose the structure and history of border regimes and connect one person's experiences to collective oppression – in the Australian prison camps and in similar situations all over the world.

Cherron A. Barnwell's analysis of Angela Davis' book resonates with this reading regarding the connection between the individual and the collective in the context of prison writing: 'The dramatization of Davis' fight to get out of isolation and back into the main population functions here as resistance to those autobiographical textures that undermine her intentions. For Davis, to be seen as part of the main population means that she belongs to a community of humans in the struggle against penal injustice – not that she has succumbed to the deindividuating routines of prison life. Hence, resistance seethes through the textures and contexts of *An Autobiography*.' (Barnwell, March 2005, p. 326) This interplay between the individual and collective is crucial for understanding the creative resistance against Australian border violence, and it can be expanded to factor in the collaborative dimensions involving supporters and collaborators such as interpreters and translators. The dynamic between the individual and the collective provides a rich lens through which to interpret and act in response to writing, art, activities on social media and other interventions in the public sphere by displaced, exiled and incarcerated peoples. Barnwell's insights into the prison writing of Davis help us understand the interdependent nature of the political, narratological and philosophical layers in this kind of work; she continues:

> Deindividuation is seized upon as a signifier and thus reconfigured to fit the con/textual demands of her autobiographical intentions. It is the pivotal point of textual resistance. Let me explain.
>
> Recalling her earlier prison writings, Davis reasserts in the Introduction to the second printing of her autobiography that members in the community of struggle understand their struggle to be a collective one; they see themselves as a collective power.10 The original idea behind her term "political autobiography" is, again, to make her autobiography a public document from which she speaks for, by, and of the people opposed to racism and political oppression. The story of Davis' prison experience can be made to fit her demands when its generic element to resist deindividuating routines through individuating discourses is turned on its axis and made to redefine deindividuating routines as collective resistance. Hence, it is textual resistance at work. (p. 326)

In relation to the projects I have been involved with, the translation products are part of a complex, polyvocal and fluid matrix of collaboration, activism, translation and storytelling. Rather than emphasise the individual or the collective aspects of these translation products, it is politically and philosophically more potent and practical to highlight and interpret different elements wholistically and as part of a unity dedicated to liberatory aims and empowerment. As a hermeneutical schema horrific surrealism attempts to bring together the individual and collective in this way by connecting factors and features characterised by fragmentation, disruption, disjointedness and shattered experiences and visions. The lives and identities of each individual and the collectives involved, the socio-political conditions, the mode of production, and the structure and content of the products, all engage in a form of reciprocal reinforcement – a kind of 'mutual scaffolding' (Tofighian, 2016). Barnwell's analysis of Davis' political autobiography carefully and skilfully builds on her reading of the connections between the individual and collective (below she employs a 'double-helix' trope). I see how her approach can be expanded for application in different texts and contexts to reflect and incorporate even more elements. I have tried to argue in this book that a wide range of diverse features and factors can be read as interwoven to make a whole (a 'multicoil-helix'). The aim here is to present a fuller notion of creative resistance in the context of border violence; one which centres collaboration, activism and storytelling practices (I add translation to these elements within the situations I describe. Also, see my study of citizen media and philosophy where I discuss Davis, the Haitian Revolution, and resistance by displaced and exiled peoples such as Boochani [2020]):

> So when Davis recounts how her hunger strike grew into a mass hunger strike among other women prisoners who sympathized with hers (42, 44), her hunger strike takes the form of a double-helix, if you will, in her dramatization of collective resistance. One end of the coil represents her individual fight to get out of isolation, a fight waged against the penal system on behalf of all political prisoners. The other end of the coil represents a shared/communal fight by many women prisoners against the dehumanization of jail life. These coils intertwine and circle each other, much like the textuality and intentionality of Davis' autobiographical enterprise.
>
> To further meet her autobiographical intentions and thus "fight the tendency to individualize [her] predicament" (28), Davis presents her prison experience as a shared one by telling other prisoners' stories. Telling others' stories about isolation, Davis avoids claiming an isolate, dehumanized, deindividuated self and resists the individuating impulse of autobiography. (Barnwell 2005, pp. 326–327)

The largest groups held in offshore and onshore immigration detention are people from Afghanistan, Sri Lanka, Iran, Iraq, the Kurdish regions, Pakistan, Myanmar, Sudan, and Somalia – many of these places have been directly affected by Australia's foreign policies with Afghanistan, Iraq, Iran and Sri Lanka the most obvious examples. Over the past twenty years Australia has had an integral role in the wars in Afghanistan and Iraq which has caused large numbers to leave those countries. The wars in these countries have significantly impacted their neighbours with many people having crossed the border from Afghanistan into Pakistan or Iran first before seeking asylum in Australia. Also, countries such as Australia implement strict international sanctions on Iran; Australia is part of the international sanctions regime, and has its own autonomous sanctions on the country that mostly impact civil society and has proven to empower the government. Rather than strategies and tactics that directly sanction dictators and oppressors and their beneficiaries and enablers, the untargeted and blanket use of sanctions – in contrast to their policy aims – help support the Iranian state in their persecution of the population with marginalized groups facing the most severe outcomes. A layered approach which factors in these geopolitical dynamics discloses the transnational and transhistorical dimensions of Australia's border regime.

In recent years, places such as the UK (regarding the Rwanda policy, formally known as the Migration and Economic Development Partnership; see Walsh, 2024) and certain European countries are looking at Australia as a model for border control. For them, Australia's externalisation of borders represents success. Also, in a 2017 leaked phone conversation with former prime minister Malcolm Turnbull, former US president Donald Trump replied to the Australian's explanation regarding the offshore indefinite detention of refugees by saying: 'That is a good idea. We should do that too. You are worse than I am.' (Guardian, 2017) It is significant that the first article I translated for Boochani was his encounter with Turnbull on the ABC program *Q&A* (Boochani, 2016). His own party replaced him as prime minister with former immigration minister Scott Morrison in 2018.

In the EU, Denmark was planning to use Lindholm Island to imprison people seeking asylum. The government does not portray or describe the island as a prison; but like Manus Prison and Nauru Prison, it is actually so much more than a prison: '… a tiny, hard-to-reach island that now holds the laboratories, stables and crematory of a center for researching contagious animal diseases.' (Selsøe Sørensen, 2018; Lopez-Hodoyan, 2018; Barker and Smith, 2021) One of the ferries people use to travel to the island is named 'Virus'. The impact on the social imaginary is clear. This example highlights the reason why changing the material conditions is only one dimension amongst many necessary for resistance against border violence. The policies and practices of Denmark here correspond with a particular narrative and ideology which is bolstered by, for instance, the history and activities of the island and the name of the ferry, in addition to a concerted effort in the mainstream media to invigorate and project racist and xenophobic government policies and socio-cultural attitudes. Therefore, opposing targeted and racist strategies to harm people seeking asylum must include challenging the epistemic factors, the symbolic aesthetic, and dimensions of the social imaginary.

The border-industrial complex – which includes the externalisation of borders, detention, deterrence and deportation – is a global and transhistorical phenomenon with Australia's recent border regime representing just one strategy (consider the influence on Australia by the US strategy in the 90s for indefinitely detaining Haitians [and later Cubans] in Guantanamo Bay and forcibly deporting large numbers [Paik, 2018 and 2016, Part II; Bochenek,

2016). Externalisation and deterrence are also practiced in perverse ways by the EU in places such as Libya and Sudan. Over the past two decades Australia's offshore prisons have held significant numbers of people fleeing from African countries. At the time of writing some are still suffering from Australia's policies and are confined in Port Moresby (PNG) and Nauru. Several refugees from African countries are among those who were transferred to Australia for medical treatment and were locked up in motels before being released and are now living on temporary visas with no clear pathway to a safe and free future (and still no adequate treatment).

Similar to Australia's complicity in the politics and economy of the counties from which people flee, the EU funded the Sudanese government for building and managing camps to hold people fleeing from different parts of sub-Saharan Africa and other places including Syria (something that has also occurred in Libya since Gaddafi was in power; Noll and Giuffré, 2011). There is clear evidence that EU funding, technology and training was redirected by the Sudanese government for domestic political control and suppression. Essentially, EU money and other forms of support helped fund the persecution of the pro-democracy movement and general civil society in Sudan. A recent study details how the variety of EU funded technologies employed in migrant camps are in turn used against Sudanese protestors during uprisings. 'The EU's action plan will involve building the capacities of Sudan's security and law enforcement agencies, including a paramilitary group known as the Rapid Support Forces (RSF), which has been branded as Sudan's primary "border force." The EU will assist the RSF and other relevant agencies with the construction of two camps with detention facilities for migrants. The EU will also equip these Sudanese border forces with cameras, scanners, and electronic servers for registering refugees.

There are legitimate concerns with these plans. Much of the EU-funded training and equipment is *dual-use*. The equipment that enables identification and registration of migrants will also reinforce the surveillance capabilities of a Sudanese government that has violently suppressed Sudanese citizens for the past 28 years.' (Baldo, 2017, p. 1; emphasis added; also see Gatekeepers of the European Union, 2022)

As these examples prove, there exists a disturbing interconnection between humanitarianism, surveillance, border control, and militarism. Dictatorships and their forms of state oppression are enabled by Western support networks; they work together to force people to flee, they create conditions where people find it impossible to live. When they leave and ask for protection and freedom in Western countries they feel the full weight of border violence.

The companies contracted by Australia's detention industry operate globally and function within Australian society and economy in significant ways. For instance, Wilson Security and Serco who have held security contracts in offshore and onshore detention for years also provide services to Australian institutions, including Australian universities. Many examples such as Wilson and Serco reflect the distressing and exploitative interconnections that exist between capital, government policies, and oppressive technologies. In recent years, the Coalition government considered privatizing visa processing when it was in power; in 2023 an inquiry was launched investigating procurement controversies which involved "tainted contracts" (Karp, 2023). There exist long and detailed paper trails that reveal many aspects of the corruption, complicity, opportunism and secrecy of the border-industrial complex which involves numerous companies, government officials, and many others. Following the money, it is not difficult to find who is benefiting from these carceral sites – they produce financial capital and political profit, in addition to ideological and neocolonial encouragement and strength.

The aim of our collective and creative resistance is to initiate collaborative projects that contribute to disrupting and redirecting the discourse pertaining to border regimes and to help expose the role of most of the major actors involved. In particular, it has always been important for us that the collective work raise critical questions about the media and academia as practices, institutions, ideologies and traditions. Holding people and organisations accountable is one dimension, but transforming the narrative and initiating a different imaginary are equally important. We plan to expand our critiques to explore other approaches appropriate for a range of different contexts; examples that need to be explored further in future include a meaningful conversation about the role of unions and professional associations who have members working in the border-industrial complex. Since people working in the detention industry are members of unions and some are part of professional associations it is reasonable to reflect on the possibilities of organising activist approaches in collaboration with the relevant bodies. What could unions and professional organisations do to support creative resistance and work with refugees in indefinite detention to help change the situation? What strategies could be employed in collaboration with unions and professional organisations to persuade people against working in the detention industry. There are no definite or simple answers to these kinds of questions and more work needs to be done, but these are conversations and actions that will eventually lead to making sustainable and systemic change. Addressing these material conditions is pivotal.

Another significant aspect of the border-industrial complex is its contribution to environmental degradation. Wherever centres are built the natural environment experiences various forms of destruction. This factor is represented in most of the collaborative projects discussed in this book. The detention industry works against nature; the situation does not only target human beings but also the animal world and the ecosystem (see Measham, Winter 2019). The new approaches we propose, the new platforms we try to create, the new possibilities we imagine, and new relationships we build, always address human and non-human relationships (also see Kabgani, 2023; Tofighian, 2023).

As mentioned, large-scale public engagements increased dramatically after the release of *No Friend but the Mountains,* especially after winning the first award: the 2019 Victorian Prize for Literature (and the 2019 Victorian Premier's Prize for Nonfiction). I received the award for Boochani while he was still imprisoned. It was a completely paradoxical experience, made even more absurd considering Boochani could not enter the country to accept the prize and could not access the prize money while still incarcerated in Manus Prison. Later in 2019 (and lasting several years) a complex network of authorities and companies were responsible for the extremely precarious situation of refugees who were evacuated from Manus Island and Nauru for medical treatment and suddenly found themselves incarcerated in Melbourne hotel detention (APODs) and detention centres during the pandemic (other cities were also included in this network). One of the detainees in this situation was Arvin who I continued to work with as translator and editor as he wrote and published throughout this dangerous time locked away in a small, window-less, suffocating room in Melbourne. From presenting an award to one writer, then amplifying the already precarious situation for another – this is horrific surrealism.

The situation was also extremely absurd for us in Sydney when *No Friend but the Mountains* won the NSW Special Award and I received the award of Highly Commended for the Translation Prize at the 2019 NSW Premier's Literary Awards. Mansoubi and I accepted the Special Award on behalf of Boochani, who was indefinitely detained at the time. The examples of horrific surrealism continue.

Over the years our group of collaborators have participated in well over 300 international and Australian events and activities. These were mainly invitations by literature festivals, universities and cultural institutions. A significant number of the public events, talks and seminars we organised ourselves through various institutions and groups. The recordings and notes from some of these experiences were later transcribed, edited and translated to become publications of various forms (for examples of my own interviews and seminars in Persian see appendix 1 in Chapter 3, and the appendix for Chapter 4); all examples of the innovation and experimentation involved collaboration, activism, translation and storytelling. These examples and the projects we are planning for the future all manifest the creativity and radical potential of fragmentation, disruption, disjointedness and shattered lives and encounters.

Bibliography

Baldo, S. (2017) *Border control from Hell: how the EU's migration partnership legitimizes Sudan's "militia state"*. The Enough Project: enoughproject.org. www.enoughproject.org/reports/border-control-hell-how-eus-migration-partnership-legitimizes-sudans-militia-state

Barker, V. and Smith, P. S. (2021) 'This is Denmark: Prison Islands and detention of immigrants', *The British Journal of Criminology* 61(6): pp. 1540–1556. https://doi.org/10.1093/bjc/azab016

Barnwell, C. A. (March 2005) 'A Prison abolitionist and her literature: Angela Davis', *CLA Journal* 48(3): pp. 308–335. www.jstor.org/stable/44325619

BBC Persian (2020) 'goftegou-ye ekhtesasi ba behrouz boochani; 'yek sher-e shaeraneh ham dar habs yek amal-e siyasi ast', *BBC News*. www.bbc.com/persian/av-embeds/arts-53067925/vpid/p08h4bmj

Bochenek, M. G. (2016) 'Guantanamo's Other Sordid Legacy', *The Hill*. www.hrw.org/news/2016/01/18/guantanamos-other-sordid-legacy

Boochani, B. (2020) 'Malcolm Turnbull, Why Didn't You Answer My Question on Q&A About Manus Island', *The Guardian*. www.theguardian.com/commentisfree/2016/jun/21/malcolm-turnbull-why-didnt-you-answer-my-question-on-qa-about-manus-island

Gatekeepers of the European Union: Sudan after El-Bashir (2022) *Borderline-europe – Menschenrechte ohne Grenzen & Bildungswerk Berlin der Heinrich Böll Stiftung*. Berlin, Germany. www.bildungswerk-boell.de/sites/default/files/2022-11/gatekeepers-of-the-european-union.pdf

Gordon, M. (2015) 'Malcolm Turnbull Urged to Fix "Weeping Sore" of Manus, Nauru Asylum Seeker Detention', *The Sydney Morning Herald*. www.smh.com.au/politics/federal/malcolm-turnbull-urged-to-fix-weeping-sore-of-manus-nauru-asylum-seeker-detention-20150925-gjv14a.html

Guardian (2017) 'Full Transcript of Trump's Phone Call with Australian Prime Minister Malcolm Turnbull', *The Guardian*. www.theguardian.com/us-news/2017/aug/04/full-transcript-of-trumps-phone-call-with-australian-prime-minister-malcolm-turnbull

Kabgani, S. (2023) 'Time and Borders, Policy and Lived Experience: A Posthuman Critique', in Boochani, B. (ed), *Freedom, Only Freedom: The Prison Writings of Behrouz Boochani*, translated and edited by Tofighian, O. and Mansoubi, M. London: Bloomsbury Academic, pp. 59–61.

Karp, P. (2023) 'Coalition Plan to Privatise Visa Processing to be Subject of New Inquiry', *The Guardian*. www.theguardian.com/australia-news/2023/nov/30/coalition-liberal-national-visa-privatisation-plan-senate-inquiry

Khalili, S. and Stavans, I. (Spring 2019) 'A Lover alone in Prison: a conversation between Ilan Stavans and Sara Khalili', *Michigan Quarterly Review* 57(6). www.sites.lsa.umich.edu/mqr/2019/04/a-lover-alone-in-prison-a-conversation-between-ilan-stavans-and-sara-khalili/

Lopez-Hodoyan, K. (2018) 'Denmark Approves Plan to Send Unwanted Migrants to "Virus" Island', *Aljazeera*. www.aljazeera.com/videos/2018/12/20/denmark-approves-plan-to-send-unwanted-migrants-to-virus-island

Measham, F. (Winter 2019) 'Love in a Time of Apocalypse', *Meanjin*. www.meanjin.com.au/essays/love-in-a-time-of-apocalypse/

Noll, G. and Giuffré, M. (2011) 'EU Migration Control: Made by Gaddafi?', *OpenDemocracy*. www.opendemocracy.net/en/eu-migration-control-made-by-gaddafi/

Paik, N. A. (2018) 'US Turned Away Thousands of Haitian Asylum-Seekers and Detained Hundreds More in the 90s', *The Conversation*. www.theconversation.com/us-turned-away-thousands-of-haitian-asylum-seekers-and-detained-hundreds-more-in-the-90s-98611

Paik, N. A. (2016) *Rightlessness: testimony and redress in U.S. prison camps since World War II*. Chapel Hill: The University of North Carolina Press.

Rachwani, M. (2023) 'Lawyers Welcome Government's Decision to Settle Negligence Case of Refugee Infant Detained on Nauru', *The Guardian*. www.theguardian.com/australia-news/2023/nov/05/lawyers-welcome-governments-decision-to-settle-negligence-case-of-infant-detained-on-nauru

Selsøe Sørensen, M. (2018) 'Denmark Plans to Isolate Unwanted Migrants on a Small Island', *The New York Times*. www.nytimes.com/2018/12/03/world/europe/denmark-migrants-island.html

Tofighian, O. (2016) *Myth and philosophy in Platonic Dialogues*. London: Palgrave Macmillan.

Tofighian, O. (2020) 'Citizen Media and Philosophy', in Pérez-González, L., Blaagaard, B. and Baker M. (eds), *Routledge Encyclopedia of Citizen Media*. New York: Routledge, pp. 286–292.

Tofighian, O. (2023) 'Manus Island and Manus Prison Theory', in Braidotti, R., Klumbyte, G. and Jones, E. (eds), *More Posthuman Glossary*. London: Bloomsbury Academic, pp. 77–80.

Walsh, P. W. (2024) 'Q&A: The UK's Policy to Send Asylum Seekers to Rwanda', *The Migration Observatory at the University of Oxford*. www.migrationobservatory.ox.ac.uk/resources/commentaries/qa-the-uks-policy-to-send-asylum-seekers-to-rwanda/

Whitlock, G (2024) *Refugee lives in the archives: a Pacific imaginary*. London: Bloomsbury Academic.

INDEX

Note: Endnotes are indicated by the page number followed by 'n' and the endnote number; e.g., 20n1 refers to endnote 1 on page 20.

abbasid 30
ABC (Australian Broadcasting Corporation) 36, 78–79, 111, 112, 183, 215
Abdalla, Saeed Qasem 178
Abdile, Hani 64, 108, 109, 113, 144
Abdul, Samad 108
abolition 17, 181
abolitionist 184
Aboriginal 110
Aboriginal and Torres Strait Islander peoples 84, 120, 142, 181, 198
Aboubakr, Randa 171
absurd 14, 18, 53, 63, 147, 158, 161, 178, 212, 218
absurdity 16, 52, 53, 92, 99, 173, 194
absurdities 44, 179
absurdly 11, 91
activism xiii, 1, 10, 15, 16, 18, 34, 35, 36, 57, 58, 68, 78, 91, 92, 96, 97, 99, 100, 102, 106, 110, 118, 121, 126n1, 140, 142, 148, 159, 172, 173, 175, 177, 182, 186, 189, 193, 199, 206, 208, 213, 214, 218
activist/s 1, 3, 4, 6, 7, 14, 15, 17, 35, 58, 59, 62, 67, 72, 74, 75, 84, 95, 97, 109, 193, 206, 217
Adam, Mohamed 64, 108, 109, 113, 144

Adamson, Peter 30
Afghanistan xiii, 60, 148–149, 214
Aghili, Hooshmand 173
Ahmed, Faysal Ishak 104, 143–145, 179
Ahmadzadeh, Hashem 155
al-Kindi 30
Alphaville: Journal of Film and Screen Media 59
America 20
American University in Cairo 64, 80, 109, 118, 121
Amnesty International award 104
Anderson, Elizabeth 85
animal/s 190, 215, 217
anti-colonial 1, 71, 197
anti-genre 58, 81–82, 106, 117, 118, 120, 155, 181, 194, 196
Anzac Day 86
Aotearoa New Zealand 45, 70
appendix/es 2–3, 8, 20, 37, 38, 39, 41, 49, 59, 78, 99, 106, 115, 117, 122, 156, 187, 188, 192, 209, 218
Arab 211
Arabic 34, 62, 64, 76, 96, 109, 122, 143, 155, 184, 185, 209
ārāmsāyesh gāh 8
Arendt, Hannah 12–13
art xiii, xiv, 9, 10, 12, 21–22n1, 34, 35, 36, 39, 58, 59, 63, 66, 73, 74, 108,

222 Index

124, 139, 160, 162, 179, 189, 191, 196, 213
art of translation 29, 31, 49
artist xi, xiii, xiv, 35, 36, 59, 66, 80
artistic 2, 4, 5, 6, 7, 15, 52, 57, 59, 61, 66, 92, 125, 126, 138, 139, 153, 176, 177, 179, 184, 185, 188
artwork xi, xiii, 34
Arvin, Mardin 21–22n1, 96, 111–112, 150–151, 156, 218
Ashraf, Noman Ahmed 64, 109
asylum 34, 36, 43, 44, 60, 96, 113, 118, 120, 121, 122, 124, 145, 146, 148, 150, 151, 173, 181, 182, 200, 212, 214
asylum seeker/s 60, 124, 146, 200
audience/s 3, 5, 6, 29, 63, 70, 74, 100, 102, 103, 111, 124, 153, 162
Australian authorities 70, 111, 174, 207
Australian Story 111
Australian Government/s 44, 93, 94, 109, 144, 151, 177, 179, 182, 207
autobiography/autobiographies 64, 69, 120, 213, 214, 140

bad faith 17, 145, 212
Baker, Mona 28, 63, 171
Ballard, Jacob (aka Izzy) 36
Barati, Reza 98, 122, 178
Barnes, Elizabeth 86
Barnwell, Cherron A. 212–214
Barseghian, Araz 30–31, 176
BBC Persian 210
Bekas, Sherko 123
Beneba Clarke, Maxine 106
Benjamin, Walter 27, 108
Bible 11, 26, 67
Biblical 67, 68
Bielsa, Esperança 7, 27, 28, 33, 63
bird/s 116, 117
blood 78, 164
Black Lives Matter 87
The Blue Eyed Boy 150, 156
boat 44, 64, 95, 111, 112, 121, 142, 150, 151, 158, 212
Boochani, Behrouz xiv, 2, 8, 9, 13, 30, 31, 32, 33, 38, 41, 44, 45, 47, 49, 50, 51, 52, 53, 59, 62, 64, 68, 69, 70, 71, 72, 75, 80, 81, 82, 83, 84, 85, 93, 94, 95, 97–98, 99, 100, 101, 102, 103, 104, 105, 106–107, 108, 109, 110, 111, 112, 113, 115, 118, 119, 120, 121, 122, 123, 124, 125, 138, 139, 141, 143, 149, 150, 151, 152, 153, 154, 156, 158, 159, 160, 161, 162, 163, 164, 165n2, 171, 173, 174, 175, 176, 177, 178, 184, 189, 192, 193, 194, 195, 196, 197, 198, 210, 214, 215, 218
border/s xii, xiii, xiv, 1, 3, 4, 6, 7, 10, 11, 12, 13, 14, 17, 18–19, 20, 21, 21–22n1, 33, 35, 36, 37, 41, 42, 44, 53, 53n1, 57, 58, 59, 60, 63, 66, 67, 68, 70, 71, 72, 73, 78, 79, 81, 83, 85, 91, 92, 93, 99, 100, 111, 113, 119, 121, 122, 123, 124, 126, 137, 139, 141, 142, 144, 146, 147, 153, 154, 157, 158, 162, 163, 171, 172, 173, 177, 178, 179, 181, 182, 183, 184, 185, 186, 190, 191, 193, 194, 195, 196, 197, 198, 199, 200, 207, 208, 209, 211, 212, 213, 214, 215, 216, 217
border-industrial complex 1, 4, 7, 10, 11, 12, 13, 14, 15, 16, 57, 58, 59, 66, 68, 70, 71, 74, 75, 147, 153, 171, 176, 179, 181, 183, 188, 190–191, 206, 207, 209, 211–212, 215, 217
Border-Industrial Complex 60
bordering xiv, 13, 17, 19, 66, 81, 87, 92, 137, 146, 179, 181, 182, 190, 211
border violence 7, 10, 11, 12, 13, 14, 17, 20, 21, 35, 36, 42, 57, 58, 59, 60, 63, 67, 68, 70, 71, 73, 78, 91, 92, 93, 111, 137, 139, 142, 146, 147, 153, 177, 178, 181, 183, 184, 185, 190, 191, 198–199, 208, 209, 211, 212, 213, 214, 215, 216
born-translated literature 33, 207, 210
Bornstein, Josh 189
British Empire 19, 145, 157–158, 181
brother 44, 143, 144, 156, 172
brotherhood 94
Du Bois, W. E. B. 20
bureaucracy 7, 19
bureaucratic 42, 157, 189, 190, 197, 210, 212
Burton, Orisanmi 17

Cairo 53, 64, 80, 97, 109, 118, 121, 156, 171
Canada 156, 157, 162, 163
carceral-border/s xiv–xv, 1, 4, 6, 8, 11, 12, 13, 14, 19, 20, 21–22n1, 42, 70, 78, 92, 145–146, 184

carceral-border archipelago 1, 6, 21–22n1, 70, 96, 108, 143, 182
celebration 86, 123, 125, 141, 172, 188
censor/ed 164n2, 210–211
Censoring an Iranian Love Story 32
censorship xiii, 209, 210–211
Cervantes 210–211
Chauka, Please Tell Us the Time (film) 59, 100, 117, 122, 152–153
Chauka–bird 116, 117
Chegani, Fazel 179
Christchurch 183
Christmas Eve 2016 143
Christmas Island 1, 6, 44, 45, 70, 96, 108, 151, 173, 178, 179
cigarettes 152, 175
citizen/s 11, 13, 14, 18, 19, 21, 61, 66, 79, 83, 86, 153, 157, 162, 178, 180, 183, 197, 209, 216
citizen media 214
citizen privilege 15, 18, 66, 73, 83, 181, 182
citizenship 41, 42, 44, 85, 109, 180, 193, 194, 199, 211
co-creation/co-create/co-created/co-creating/co-creative/co-createdness 6, 9, 27, 33, 41, 58, 71, 101, 108, 152, 153
collaboration/s xiii, xiv, 1, 2, 3, 4, 5, 6, 7, 8, 10, 13, 14, 19, 26, 30, 31, 32, 33, 36, 38, 42, 53, 59, 64, 65, 66, 70, 72, 78, 82, 86, 91, 92, 93, 94, 95, 96, 97, 99, 100, 101, 102, 106, 109, 110, 111, 113, 117, 123, 137, 138, 139, 140, 141, 147, 148, 152, 154, 175, 176, 180, 182, 187, 188, 189, 193, 197, 206, 208, 210, 211, 213, 214, 217, 218
collaborative 2, 4, 5, 6, 8, 9, 10, 12, 21, 36, 51, 57, 91, 92, 93, 97, 99, 100, 101, 114, 123, 137, 138, 139, 140, 146, 149, 151, 172, 177, 178, 179, 184, 186, 191, 194, 196, 213, 217
collaboratively 1, 67
collective/s xii, 1, 2, 4, 6, 7, 8, 11, 12, 19, 29, 33, 34, 37, 57, 83, 91, 93, 95, 97, 106, 109, 115, 124, 138, 139, 140, 141, 179, 183, 188, 189, 194, 196, 197, 198, 199, 209, 212, 213, 214, 217
colonial 11, 14, 19, 20, 26, 27, 36, 40, 60, 71, 72, 73, 78, 92, 120, 138, 141, 142, 143, 145, 146, 162, 163, 176, 178, 180, 181, 182, 183, 184, 196, 197, 198
colonialism 11, 12, 14, 36, 68, 71, 117, 120, 157, 163, 198, 199
coloniality 10, 13, 68, 142, 179, 181, 185, 188, 190
colonisation 26, 181, 196
community/communities xiv, 1, 3, 6, 9, 14, 15, 18, 19, 20, 21, 35, 59, 72, 74, 80, 83, 87, 114, 115, 120, 125, 139, 142, 145, 147, 148, 157, 158, 159, 162, 163, 171, 173, 180, 184, 190, 192, 199, 200, 206, 208, 213
Continuum: Journal of Media and Cultural Studies 106, 107
corruption 61, 176, 217
creative resistance 1, 3, 4, 5, 6, 8, 33, 57, 59, 63, 73, 91, 96, 97, 106, 110, 111, 123, 137, 138, 139, 140, 153, 175, 177, 179, 186, 188, 189, 190, 206, 208, 209, 213, 214, 217
crime 148
Critical Legal Thinking 112
Cubans 215
Cutting, Lucille 37, 49

Dana, Erfan 60, 61, 96, 148
Darfur 64
Darwin 185
Davidson, Maria Del Guadalupe 16
Davies Hayon, Kaya 122
Davis, Angela 212–214
Davis, Dick 172
death xiii, xiv, xv, 34, 78, 98, 111, 143, 144, 150, 151, 156, 172, 174, 177, 178
debordering 8, 15, 17, 21, 81, 141, 146, 149, 155, 181
decolonial 12, 68, 71, 72, 155, 181, 182, 191, 198
decoloniality 68
decolonisation 181
deficit/surplus dichotomy 18, 66
democracy 13, 157, 189, 216
Denmark 215
deportation xv, 215
deported 149, 178
deporting 215
detained 21, 62, 74, 97, 110, 112, 113, 124, 143, 144, 146, 148, 157, 218
detainees 34, 94, 190, 218
dialectic/al 2, 70

dialogue/s 2, 3, 8, 28, 31, 34, 38, 40, 42, 70, 74, 78, 82, 102, 113, 118, 140, 141, 147, 152, 157, 206, 210
dignity 13, 33
discrimination xiii, xiv, 1, 7, 10, 19, 33, 37, 44, 58, 68, 73, 75, 118, 120, 126n1, 145, 147, 172, 179, 185, 186, 188, 211
displaced xv, 1, 2, 3, 5, 6, 12, 14, 15, 17, 18, 35, 44, 66, 72, 73, 75, 78, 83, 85, 86, 87, 118, 138, 141, 193, 199, 213, 214
displacement xiii, 1, 4, 10, 15, 33, 42, 84, 85, 86, 87, 94, 117, 118, 119, 121, 139, 145, 159, 177, 180, 181, 188, 193, 195, 198, 199
disjointed/ness xiii, 14, 38, 40, 41, 92, 93, 97, 98, 99, 102, 106, 110, 160, 189, 194, 208, 213, 218
disrupted/disruption xiii, 14, 38, 40, 41, 52, 53, 73, 81, 85, 92, 93, 97, 98, 99, 102, 106, 110, 160, 176, 189, 194, 208, 213, 218
Dodson, Patrick 184
Doha Debates 112
domination 7, 10, 11, 12, 13, 15, 18, 26, 68, 84, 92, 99, 124, 139, 145, 180, 185, 194, 195, 196
Don Quixote 210–211
Dotson, Kristie 74, 85
draft/s xii, 59, 61–62, 82, 98, 110, 116, 117, 140, 141, 160, 171, 175, 206

East Lorengau 45, 94
ecosystem/s 1, 15, 59, 115, 180, 182, 212, 217
editor/s 7, 30, 31, 59, 64, 94, 100, 101, 102, 103, 105, 106, 107, 108, 164, 165, 165n2, 171, 172, 218
education 9, 51, 71, 92, 161, 199
educational 69, 147, 191
Egypt 35, 97, 156, 163
Egyptian 63
Elphick, Jeremy 59, 122
English xii, 9, 30, 31, 32, 33, 34, 38, 40, 45, 46, 47, 50, 51, 52, 61, 62, 69, 71, 72, 76, 77, 78, 96, 97, 106, 108, 110, 111, 114, 116, 117, 119, 120, 122, 123, 124, 139, 140, 141, 143, 152, 154, 155, 156, 158, 163, 164, 165, 165n1, 172, 175, 177, 184, 185, 191, 192, 208, 209, 210
environment/s xiv, 15, 17, 40, 44, 66, 69, 92, 99, 106, 115, 142, 146, 147, 180, 190, 194, 199, 217
environmental 212, 217

epic 82, 120, 172
epistemic 2, 4, 13, 15, 17, 20, 21, 42, 65, 67, 72, 73, 81, 86, 87, 91, 93, 99, 103, 106, 110, 139, 140, 141, 145, 194, 198, 209, 215
epistemic injustice 7, 8, 9, 59, 74, 78, 79, 86, 100, 144
epistemology/epistemologies 9, 12, 16, 20, 74, 85, 119, 122, 191, 200
epistemological 29, 67, 74, 196
epitext/s 98, 100, 101, 106, 150
Europe xiii, 30, 35, 159, 199
European 27, 40, 71, 120, 215
European Renaissance 30
exile/exiles/exiled xiii, 1, 2, 3, 4, 5, 6, 10, 12, 14, 15, 17, 18, 19, 33, 35, 42, 43, 44, 49, 53, 66, 70, 72, 73, 75, 78, 83, 84, 85, 86, 87, 94, 117, 118, 119, 137, 139, 141, 142, 151, 159, 172, 173, 174, 176, 180, 188, 193, 195, 198, 199, 212, 213, 214
experimental xii, xiii, 8, 10, 35, 57, 58, 72, 91, 92, 98, 122–123, 137, 152, 155, 175, 176, 177, 188, 194
experimentation 4, 8, 21, 33, 52, 93, 149, 171, 193, 210, 218
externalisation 215–216
extralegal 142, 145, 182, 212
extraterritorial 19, 142, 212

Facebook 125, 193, 207
father/s xiii, 38, 39, 43, 46, 54n1, 62, 85, 158, 160, 172
feminist/s 11, 68, 69, 120, 141, 164, 165, 186, 196
First Nations 36, 145, 158, 181, 182
folklore 69, 82, 195
fragmented/fragmentation xii, xiii, 14, 27, 38, 40, 41, 52, 53, 62, 76, 92, 93, 97, 98, 99, 102, 106, 110, 113, 151, 160, 189, 194, 208, 213, 218
frame narrative/s 97, 100, 106
Frankl, Viktor 140
Fraser, Malcolm 43
freedom xiii, 1, 13, 16, 19, 33, 51, 79, 83, 87, 94, 109, 110, 114, 115, 162, 197, 198, 209, 216
Freedom, Only Freedom: The Prison Writings of Behrouz Boochani 94, 107, 108, 111, 115, 123, 153, 155
Fricker, Miranda 85

Galbraith, Janet 59, 64, 108, 109, 122
genre/s xiii, 14, 26, 47, 52, 58, 71, 73, 91, 160, 181, 194

German xi, xii, 38
Germian, Roza 122, 123
Gaddafi, Muammar 216
Gholami, Mohammad Ali (aka Mamali, aka Silas) 36
Gilbert, Helen 184
global xiv, 1, 3, 6, 7, 14, 33, 60, 63, 72, 73, 92, 99, 111, 119, 146, 149, 179, 184, 194, 200, 209, 212, 215
Globalizations 154
Gordon, Michael 209
Gorman, Amanda 33
Grossman, Edith 28, 30, 187
Guantanamo Bay 215
Guardian, The 50, 97, 101, 102, 103, 104, 105, 106, 112, 113, 143, 193

Haitians 215
Haitian Revolution 214
Hashemi, Fatemeh 117, 118, 156
Hass, Hassaballa 108, 109, 110, 113, 144
Hawke, Bob 43
Hazara 148–149
Hemelryk Donald, Stephanie 122
hermeneutic/s 11, 27, 40, 68, 69, 186, 196
hermeneutical 13, 14, 39, 41, 42, 74, 178, 213
heteronormativity 10
hierarchy/hierarchies 100, 108, 178, 192
Hillside Haus 94
history/histories 7, 10, 11, 12, 14, 15, 16, 19, 21, 28, 29, 30, 33, 37, 39, 42, 50, 66, 69, 71, 73, 83, 84, 87, 99, 104, 118, 119, 120, 123, 137, 139, 143, 145, 146, 147, 148, 149, 152, 162, 177, 179, 180, 182, 183, 188, 190, 193, 195, 199, 206, 212, 215; oral history/histories 97, 101, 114, 151, 206
home 142, 148
homeland/s xiii, 46, 69, 76, 83, 123, 139, 148, 196
hope/s 7, 31, 37, 44, 65, 105, 109, 118, 120–121, 125, 126, 141, 144, 148, 152, 188, 193, 200
Horace 30
horrific 21, 41, 52, 53, 105, 120, 142, 146, 148, 194
horrific surrealism xiii, 13–14, 16, 41, 42, 52, 99, 100, 102, 105, 110, 120, 161, 178, 188, 194, 199, 213, 218
Huffington Post 101, 105, 106
Huitema, Stephanie 172

human being/s xiv, 18, 67, 69, 76, 116, 117, 142, 145, 162, 197, 208, 217
human rights 34, 62, 113
humiliation 207
hunger strike 214
Hussain, Kamil 179
Hussain, Yasir 115
Hussein, Seyed Ibrahim 179

identity xiii, 8, 9, 33, 36, 46, 49, 50, 51, 52, 83, 99, 119, 123, 124, 139, 145, 148, 159, 162, 189–190, 194
identity politics 33
International Criminal Court (ICC) 207
International Health and Medical Services (IHMS) 69, 76, 143, 144
Ilam 69, 150, 210
Ilic, Dan 212–113
imaginary/imaginaries 1, 12, 13, 19, 20, 65, 67, 72, 73, 86, 141, 178, 180, 181, 182, 184, 198, 200, 209, 215, 217
imagination 40, 65, 161, 183, 190, 193, 211
immigrants 19, 181
immigration 60, 95, 145, 162, 181, 182, 207, 215
immigration detention 1, 17, 21–22n1, 34, 36, 42, 45, 59, 60, 80, 141, 142, 144, 151, 162, 180, 181, 183, 214
imperialism 158
imprison/ed xiii, 30, 62, 66, 69, 74, 78, 101, 106, 108, 112, 139, 140, 143, 151, 161, 184, 206, 212, 215, 218
imprisonment 1, 19, 21–22n1, 41, 45, 59, 96, 114, 142, 179, 194, 207, 212
incarcerated xiii, 1, 2, 3, 4, 5, 6, 7, 14, 15, 17, 18, 21, 41, 44, 59, 64, 66, 69, 70, 75, 78, 80, 84, 94, 126n1, 137, 138, 139, 140, 141, 148, 174, 180, 181, 184, 185, 193, 197, 207, 208, 213, 218
incarceration 15, 17, 19, 33, 70, 71, 78, 79, 94, 137, 142, 143, 152, 159, 180, 184, 185, 195, 198
indefinite 3, 15, 20, 36, 37, 39, 59, 60, 62, 65, 66, 70, 92, 114, 115, 124, 138, 139, 142, 144, 145, 147–148, 153, 173, 174, 176, 177, 178, 180, 183, 186, 189, 212, 215, 217, 218
indeterminate 148
Indigenous 10, 36, 87, 120, 145, 157, 158, 181, 182, 184, 185, 200
Indonesia/n 1, 6, 14, 44, 60, 61, 64, 96, 108, 111, 142, 148, 150, 151, 156, 178, 186

intellectual 1, 2, 3, 4, 7, 10, 14, 15, 21, 28, 30, 42, 57, 66, 67, 69, 87, 91, 92, 99, 110, 113, 137, 139, 141, 142, 147, 148, 152, 153, 171, 172, 180, 184, 189, 190, 193, 194, 196, 198, 200
interdependent 5, 6, 14, 20, 42, 58, 182, 183, 213
interlingual 28, 58, 141
international 1, 6, 7, 35, 44, 61, 69, 76, 78, 93, 96, 102, 104, 111, 113, 114, 119, 143, 145, 151, 152, 153, 154, 158, 174, 182, 184, 185, 189, 207, 210, 212, 214, 218
interpret/ed 3, 9, 10, 11, 12, 16, 17, 27, 28, 30, 36, 42, 44, 49, 57, 58, 61, 65, 74, 82, 99, 114, 123, 125, 140, 141, 143, 145, 146, 179, 184, 188, 190, 196, 208, 210, 213
interpreting xi, 7, 13, 33, 34, 39, 40, 49, 62, 96, 97, 98, 99, 102, 112, 113, 114, 139, 140, 147, 159, 187, 194, 206, 208, 209
intersectional 1, 7, 19, 42, 62, 65, 68, 72, 120, 138, 181, 186, 188, 211
intersectionality 68, 186
intersemiotic xi, xii, 58
intralingual 30, 58, 141, 176
Iran xiii, xiv, 9, 30, 31, 34, 35, 36, 37, 38, 39, 43, 46, 49, 51, 52, 59, 69, 82, 85, 108, 126n1, 159, 165n2, 172, 173, 174, 175, 177, 195, 210, 214
Iranian/s xi, xiii, xiv, 9, 31, 32, 33, 34, 36, 37, 39, 43, 49, 84, 85, 111, 126n1, 163, 165n2, 172, 173, 193, 195, 206, 209, 210, 215
Iraq/i 34, 37, 43, 52, 155, 214
Irfani, Fatima 178
Isfahan xi, xiii, xiv, 173

Jahangir, Mohammad 179
Japanese 155
Jensen, Erik 105, 108
journalism 45, 50, 60, 62, 63, 73, 74, 81, 84, 93, 100, 101, 104, 123, 152, 154, 159, 160, 162, 209
journalist/s 31, 49, 50, 59, 67, 80, 95, 97, 105, 119, 123, 174, 175, 193, 209
Jurrungu Ngan-ga 184

Kabgani, Sajad 9, 51, 82, 160, 165, 176, 217
Kamali Sarvestani, Arash 59, 119, 122, 152, 156, 162, 174

Kanapathi, Shaminda 94, 95, 108, 111, 113
Karami, Fariborz 179
Khalili, Sarah 30, 31–32, 210–211
Khan, Rakib 179
Khayyam, Omar 31, 172
Khazaei, Hamid 179
knowing 30, 65, 79, 83, 93, 137, 146, 147, 148, 181, 191, 196, 211
knowledge 1, 4, 6, 7, 9, 12, 14, 15, 21, 27, 29, 34, 35, 42, 57, 59, 65, 67, 73, 79–80, 80, 81, 84, 86, 87, 91, 92, 96, 102, 103, 106, 110, 112, 115, 119, 121, 137, 139, 140, 141, 146, 147, 163, 176, 179, 198, 199, 200, 211
Kurd/s 34, 46, 69, 85, 123, 210
Kurdish 13, 34, 46, 52, 69, 96, 123, 155, 195, 196, 206, 209, 214
Kurdish Iranian 34, 80, 98, 111, 115, 193
Kyawning, Salim 179
kyriarchal 1, 10, 11–13, 145, 178, 187
Kyriarchal System xiv, 4, 8, 11–12, 17, 18, 19, 68–70, 71, 76, 78, 117, 119, 120, 145, 146, 154, 164, 165, 184, 185–187, 188, 189, 190, 195, 196, 199, 209
kyriarchy 4, 10–13, 15, 18, 68, 71, 120, 181, 184, 185, 186, 187, 189, 196
kyriocentric/kyriocentrism 10, 11, 12, 13, 67
Kukathas, Chandran 13

Labor Party/government 43, 151, 183
law/s 19, 145, 146, 151, 157, 158, 181, 182, 212, 216
leader/s 5, 7, 15, 21, 43, 95, 96, 97, 101, 114, 115, 154, 183
Lee, Bri 186–187, 188, 189
Lefevre, André 28
liberal humanitarianism 14, 15, 66, 188
Liberal Party/government (Liberal-National Coalition) 42, 183
limbo xv, 39, 147, 157
lived experience/s xii, 1, 5, 6, 10, 15, 33, 36, 38, 41, 42, 59, 62, 63, 66, 67, 71, 73, 139, 141, 145, 147, 164, 193, 194, 195, 196
local/s 3, 27, 33, 35, 63, 95, 112, 114, 124, 142, 176
Lombrum Naval Base/centre (RPC) 45, 93, 94, 100, 101, 105, 176
Lorengau 94, 95, 102, 105, 149, 174, 175, 176

love 64, 83, 109, 141, 172, 188
Lucashenko, Melissa 109
Luong, Louisa 187, 192, 193
Libya 216

Mandanipour, Shahriar 30, 32
mandatory 145
Mansoubi, Moones 9, 51, 82, 94, 97, 98, 103, 104, 107, 119, 152, 160, 164, 176, 210, 218
Manus Island 1, 6, 13, 30, 44, 45, 49, 51, 53, 62, 64, 70, 80, 84, 93, 95, 96, 104, 105, 106, 109, 110, 111, 112, 113, 114, 116, 117, 119, 124, 126n1, 141, 142, 149, 151, 160, 161, 164, 171, 173, 174, 175, 176, 190, 193, 194, 196, 206, 207, 208, 210, 218
Manus Prison 4, 41, 44, 49, 62, 69, 70, 80, 91, 94, 96, 100, 103, 108, 111, 112, 115, 126n1, 138, 139, 141, 142, 143, 146, 149, 151, 152, 154, 157, 158, 161, 172, 173, 174, 175, 176, 177, 178, 180, 186, 189, 196, 206, 207, 208, 209, 215, 218
Manus Prison Theory 8, 19, 70, 138, 141, 146, 149, 173, 179
Manusian 111, 112
marginalise/d 15, 29, 37, 93, 158, 159, 164, 180, 198, 200
Marrugeku 184, 185
Masoumali, Omid 179
Mbuvi, Andrew 26
McGill University 156, 157, 163
McNevin, Anne 177
Meanjin 98, 112, 150
Measham, Fatima 153
Medevac 112
media 14, 39, 59, 63, 66, 74, 92, 100, 101, 102, 103, 108, 109, 111, 114, 121, 125, 142, 148, 149, 152, 153, 174, 209, 215, 217
Medina, José 85
medical 69, 76, 112, 143, 144, 145, 216, 218
Mehrez, Samia 171
Melbourne 34, 49, 106, 111, 112, 122, 126, 218
Melbourne Bach Choir 122
memorial 144, 172, 173
method/s/methodology/methodologies 3, 5, 6, 14, 15, 19, 27, 34, 35, 41, 42, 44, 67, 70, 73, 92, 99, 118, 119, 120, 121, 123, 124, 125, 139, 142, 146, 147, 148, 150, 163, 173, 176, 177, 180, 195, 197, 199, 200
metaphor/s/metaphorical/metaphorically xiii, 18, 20, 21n1, 28, 57, 68
Middle East 13, 35, 159, 195
Middle East and North Africa 35, 199
migration xiv, 4, 22n1, 33, 36, 37, 38, 39, 40, 42, 43, 44, 85, 99, 118, 119, 121, 122, 123, 142, 151, 159, 180, 192, 215
militarisation 184, 209
military 22, n1, 95, 161, 184
Mills, Charles 20, 74, 85
minority/minorities xiv, 43, 157
Mira 139–141
Missaghi, Poupeh 32
Mohammadzadeh, Navid 210
Mohammed, Abdirahman Ahmed 179
Jack, Omar 113
Montreal 156
Morrison, Scott 215
mother xiii, xiv, 53n1, 158, 159, 172, 173, 208
Muhamat, Abdul Aziz 113, 115
multicultural/ism 17, 43, 158
multilingual 2, 61, 62, 208, 209
multiplication 12, 13
multiplicative 11, 13, 18, 42, 72
multiply/ing xiv, 17, 18, 67, 72
music/al 28, 36, 115, 122, 123, 124–126, 147, 158, 160
mutual scaffolding 40, 42, 214
Myanmar 214
myth/s/mythical/mythological/mythmaking 16, 40, 42, 50, 82, 120, 145, 158, 172, 180, 181, 182, 192

naming 67, 137, 180
narrative/s 2, 3, 4, 7, 11, 12, 14, 20, 21, 26, 27, 28, 29, 33, 36, 38, 39, 40, 41, 42, 45, 52, 57, 63, 66, 67, 72, 73, 75, 76, 83, 84, 85, 86, 87, 91, 96, 97, 98, 100, 101, 102, 103, 106, 112, 118, 119, 137, 139, 140, 141, 145, 146, 147, 150, 151, 154, 157, 158, 160, 172, 173, 174, 177, 180, 181, 182, 184, 186, 189, 191, 193, 196, 197, 198, 200, 206, 208, 209, 211, 215, 217
narratological 72, 213
Nashr-e Cheshmeh 45, 163, 175
national security 143
Nauru, Republic of 1, 6, 21, 45, 59, 60, 62, 75, 96, 108, 114, 119, 138,

139, 140, 141, 142, 144, 151, 158, 178–179, 190, 206, 207, 208, 212, 216, 218
Nauru Imprisoned Exiles Collective 8, 141
Nauru Prison 139, 141, 142, 143, 146, 180, 207, 215
Nauru Prison Theory 8, 19, 21, 70, 138, 139, 146, 179
navy 95, 150, 151
neocolonial 19, 70, 142, 145, 146, 180, 183, 190, 217
neoliberal/ism 12, 16, 164, 184, 196
Netherlands 59, 119
New Zealand 45, 70, 98, 150, 157, 163, 183, 212
Nida, Eugene 26
1951 Refugee Convention and Protocol Relating to the Status of Refugees 182
19 July 2013 151
Nkechi, Anele 49
No Friend but the Mountains: A Journey Through Song 123
No Friend but the Mountains: a Symphonic Song Cycle 122, 126
No Friend but the Mountains: Writing from Manus Prison xiv, 2, 3, 4, 8, 9, 13, 15, 20, 30, 32, 33, 38, 41, 44, 45, 47, 49, 66, 68, 71, 72, 75, 76, 78, 82, 93, 98, 99, 100, 101, 102, 106, 108, 109, 111, 115, 117, 118, 122, 123, 138, 149, 150, 151, 152, 154, 155, 159, 162, 171, 175, 177, 178, 181, 186, 187, 188, 189, 191, 192, 193, 209, 210, 218
Northern Territory 184

Öcalan, Abdullah 69
officer/s 95
offshore 14, 19, 22n1, 44, 45, 59, 62, 99, 109, 139, 142, 143, 145, 147, 151, 153, 158, 173, 176, 177, 178, 180, 182, 183, 190, 192, 207, 212, 214, 215, 216
onshore 14, 19, 45, 142, 143, 145, 147, 173, 177, 178, 190, 214, 216
Operation Sovereign Borders 6, 178
oppressed 11, 124
oppression 7, 10, 11, 13, 15, 17, 18, 33, 36, 43, 58, 60, 67, 68, 70, 73, 74, 92, 99, 123, 124, 139, 142, 145, 146, 178, 180, 185, 186, 194, 195, 196, 198, 212, 213, 216

oppressive 33, 60, 71, 92, 119, 212, 217
oppressors 67, 97, 195, 215
Osman, Bashir 115
Overland 112

Pacific Solution 6, 178
pain 46, 72
painting/s xi, xii, 10, 60, 73
Pakistan xiii, 214
Pakistani 115
Papua New Guinea (PNG) 1, 6, 44, 45, 93, 94, 95, 96, 98, 108, 111, 114, 144, 149, 151, 156, 165, 173, 174, 178, 192, 206, 207, 208, 212, 216
paratexts 102, 150, 155
penal colony 19, 84, 145, 158
people seeking asylum 34, 36, 44, 118, 120, 145, 150, 182, 183, 215
peritext 150
persecuted xiv, 34, 148, 180
persecution xii, xiii, 33, 37, 44, 69, 126n1, 148, 172, 180, 195, 198, 215, 216
Persian/Farsi xi, xii, xiv, 3, 9, 30, 31, 32, 34, 38, 45, 47, 61, 62, 68, 69, 72, 75, 76, 77, 78, 96, 101, 106, 107, 108, 116, 117, 119, 122, 138, 139, 140, 141, 143, 152, 155, 156, 159, 160, 163, 164, 165n1 & 2, 172, 175, 176, 177, 185, 191, 195, 207, 208, 209, 210, 218
Persian literature 31
personhood 190
The Philosopher 21
The Philosopher's Zone 78, 79
philosophy xiii, 5, 6, 9, 30, 35, 36, 38, 40, 42, 58, 59, 68, 69, 70, 78, 80, 81, 82, 83, 85, 117, 118, 119, 120, 121, 160, 173, 186, 192, 193, 196, 214
phone/s xiv, 4, 6, 30, 49, 82, 97, 107, 112, 114, 119, 143, 146, 149, 175, 176, 193, 215
Picador-Pan Macmillan 152, 165
Pigram, Dalisa 184
place-based 42, 68, 92, 137, 146, 180
plan/s xiii, 2, 3, 10, 26, 27, 28, 29, 30, 31, 36, 37, 38, 39, 40, 41, 42, 43, 45, 52, 58, 69, 94, 108, 111, 141, 162, 163, 173, 175, 176, 188, 206, 208, 210, 216, 217
Plato 20, 41, 42, 82
poetic 45, 46, 50, 100, 101, 106, 115, 117, 122, 123, 177
poetics 194

poetry xi, xii, 31, 33, 45, 46, 50, 73, 77, 106, 109, 113, 117, 120, 124, 154, 155, 156, 158, 160, 172, 175, 193
Pohlhaus, Gaile, Jr 74
police 95, 98, 115, 173, 183, 185
policies 27, 36, 42, 43, 72, 74, 84, 120, 145, 157, 162, 177, 183, 184, 214, 215, 216, 217
policy 17, 19, 27, 43, 53, 85, 157, 215
Port Moresby 1, 6, 45, 70, 96, 108, 114, 156, 157, 173, 178, 216
positionality/positionalities 5, 6, 11, 14, 20, 27, 33, 65, 66, 70, 146, 147, 173, 212
posthumanism 9
Post Traumatic Growth (PTG) 140
pride 52, 86–87, 123, 141, 172, 188
prisoner/s 62, 69, 76, 78, 79–80, 178, 192, 214
pro-refugee/anti-refugee disposition 14, 15–16, 16, 17, 18, 66, 72, 74, 188, 199
process/es 2, 3, 4, 5, 6, 7, 8, 9, 10, 13, 16, 17, 21, 26, 27, 28, 29, 31, 33, 37, 38, 39, 41, 42, 44, 45, 51, 54n1, 57, 58, 60, 61, 68, 76, 83, 85, 91, 92, 93, 98, 99, 100, 101, 102, 103, 108, 138, 139, 140, 141, 142, 145, 146, 149, 150, 151, 152, 157, 160, 164–165, 171, 175, 176, 177, 180, 181, 186, 187, 188, 189, 194, 195, 196, 206, 207, 208, 210, 212
product/s 2, 3, 4, 6, 7, 10, 26, 27, 28, 29, 31, 33, 36, 39, 41, 42, 58, 91, 92, 99, 100, 102, 103, 108, 112, 141, 176, 181, 186, 188, 206, 210, 213
prose 32, 45, 47, 76, 77, 106, 117, 122, 154, 155, 156
protest/s 69, 94, 95, 96, 101, 108, 113, 114, 115, 126n1, 154, 216
psychoanalysis 9, 120
psychoanalytic 81
psychology 142
public philosophy 1, 2, 4, 5, 8, 10, 21, 57, 71, 137, 138, 140, 186, 187, 189, 206
punish/ed 145, 148
punishment 1, 68, 144, 145, 189

quarantine 183

race 18, 36, 49, 68, 75, 85
racialised 17, 199, 200
racialisation 146, 209

racism 10, 16, 17, 18, 20, 120, 143, 147, 196, 209, 213
racist/s 12, 16, 72, 183, 215
Rajendran, Rajeev 179
Rancière, Jacques 177
Rapid Support Forces (RSF) 216
Razivand, Ali (aka King Ali) 36
reception xii, 2, 4, 14, 21, 26, 100, 102, 106, 123, 146, 152, 153, 176, 177
refugeehood 15, 18, 181, 182
resettle/d 94, 96, 114, 212
resettlement 208
Rohani, Sayed Mirwais 179
Rojava 69
Rooney, Michelle Nayahamui 176
Roy, Arundhati 80
Rudd, Kevin 151
Rutledge, David 78, 79
Rwanda 221

Sadatsharifi, Farshid 156, 157
Sarwar, Mohammed 178
Sarwari, Sadiqa 96
Satah, Benham 96, 97, 98, 101, 112, 113–114, 115, 126n1, 151, 174–175, 206–209
The Saturday Paper 50, 94, 101, 105, 106, 108
SBS Kurdish 122, 123
SBS Persian 59, 117, 118, 156
Schüssler Fiorenza, Elisabeth 10, 11, 67, 68, 69, 120, 186, 196
Serco 216, 217
settler colonial 14, 19, 80, 163
Shamshiripour, Hamed 178, 179, 184
shared philosophical activity 2, 4, 5, 6, 8, 9, 10, 15, 19, 21, 33, 51, 70, 82, 84, 93, 138, 139, 140, 149, 188, 193, 196, 197, 206
shattered xiii, 14, 38, 39, 40, 41, 53, 92, 93, 97, 98, 99, 102, 106, 110, 160, 189, 208, 213, 218
Silverstein, Jordana 153
sister-in-law 172
situation-specific 42, 68, 92, 137, 146
smuggle/d 49, 95, 112, 152
smuggler 151
social media 4, 6, 108, 110, 113, 125, 208, 213
Somalia 214
Sorbera, Lucia 122
Southerly 22n1, 64, 108, 109, 112, 148
Spicy (aka Helal Uddin) 95
Sri Lanka 214

Stavans, Ilan 31, 210
stigmatisation 7, 10, 146, 172, 195, 199
stigmatise/stigmatised xiv, 37, 39, 159
storytelling xiii, 3, 4, 13, 49, 86, 91, 92, 96, 97, 99, 100, 106, 110, 124, 140, 158, 160, 171, 172, 173, 181, 182, 188, 189, 193, 197, 198, 208, 213, 214, 218
strategy/ies 36, 58, 63, 66, 70, 73, 93, 96, 107, 121, 137, 144, 145, 148, 153, 154, 189, 190, 191, 193, 197, 200, 215, 217
subjugated 27
subjugation 7, 10, 84, 92, 124, 190
Sudan 62, 64, 143, 214, 216
Sudanese 115, 143, 216
suicide 34, 53, 157, 207
Surma, Anne 106, 107
surreal 21, 41, 53, 194
surveillance xiv, 19, 22n1, 61, 209, 216
survival 124, 125, 139
survive/s 27, 124, 140, 142, 212
Swain, Rachael 184
Sydney Film Festival 153
Styles, Luke 122, 125
symbolic 15, 17, 42, 72, 81, 100, 145, 195
symbolic aesthetic 13, 18, 72, 91, 141, 215
synecdoche 178
synecdochic 182, 183, 184, 190
synonym/s 71, 72, 185, 186
Syria 52, 216
systematic torture 15, 59, 60, 72, 73, 94, 117, 119, 124, 138, 142, 144, 147, 174, 176, 189, 199, 209
system-e hākem 68, 69, 70, 71, 119, 120, 164, 165, 185, 196
systemic xiv, 2, 7, 19, 37, 44, 68, 72, 86, 93, 98, 141, 145, 147, 159, 162, 185, 190, 195, 200, 207, 217

tactic/s 14, 58, 70, 73, 94, 145, 182, 184, 189, 190, 197, 200, 215
Tahirih Qurrat al-Ayn 172
Tall Fences, Taller Trees 174
Tamborini, Adrian 122
Tehran xiii, 31, 39, 43, 53n1, 85
terra nullius 145, 158, 181
terrorist 183
temporal 27
testimonial injustice 145
testimony 145, 147, 191, 193

Tofighian, Akhtar 172
Tofighian, Manoutchehr 172, 173
Tofighian, Navid 172
Tofighian, Naysan 172
Tofighian, Omid 49, 53, 79, 80, 102, 104, 105, 107, 118, 123, 126, 141, 156, 158, 159, 187, 192, 193, 208
Towfighian, Iradj 172
Tok Pisin 96, 111, 112
tragedy 34, 105, 143, 150
tragic 14, 18, 67
transhistorical 92, 146, 149, 184, 215
Transition: the magazine of Africa and the diaspora 109, 113, 144
translate 27, 32, 34, 40, 49, 50, 52, 53, 62, 72, 76, 97, 102, 103, 104, 105, 107, 112, 143, 154, 157, 159, 165, 189, 192, 193, 208
translated 3, 8, 9, 27, 29, 30, 31, 32, 34, 36, 40, 44, 47, 50, 51, 59, 60, 62, 64, 71, 72, 76, 94, 95, 97, 98, 99, 100, 101, 102, 103, 104, 105, 106, 107, 109, 110, 112, 115, 116, 117, 118, 119, 121, 122, 123, 141, 143, 148, 150, 152, 153, 155, 156, 164, 173, 175, 177, 184, 193, 196, 207, 208, 209, 210, 211, 215, 218
translating 8, 10, 12, 26, 31, 32, 33, 41, 42, 45, 49, 50, 51, 53, 60, 62, 63, 68, 74, 81, 97, 99, 105, 106, 112, 113, 117, 138, 147, 149, 151, 159, 160, 176, 183, 192, 193, 194, 195, 196
transnational 1, 3, 4, 6, 15, 33, 35, 36, 70, 73, 92, 118, 141, 182, 184, 185, 191, 195, 196, 212, 215
trauma 41, 191, 194, 195, 197
traumatic 99, 195
trope/s xiii, 4, 14, 18, 40, 52, 66, 67, 73, 99, 123, 148, 182, 191, 194, 195, 198, 214
Trump, Donald 215
Turkey 52
Turnbull, Malcolm 215
23-day siege 4, 91, 93, 97, 99, 100, 106, 108, 116, 122, 154, 174
two islands thought experiment 18–20, 79–80, 190
2019 Australian Book Industry Award 3, 161
2019 National Biography Award 3, 161
2019 New South Wales (NSW) Premier's Literary Awards 3, 161, 218

2019 New South Wales (NSW) Premier's Special Award 3, 161, 218
2019 New South Wales (NSW) Premier's Translation Prize 3, 218
2019 Victorian Prize for Literature 3, 38, 49, 111, 117, 153, 161, 218
2019 Victorian Premier's Award for Nonfiction 3, 38, 218
2020 Australia Book Industry Awards (ABIA) Audiobook of the Year 3
Tymoczko, Maria 28, 57, 58, 67

Ubud Writers and Readers Festival 186
UK 122, 199, 215
unconstitutional 93, 149, 173
Urdu 96, 209
US 33, 37, 38, 39, 42, 43, 54n1, 59, 64, 85, 109, 157, 159, 163, 173, 215
UTS Data Arena 60

Venuti, Lawrence 57, 63
verse 45, 47, 76, 117, 122, 156
visa/s 19, 37, 39, 42, 43, 44, 45, 53–54n1, 140, 145, 147, 190, 216, 217
Voller, Dylan 184–185

war 37, 43, 44, 46, 64, 70, 78, 214
weaponisation 8, 139, 190
Weapons of Slow Destruction 60

West Lorengau Haus 94
WhatsApp xiv, 30, 45, 49, 50, 51, 53, 59, 61, 62, 76, 82, 97, 98, 101, 103, 107, 112, 113, 114, 119, 125, 141, 143, 146, 151, 161, 164, 175, 176, 193, 210
Wheeler Centre 153
White Australia policy 43, 85
whiteness 16, 17, 18
Whitlock, Gillian 60, 100, 101, 102, 206
Who Gets to be Smart: Privilege, Power and Knowledge 186
Wilson Security 216
Wittgenstein, Ludwig 58
Woman, Life, Freedom; *jin, jiyān, āzādi*; *zan, zendegi, āzādi* 69
Woodward, Will 101, 102
WORD Christchurch Festival 45
Writing Through Fences 109
Writing Through Fences: Archipelago of Letters 64, 108

Yancy, George 16–18

Zamiri, Homaira 96
Zazai, Walid 108
Zelman Symphony Orchestra 122
Zivardar, Elahe 8, 21, 59–60, 71, 74, 96, 138–139, 206

For Product Safety Concerns and Information please contact our EU
representative GPSR@taylorandfrancis.com
Taylor & Francis Verlag GmbH, Kaufingerstraße 24, 80331 München, Germany

www.ingramcontent.com/pod-product-compliance
Lightning Source LLC
Chambersburg PA
CBHW050302010526
44108CB00040B/2019